MANKIND
IN THE MAKING

H. G. WELLS

1st WORLD
LIBRARY
Literary Society

Mankind in the Making

H. G. Wells

© 1st World Library, 2006
PO Box 2211
Fairfield, IA 52556
www.1stworldlibrary.com
First Edition

LCCN: 2006909917

Softcover ISBN: 978-1-4218-3339-2
Hardcover ISBN: 978-1-4218-3239-5
eBook ISBN: 978-1-4218-3439-9

Purchase *"Mankind in the Making"*
as a traditional bound book at:
www.1stWorldLibrary.com/purchase.asp?ISBN=978-1-4218-3339-2

1st World Library Literary Society

Giving Back to the World

"If you want to work on the core problem, it's early school literacy."

- James Barksdale, former CEO of Netscape

"No skill is more crucial to the future of a child, or to a democratic and prosperous society, than literacy."

- Los Angeles Times

Literacy... means far more than learning how to read and write... The aim is to transmit... knowledge and promote social participation."

- UNESCO

"Literacy is not a luxury, it is a right and a responsibility. If our world is to meet the challenges of the twenty-first century we must harness the energy and creativity of all our citizens."

- President Bill Clinton

"Parents should be encouraged to read to their children, and teachers should be equipped with all available techniques for teaching literacy, so the varying needs and capacities of individual kids can be taken into account."

- Hugh Mackay

CONTENTS

PREFACE 7

I. THE NEW REPUBLIC 10

II. THE PROBLEM OF THE BIRTH SUPPLY 32

III. CERTAIN WHOLESALE ASPECTS OF
    MAN-MAKING 60

IV. THE BEGINNINGS OF THE MIND AND
    LANGUAGE 87

V. THE MAN-MAKING FORCES OF THE
    MODERN STATE 118

VI. SCHOOLING 145

VII. POLITICAL AND SOCIAL INFLUENCES 171

VIII. THE CULTIVATION OF THE IMAGINATION 204

IX. THE ORGANIZATION OF THE HIGHER
    EDUCATION 221

X. THOUGHT IN THE MODERN STATE 247

XI. THE MAN'S OWN SHARE 271

APPENDIX - A PAPER ON ADMINISTRATIVE
AREAS READ BEFORE THE FABIAN SOCIETY 275

PREFACE

It may save misunderstanding if a word or so be said here of the aim and scope of this book. It is written in relation to a previous work, *Anticipations*, [Footnote: Published by Harper Bros.] and together with that and a small pamphlet, "The Discovery of the Future," [Footnote: Nature, vol. lxv. (1901-2), p. 326, and reprinted in the Smithsonian Report for 1902] presents a general theory of social development and of social and political conduct. It is an attempt to deal with social and political questions in a new way and from a new starting-point, viewing the whole social and political world as aspects of one universal evolving scheme, and placing all social and political activities in a defined relation to that; and to this general method and trend it is that the attention of the reader is especially directed. The two books and the pamphlet together are to be regarded as an essay in presentation. It is a work that the writer admits he has undertaken primarily for his own mental comfort. He is remarkably not qualified to assume an authoritative tone in these matters, and he is acutely aware of the many defects in detailed knowledge, in temper, and in training these papers collectively display. He is aware that at such points, for example, as the reference to authorities in the chapter on the biological problem, and to books in the educational chapter, the lacunar quality of his reading and knowledge is only too evident; to fill in and complete his design—notably in the fourth paper—he has had quite frankly to jerry-build here and there. Nevertheless, he ventures to publish this book. There are phases in the development of every science when an incautious outsider may think himself almost necessary, when sketchiness ceases to be a sin, when the mere facts of irresponsibility and an untrained interest may permit a freshness, a freedom of mental gesture that would be inconvenient and compromising for the specialist; and such a phase, it is submitted, has been reached in this field of speculation. Moreover, the work attempted is not so much special and technical as a work of reconciliation, the suggestion of broad generalizations upon which divergent specialists may meet, a business for non-technical expression, and in which a man who knows a little of biology, a little of physical science, and a little in a practical way of social stratification, who has concerned himself with education and aspired to creative art, may claim in his very amateurishness a special qualification. And in addition, it is particularly a business for some irresponsible writer, outside the complications of practical politics, some man who, politically, "doesn't matter," to provide the first tentatives of a political doctrine that shall be equally available for application in the British Empire and in the United States. To that we must come, unless our talk of co-operation, of reunion, is no more than sentimental dreaming. We have to get into line, and that we cannot do while over here and over there men hold themselves bound by old party formulae, by loyalties and institutions, that are becoming, that have become, provincial in proportion to our new and wider needs. My instances are commonly British, but all the broad project of this book—the discussion of the quality of the average birth and of the average home, the educational scheme, the suggestions for the organization of literature and a common language, the criticism of polling and the jury system, and the ideal of a Republic with an apparatus of honour—is, I submit, addressed to, and could be adopted by, any English-reading and English-speaking man. No doubt the spirit of the inquiry is more British than American, that the abandonment of Rousseau and anarchic democracy is more complete than American thought is yet prepared for, but that is a difference not of quality but of degree. And even the appendix, which at a hasty glance may seem to be no more than the discussion of British parochial boundaries, does indeed develop principles of primary importance in the fundamental schism of American politics between the local State government and the central power. So much of apology and explanation I owe to the reader, to the contemporary specialist, and to myself.

These papers were first published in the British *Fortnightly Review* and in the American *Cosmopolitan*. In the latter periodical they were, for the most part, printed from uncorrected proofs set up from an early version. This periodical publication produced a considerable correspondence, which has been of very great service in the final revision. These papers have indeed been honoured by letters from men and women of almost every profession, and by a really very considerable amount of genuine criticism in the British press. Nothing, I think, could witness more effectually to the demand for such discussions of general principle, to the need felt for some nuclear matter to crystallize upon at the present time, however poor its quality, than this fact. Here I can only thank the writers collectively, and call their attention to the more practical gratitude of my frequently modified text.

I would, however, like to express my especial indebtedness to my friend, Mr. Graham Wallas, who generously toiled through the whole of my typewritten copy, and gave me much valuable advice, and to Mr. C. G. Stuart Menteath for some valuable references.

H. G. WELLS.
SANDGATE, *July*, 1903.

I

THE NEW REPUBLIC

Toleration to-day is becoming a different thing from the toleration of former times. The toleration of the past consisted very largely in saying, "You are utterly wrong and totally accurst, there is no truth but my truth and that you deny, but it is not my place to destroy you and so I let you go." Nowadays there is a real disposition to accept the qualified nature of one's private certainties. One may have arrived at very definite views, one may have come to beliefs quite binding upon one's self, without supposing them to be imperative upon other people. To write "I believe" is not only less presumptuous and aggressive in such matters than to write "it is true," but it is also nearer the reality of the case. One knows what seems true to one's self, but we are coming to realize that the world is great and complex, beyond the utmost power of such minds as ours. Every day of life drives that conviction further home. And it is possible to maintain that in perhaps quite a great number of ethical, social, and political questions there is no absolute "truth" at all—at least for finite beings. To one intellectual temperament things may have a moral tint and aspect, differing widely from that they present to another; and yet each may be in its own way right. The wide differences in character and quality between one human being and another may quite conceivably involve not only differences in moral obligation, but differences in fundamental moral aspect—we may act and react upon each other towards a universal end, but without any universally applicable rule of conduct whatever. In

H. G. Wells

some greater vision than mine, my right and wrong may be no more than hammer and anvil in the accomplishment of a design larger than I can understand. So that these papers are not written primarily for all, nor with the same intention towards all who read them. They are designed first for those who are predisposed for their reception. Then they are intended to display in an orderly manner a point of view, and how things look from that point of view, to those who are not so predisposed. These latter will either develop into adherents as they read, or, what is more likely, they will exchange a vague disorderly objection for a clearly defined and understood difference. To arrive at such an understanding is often for practical purposes as good as unanimity; for in narrowing down the issue to some central point or principle, we develop just how far those who are divergent may go together before separation or conflict become inevitable, and save something of our time and of our lives from those misunderstandings, and those secondary differences of no practical importance whatever, which make such disastrous waste of human energy.

Now the point of view which will be displayed in relation to a number of wide questions in these pages is primarily that of the writer's. But he hopes and believes that among those who read what he has to say, there will be found not only many to understand, but some to agree with him. In many ways he is inclined to believe the development of his views may be typical of the sort of development that has gone on to a greater or lesser extent in the minds of many of the younger men during the last twenty years, and it is in that belief that he is now presenting them.

And the questions that will be dealt with in relation to this point of view are all those questions outside a man's purely private self—if he have a purely private self—in which he interacts with his fellow-man. Our attempt will be to put in order, to reduce to principle, what is at present in countless instances a mass of inconsistent proceedings, to frame a general theory in accordance with modern conditions of social and political activity.

This is one man's proposal, his attempt to supply a need that has oppressed him for many years, a need that he has not only found in his own schemes of conduct, but that he has observed in the thought of numberless people about him, rendering their action fragmentary, wasteful in the gross, and ineffective in the net result, the need for some general principle, some leading idea, some standard, sufficiently comprehensive to be of real guiding value in social and political matters, in many doubtful issues of private conduct, and throughout the business of dealing with one's fellow-men. No doubt there are many who do not feel such a need at all, and with these we may part company forthwith; there are, for example, those who profess the artistic temperament and follow the impulse of the moment, and those who consult an inner light in some entirely mystical manner. But neither of these I believe is the most abundant type in the English-speaking communities. My impression is that with most of the minds I have been able to examine with any thoroughness, the attempt to systematize one's private and public conduct alike, and to reduce it to spacious general rules, to attempt, if not to succeed, in making it coherent, consistent, and uniformly directed, is an almost instinctive proceeding.

There is an objection I may anticipate at this point. If I am to leave this statement unqualified, it would certainly be objected that such a need is no more nor less than the need of religion, that a properly formulated religion does supply a trustworthy guide at every fork and labyrinth in life. By my allusion to the failure of old formulae and methods to satisfy now, I am afraid many people will choose to understand that I refer to what is often spoken of as the conflict of religion and science, and that I intend to propound some contribution to the conflict. I will at any rate anticipate that objection here, in order to mark out my boundaries with greater precision.

Taken in its completeness, I submit that it is a greater claim than almost any religion can justifiably make, to satisfy the need I have stated. No religion prescribes rules that can be immediately applied to every eventuality. Between the general rules laid down and the particular instance there is always a wide gap, into which doubts and alternatives enter and the private judgment has play. No doubt upon certain defined issues of every-day life some religions are absolutely explicit; the Mahomedan religion, for example, is very uncompromising upon the use of wine, and the law of the Ten Commandments completely prohibits the making of graven images, and almost all the great variety of creeds professed among us English-speaking peoples prescribe certain general definitions of what is righteous and what constitutes sin. But upon a thousand questions of great public importance, on the question of forms of government, of social and educational necessities, of one's course and attitude towards such great facts as the press, trusts, housing, and the like, religion, as it is generally understood, gives by itself no conclusive light. It may, no doubt, give a directing light in some cases, but not a conclusive light. It leaves us inconsistent and uncertain amidst these unavoidable problems. Yet upon these questions most people feel that something more is needed than the mood of the moment or the spin of a coin. Religious conviction may help us, it may stimulate us to press for clearer light upon these matters, but it certainly does not give us any decisions.

It is possible to be either intensely religious or utterly indifferent to religious matters and yet care nothing for these things. One may be a Pietist to whom the world is a fleeting show of no importance whatever, or one may say, "Let us eat, drink, and be merry, for to-morrow we die": the net result in regard to my need is the same. These questions appear to be on a different plane from religion and religious discussion; they look outward, while essentially religion looks inward to the soul, and, given the necessary temperament, it is possible to approach them in an unbiassed manner from almost any starting-point of religious profession. One man may believe in the immortality of the soul and another may not; one man may be a Swedenborgian, another a Roman Catholic, another a Calvinistic Methodist, another an English High Churchman, another a Positivist, or a Parsee, or a Jew; the fact remains that they must go about doing all sorts of things in common every day. They may derive their ultimate motives and sanctions from the most various sources, they may worship in the most contrasted temples and yet meet unanimously in the market-place with a desire to shape their general activities to the form of a "public spirited" life, and when at last the life of every day is summed up, "to leave the world better than they found it." And it is from that most excellent expression I would start, or rather from a sort of amplified restatement of that expression —outside the province of religious discussion altogether.

A man who will build on that expression *as his foundation* in political and social matters, has at least the possibility of agreement in the scheme of action these papers will unfold. For though we theorize it is at action that our speculations will aim. They will take the shape of an organized political and social doctrine. It will be convenient to give this doctrine a name, and for reasons that will be clear enough to those who have read my book *Anticipations* this doctrine will be spoken of throughout as "New Republicanism," the doctrine of the New Republic.

The central conception of this New Republicanism as it has shaped itself in my mind, lies in attaching pre-eminent importance to certain aspects of human life, and in subordinating systematically and always, all other considerations to these cardinal aspects. It begins with a way of looking at life. It insists upon that way, it will regard no human concern at all except in that way. And the way, putting the thing as compactly as possible, is to reject and set aside all abstract, refined, and intellectualized ideas as starting propositions, such ideas as Right, Liberty, Happiness, Duty or Beauty, and to hold fast to the assertion of the fundamental nature of life as a tissue and succession of births. These other things may be important, they may be profoundly important, but they are not primary. We cannot build upon any one of them and get a structure that will comprehend all the aspects of life.

For the great majority of mankind at least it can be held that life resolves itself quite simply and obviously into three cardinal phases. There is a period of youth and preparation, a great insurgence of emotion and enterprise centering about the passion of Love, and a third period in which, arising amidst the warmth and stir of the second, interweaving indeed with the second, the care and love of offspring becomes the central interest in life. In the babble of the grandchildren, with all the sons and daughters grown and secure, the typical life of humanity ebbs and ends. Looked at thus with a primary regard to its broadest aspect, life is seen as essentially a matter of reproduction; first a growth and training to that end, then commonly mating and actual physical reproduction, and finally the consummation of these things in parental nurture and education. Love, Home and Children, these are the heart-words of life. Not only is the general outline of the normal healthy human life reproductive, but a vast proportion of the infinitely complex and interwoven interests that fill that outline with incessant interest can be shown by a careful analysis to be more or less directly reproductive also. The toil of a man's daily work is rarely for himself alone, it goes to feed, to clothe, to educate those cardinal consequences of his being, his children; he builds for them, he plants for them, he plans for them, his social intercourse, his political interests, whatever his immediate motives, tend finally to secure their welfare. Even more obviously is this the case with his wife. Even in rest and recreation life still manifests its quality; the books the ordinary man reads turn enormously on love-making, his theatre has scarcely ever a play that has not primarily a strong love interest, his art rises to its most consummate triumphs in Venus and Madonna, and his music is saturated in love suggestions. Not only is this so with the right and proper life, but the greater portion of those acts we call vice draw their stimulus and pleasure from the impulses that subserve this sustaining fact of our being, and they are vicious only because they evade or spoil their proper end. This is really no new discovery at all, only the stripping bare of it is new. In nearly every religious and moral system in the world indeed, the predominant mass of the exposition of sin and saving virtue positively or negatively centres upon birth. Positively in the enormous stresses, the sacramental values which are concentrated upon marriage and the initial circumstances of being, and negatively in a thousand significant repudiations. Even when the devotee most strenuously renounces this world and all its works, when St. Anthony flees into the desert or the pious Durtal wrestles in his cell, when the pale nun prays in vigil and the hermit mounts his pillar, it is Celibacy, that great denial of life, that sings through all their struggle, it is this business of births as the central fact of life they still have most in mind.

This is not human life merely, it is all life. This living world, as the New Republican will see it, is no more than a great birth-place, an incessant renewal, an undying fresh beginning and unfolding of life. Take away this fact of birth and what is there remaining? A world without flowers, without the singing of birds, without the freshness of youth, with a spring that brings no seedlings and a year that bears no harvest, without beginnings and without defeats, a vast stagnation, a universe of inconsequent matter—Death. Not only does the substance of life vanish if we eliminate births and all that is related to births, but whatever remains, if anything remains, of aesthetic and intellectual and spiritual experience, collapses utterly and falls apart, when this essential substratum of all experience is withdrawn. So at any rate the world presents itself in the view the New Republican takes. And if it should chance that the reader finds this ring untrue to him, then he may take it that he stands outside us, that the New Republic is not for him.

It may be submitted that this statement that Life is a texture of births may be accepted by minds of the most divergent religious and philosophical profession. No fundamental or recondite admissions are proposed here, but only that the every-day life for every-day purposes has this shape and nature. The utter materialist may say that life to him is a fortuitous concurrence of atoms, a chance kinking in the universal fabric of matter. It is not our present business to confute him. The fact remains this is the form the kinking has taken. The believer, sedulous for his soul's welfare, may say that Life is to him an arena of spiritual conflict, but this is the character of the conflict, this is the business from which all the tests and exercises of his soul are drawn. It matters not in this present discussion if Life is no more than a dream; the dream is this.

And now one comes to another step. The reader may give his assent to this statement as obvious or he may guard his assent with a qualification or so, but I doubt if he will deny it. No one, I expect, will categorically deny it. But although no one will do that, a great number of people who have not clearly seen things in this light, do in thought and in many details of their practice follow a line that is, in effect, a flat denial of what is here proposed. Life no doubt is a fabric woven of births and the struggle to maintain and develop and multiply lives. It does not follow that life is *consciously* a fabric woven of births and the struggle to maintain and develop and multiply lives. I do not suppose a cat or a savage sees it in that light. A cat's standpoint is probably strictly individualistic. She sees the whole universe as a scheme of more or less useful, pleasurable and interesting things concentrated upon her sensitive and interesting personality. With a sinuous determination she evades disagreeables and pursues delights; life is to her quite clearly and simply a succession of pleasures, sensations and interests, among which interests there happen to be—kittens!

And this way of regarding life is by no means confined to animals and savages. I would even go so far as to suggest that it is only within the last hundred years that any considerable number of thoughtful people have come to look at life steadily and consistently as being shaped to this form, to the form of a series of births, growths and births. The most general truths are those last apprehended. The universal fact of gravitation, for example, which pervades all being, received its complete recognition scarcely two hundred years ago. And again children and savages live in air, breathe air, are saturated with air, die for five minutes' need of it, and never definitely realize there is such a thing as air at all. The vast mass of human expression in act and art and literature takes a narrower view than we have here formulated; it presents each man not only as isolated from and antagonized with the world about him, but as cut off sharply and definitely from the past before he lived and the future after he is dead; it puts what is, in relation to the view we have taken, a disproportionate amount of stress upon his egotism, upon the pursuit of his self-interest and his personal virtue and his personal fancies, and it ignores the fact, the familiar rediscovery which the nineteenth century has achieved, that he is after all only the transitory custodian of an undying gift of life, an inheritor under conditions, the momentary voice and interpreter of a being that springs from the dawn of time and lives in offspring and thought and material consequence, for ever.

This over-accentuation in the past of man's egoistic indivi-duality, or, if one puts it in another way, this unsuspicious ignorance of the real nature of life, becomes glaringly conspicuous in such weighed and deliberate utterances as *The Meditations of Marcus Aurelius*. Throughout these frank and fundamental discourses one traces a predominant desire for a perfected inconsequent egotism. Body is repudiated as a garment, position is an accident, the past that made us exists not since it is past, the future exists not for we shall never see it; at last nothing but the abstracted ego remains,—a sort of complimentary Nirvana. One citation will serve to show the colour of all his thought. "A man," he remarks, "is very devout to prevent the loss of his son. But I would have you pray rather against the fear of losing him. Let this be the rule for your devotions." [Footnote: *The Meditations of M. A. Antoninus*, ix. 40.] That indeed is the rule for all the devotions of that departing generation of wisdom. Rather serenity and dignity than good ensuing. Rather a virtuous man than any resultant whatever from his lifetime, for the future of the world. It points this disregard of the sequence of life and birth in favour of an abstract and fruitless virtue, it points it indeed with a barbed point that the son of Marcus Aurelius was the unspeakable Commodus, and that the Roman Empire fell from the temporizing detachment of his rule into a century of disorder and misery.

To the thoughtful reader to whom these papers appeal, to the

H. G. Wells

reader whose mind is of the modern cast, who has surveyed the vistas of the geological record and grasped the secular unfolding of the scheme of life, who has found with microscope and scalpel that the same rhythm of birth and re-birth is woven into the minutest texture of things that has covered the earth with verdure and shaped the massifs of the Alps, to such a man the whole literature the world produced until the nineteenth century had well progressed, must needs be lacking in any definite and pervading sense of the cardinal importance in the world of this central reproductive aspect, of births and of the training and preparation for future births. All that literature, great and imposing as we are bound to admit it is, has an outlook less ample than quite common men may have to-day. It is a literature, as we see it in the newer view, of abstracted personalities and of disconnected passions and impressions.

To one extraordinary and powerful mind in the earlier half of the nineteenth century this realization of the true form of life came with quite overwhelming force, and that was to Schopenhauer, surely at once the most acute and the most biassed of mortal men. It came to him as a most detestable fact, because it happened he was an intensely egotistical man. But his intellect was of that noble and exceptional sort that aversion may tint indeed but cannot blind, and we owe to him a series of philosophical writings, written with an instinctive skill and a clearness and a vigour uncommon in philosophers, in which a very complete statement of the new view is presented to the reader in terms of passionate protest. [Footnote: *Die Welt als Wille und Vorstellung.*] "Why," he asked, "must we be for ever tortured by this passion and desire to reproduce our kind, why are all our pursuits tainted with this application, all our needs deferred to the needs of the new generation that tramples on our heels?" and he found the answer in the presence of an overwhelming Will to Live manifesting itself throughout the universe of Matter, thrusting us ruthlessly before it, as a strong swimmer thrusts a wave before him as he swims. That the personal egotism should be subordinated to and overwhelmed by a pervading Will to Live filled his soul with passionate rebellion and coloured his exposition with the hues of despair. But to minds temperamentally different from his, minds whose egotism is qualified by a more unselfish humour, it is possible to avail one's self of Schopenhauer's vision, without submitting one's self to his conclusions, to see our wills only as temporary manifestations of an ampler will, our lives as passing phases of a greater Life, and to accept these facts even joyfully, to take our places in that larger scheme with a sense of relief and discovery, to go with that larger being, to serve that larger being, as a soldier marches, a mere unit in the larger being of his army, and serving his army, joyfully into battle.

However, it is not to Schopenhauer and his writings, at least among the English-speaking peoples, that this increasing realization of life as essentially a succession of births, is chiefly ascribed. It is mainly, as I have already suggested, the result of that great expansion of our sense of time and causation that has ensued from the idea of organic Evolution. In the course of one brief century, the human outlook upon the order of the world has been profoundly changed. It is not simply that it has become much more spacious, it is not only that it has opened out from the little history of a few thousand years to a stupendous vista of ages, but, in addition to its expanded dimensions, it has experienced a change in character. That wonderful and continually more elaborate and penetrating analysis of the evolutionary process by Darwin and his followers and successors and antagonists, the entire subordination of the individual lot to the specific destiny that these criticisms and researches have emphasized, has warped and altered the aspect of a thousand human affairs. It has made reasonable and in order what Schopenhauer found so suggestively perplexing, it has dispelled problems that have seemed insoluble mysteries to many generations of men. I do not say it has solved them, but it has dispelled them and made them irrelevant and uninteresting. So long as one believed that life span unprogressively from generation to generation, that generation followed generation unchangingly for ever, the enormous preponderance of sexual needs and emotions in life was a distressing and inexplicable fact—it was a mystery, it was sin, it was the work of the devil. One asked, why does man build houses that others may live therein; plant trees whose fruit he will never see? And all the toil and ambition, the stress and hope of existence, seemed, so far as this life went, and before these new lights came, a mere sacrifice to this pointless reiteration of lives, this cosmic *crambe repetita*. To perceive this aspect, and to profess an entire detachment from the whole vacuous business was considered by a large proportion of the more thoughtful people of the world the supreme achievement of philosophy. The acme of old-world wisdom, the ultimate mystery of Oriental philosophy is to contemn women and offspring, to abandon costume, cleanliness, and all the decencies and dignities of life, and to crawl, as scornfully as possible, but at any rate to crawl out of all these earthly shows and snares (which so obviously lead to nothing), into the nearest tub.

And the amazing revelation of our days is that they do not lead to nothing! Directly the discovery is made clear—and it is, I firmly believe, the crowning glory of the nineteenth century to have established this discovery for all time—that one generation does not follow another in *fac simile*, directly we come within sight of the reasonable persuasion that each generation is a step, a definite measurable step, and each birth an unprecedented experiment, directly it grows clear that instead of being in an eddy merely, we are for all our eddying moving forward upon a wide voluminous current, then all these things are changed.

That change alters the perspective of every human affair. Things that seemed permanent and final, become unsettled and provisional. Social and political effort are seen from a new view-point. Everywhere the old direction posts, the old guiding marks, have got out of line and askew. And it is out of the conflict of the new view with the old institutions and formulae, that there arises the discontent and the need, and the attempt at a wider answer, which this phrase and suggestion of the "New Republic" is intended to express.

Every part contributes to the nature of the whole, and if the whole of life is an evolving succession of births, then not only must a man in his individual capacity (*physically* as parent, doctor, food dealer, food carrier, home builder, protector, or *mentally* as teacher, news dealer, author, preacher) contribute to births and growths and the future of mankind, but the collective aspects of man, his social and political organizations must also be, in the essence, organizations that more or less profitably and more or less intentionally, set themselves towards this end. They are finally concerned with the birth and with the sound development towards still better births, of human lives, just as every implement in the toolshed of a seedsman's nursery, even the hoe and the roller, is concerned finally with the seeding and with the sound development towards still better seeding of plants. The private and personal motive of the seedsman in procuring and using these tools may be avarice, ambition, a religious belief in the saving efficacy of nursery keeping or a simple passion for bettering flowers, that does not affect the definite final purpose of his outfit of tools.

And just as we might judge completely and criticise and improve that outfit from an attentive study of the welfare of plants and with an entire disregard of his remoter motives, so we may judge all collective human enterprises from the standpoint of an attentive study of human births and development. *Any collective human enterprise, institution, movement, party or state, is to be judged as a whole and completely, as it conduces more or less to wholesome and hopeful births, and according to the qualitative and quantitative advance due to its influence made by each generation of citizens born under its influence towards a higher and ampler standard of life.*

Or putting the thing in a slightly different phrasing, the New Republican idea amounts to this: the serious aspect of our private lives, the general aspect of all our social and co-operative undertakings, is to prepare as well as we possibly can a succeeding generation, which shall prepare still more capably for still better generations to follow. We are passing as a race out of a state of affairs when the unconscious building of the future was attained by individualistic self-seeking (altogether unenlightened or enlightened only by the indirect moralizing influence of the patriotic instinct and religion) into a clear consciousness of our co-operative share in that process. That is the essential idea my New Republic would personify and embody. In the past man was made, generation after generation, by forces beyond his knowledge and control. Now a certain number of men are coming to a provisional understanding of some at least of these forces that go to the Making of Man. To some of us there is being given the privilege and responsibility of knowledge. We may plead lack of will or lack of moral impetus, but we can no longer plead ignorance. Just as far as our light upon the general purpose goes, just so far goes our responsibility (whether we respect it or not) to shape and subdue our wills to the Making of Mankind.

Directly the man, who has found akin to himself and who has accepted and assimilated this new view, turns to the affairs of the political world, to the general professions of our great social and business undertakings, and to the broad conventions of human conduct, he will find, I think, a very wide discrepancy from the implications of this view. He will find—the New Republican finds—that the declared aims and principles of the larger amount of our social and political effort are astonishingly limited and unsatisfactory, astonishingly irrelevant to the broad reality of Life. He will find great masses of men embarked collectively upon enterprises that will seem to his eyes to have no definable relation to this real business of the world, or only the most accidental relationship, he will find others in partial lop-sided co-operation or unintelligently half helpful and half obstructive, and he will find still other movements and developments which set quite in the opposite direction, which make neither for sound births nor sound growth, but through the thinnest shams of excuse and purpose, through the most hypnotic and unreal of suggestions and motives, directly and even plainly towards waste, towards sterility, towards futility and death and extinction.

But not deliberately towards Death. It is only in the theoretical aspirations of Schopenhauer that he will find an expression of conscious and resolved opposition to the pervading will and purpose in things. In the common affairs of the world he will find neither deliberate opposition nor deliberate co-operation, chance opposition indeed and chance co-operation, but for the most part only a complete unconsciousness, a blind irrelevance or a purely accidental accordance to the essential aspect of Life.

Take, for example, the great enthusiasm that set all England waving bunting in June, 1902. It was made clear to the most unwilling observer that the great mass of English people consider themselves aggregated together in one nation mainly to support, honour, and obey a King, and that they rejoice in this conception of their national purpose. Great sums of money were spent to emphasize this purpose, public work of all sorts was dislocated, and the channels of public discussion clogged and choked. A discussion of the education of the next generation, a matter of supreme interest from the New Republican point of view, passed from public sight amidst the happy tumults and splendours of the time. The land was filled with poetry in the Monarch's praise, bad beyond any suspicion of insincerity. All that was certainly great in the land, all that has any hold upon the motives and confidence of the English, gathered itself into a respectful proximity, assumed attitudes of reverent subordination to the Monarch. All that was eminent in science and literature and art, the galaxy of the episcopate, the crowning intellectualities of the army, came to these rites, clad in robes and raiment that no sane person would ever voluntarily assume in public except under circumstances of extreme necessity. The whole business was conducted with a zest and gravity that absolutely forbids the theory that it was a mere formality, a curious survival of mediævalism cherished by a country that makes no breaks with its past. The spirit and idea of the whole thing was intensely real and contemporary; one could believe only that those who took part in it regarded it as a matter of primary importance, as one of the cardinal things for which they existed. The alternative is to imagine that they believe nothing to be of primary importance in this world; a quite incredible levity of soul to ascribe to all those

H. G. Wells

great and distinguished people.

But it reflects not at all upon the high intelligence, the unobtrusive but sterling moral qualities, the tact, dignity, and personal charm of the central figure in their pageantries, a charm the pathetic circumstances of his unseasonable illness very greatly enhanced, if the New Republican fails to consider these ceremonials of primary importance, if he declines to see them as of any necessary importance at all, until it has been conclusively shown that they do minister to the bettering of births and of the lives intervening between birth and birth. On the surface they do not do that. Unless they can be shown to do that they are dissipations of energy, they are irrelevant and wrong, from the New Republican point of view. The New Republican can take no part in these things, or only a very grudging and qualified part, on his way to real service. He may or he may not, after deliberate examination, leave these things on one side, unchallenged but ignored.

It may be urged that all the subserviences that distinguish our kingdom and that become so amazingly conspicuous about a coronation, the kissing of hands, the shambling upon knees, the crawling of body and mind, the systematic encouragement of that undignified noisiness that nowadays distinguishes the popular rejoicings of our imperial people, are simply a proof of the earnest preoccupation of our judges, bishops, and leaders and great officers of all sorts with remoter and nobler aims. The kingdom happens to exist, and it would be complex and troublesome to get rid of it. They stand these things, they get done with these things, and so are able to get to their work. The paraphernalia of a Court, the sham scale of honours, the submissions, the ceremonial subjection, are, it is argued, entirely irrelevant to the purpose and honour of our race, but then so would rebellion against these things be also irrelevant and secondary. To submit or to rebel is a diversion of our energies from the real purpose in things, and of the two it is infinitely less bother to submit. In private conversation, I find, this is the line nine out of ten of the King's servants will take. They will tell you the public understands; the thing is a mere excuse for festivity and colour; their loyalty is of a piece with their Fifth of November anti-popery. They will tell you the peers understand, the bishops understand, the coronating archbishop has his tongue in his cheek. They all understand—men of the world together. The King understands, a most admirable gentleman, who submits to these traditional things, but who admits his preference is for the simple, pure delight of the incognito, for being "plain Mr. Jones."

It may be so. Though the psychologist will tell you that a man who behaves consistently as though he believed in a thing, will end in believing it. Assuredly whatever these others do, the New Republican must understand. In his inmost soul there must be no loyalty or submission to any king or colour, save only if it conduces to the service of the future of the race. In the New Republic all kings are provisional, if, indeed—and this I shall discuss in a later paper—they can be regarded as serviceable at all.

And just as kingship is a secondary and debatable thing to the New Republican, to every man, that is, whom the spirit of the new knowledge has taken for its work, so also are the loyalties of nationality, and all our local and party adhesions.

Much that passes for patriotism is no more than a generalized jealousy rather gorgeously clad. Amidst the collapse of the old Individualistic Humanitarianism, the Rights of Man, Human Equality, and the rest of those broad generalizations that served to keep together so many men of good intention in the age that has come to its end, there has been much hasty running to obvious shelters, and many men have been forced to take refuge under this echoing patriotism—for want of a better gathering place. It is like an incident during an earthquake, when men who have abandoned a cleft fortress will shelter in a drinking bothy. But the very upheavals that have shattered the old fastnesses of altruistic men, will be found presently to be taking the shape of a new gathering place—and of this the New Republic presents an early guess and anticipation. I do not see how men, save in the most unexpected emergency, can be content to accept such an artificial convention as modern patriotism for one moment. On the one hand there are the patriots of nationality who would have us believe that the miscellany of European squatters in the Transvaal are one nation and those in Cape Colony another, and on the other the patriots of Empire who would have me, for example, hail as my fellow-subjects and collaborators in man-making a host of Tamil-speaking, Tamil-thinking Dravadians, while separating me from every English-speaking, English-thinking person who lives south of the Great Lakes. So long as men are content to work in the grooves set for them by dead men, to derive all their significances from the past, to accept whatever is as right and to drive along before the compulsions of these acquiescences, they may do so. But directly they take to themselves the New Republican idea, directly they realize that life is something more than passing the time, that it is constructive with its direction in the future, then these things slip from them as Christian's burthen fell from him at the very outset of his journey. Until grave cause has been shown to the contrary, there is every reason why all men who speak the same language, think the same literature, and are akin in blood and spirit, and who have arrived at the great constructive conception that so many minds nowadays are reaching, should entirely disregard these old separations. If the old traditions do no harm there is no reason to touch them, any more than there is to abolish the boundary between this ancient and invincible kingdom of Kent in which I write and that extremely inferior country, England, which was conquered by the Normans and brought under the feudal system. But so soon as these old traditions obstruct sound action, so soon as it is necessary to be rid of them, we must be prepared to sacrifice our archaeological emotions ruthlessly and entirely.

And these repudiations extend also to the political parties that struggle to realize themselves within the forms of our established state. There is not in Great Britain, and I understand there is not in America, any party, any section, any group, any single politician even, based upon the manifest trend and purpose of life as it appears in the modern view. The necessities of continuity in public activity and of a glaring consistency in public profession, have so far prevented any such fundamental reconstruction as the new generation requires. One hears of Liberty, of Compromise, of Imperial Destinies and Imperial Unity, one hears of undying loyalty to the Memory of Mr. Gladstone and the inalienable right of Ireland to a separate national existence. One hears, too, of the sacred principle of Free Trade, of Empires and Zollvereins, and the Rights of the Parent to blockade the education of his children, but one hears nothing of the greater end. At the best all the objects of our political activity can be but means to that end, their only claim to our recognition can be their adequacy to that end, and none of these vociferated "cries," these party labels, these programme items, are ever propounded to us in that way. I cannot see how, in England at any rate, a serious and perfectly honest man, holding as true that ampler view of life I have suggested, can attach himself loyally to any existing party or faction. At the utmost he may find their faction-fighting may be turned for a time towards his remoter ends. These parties derive from that past when the new view of life had yet to establish itself, they carry faded and obliterated banners that the glare and dust of conflict, the vote-storms of great campaigns, have robbed long since of any colour of reality they once possessed. They express no creative purpose now, whatever they did in their inception, they point towards no constructive ideals. Essentially they are things for the museum or the bonfire, whatever momentary expediency may hold back the New Republican from an unqualified advocacy of such a destination. The old party fabrics are no more than dead rotting things, upon which a great tangle of personal jealousies, old grudges, thorny nicknames, prickly memories, family curses, Judas betrayals and sacred pledges, a horrible rubbish thicket, maintains a saprophytic vitality.

It is quite possible I misjudge the thing altogether. Sir Henry Campbell-Bannerman, for example, may hide the profoundest and most wide-reaching aims beneath his superficial effect of utter superficiality. His impersonation of an amiable, spirited, self-conscious, land-owning gentleman with a passion for justice in remote places and a whimsical dislike of motor cars in his immediate neighbourhood, may veil the operations of a stupendous intelligence bent upon the regeneration of the world. It may do, but if it does, it is a very amazing and purposeless impersonation. I at any rate do not believe that it does. I do not believe that he or any other Liberal leader or any Conservative minister has any comprehensive aim at all—as we of the new generation measure comprehensiveness. These parties, and the phrases of party exposition—in America just as in England—date from the days of the limited outlook. They display no consciousness of the new dissent. They are absorbed in the long standing game, the getting in, the turning out, the contests and governments, that has just about the same relation to the new perception of affairs, to the real drift of life, as the game of cricket with the wheel as a wicket would have to the destinies of a ship. They find their game highly interesting and no doubt they play it with remarkable wit, skill and spirit, but they entirely disregard the increasing number of passengers who are concerning themselves with the course and destination of the ship.

Those particular passengers in the figure, present the New Republic. It is a dissension, an inquiry, it is the vague unconsolidated matter for a new direction. "We who are young," says the spirit of the New Republic, "we who are in earnest can no more compass our lives under these old kingships and loyalties, under these old leaders and these old traditions, constitutions and pledges, with their party liabilities, their national superstitions, their rotting banners and their accumulating legacy of feuds and lies, than we can pretend we are indeed impassioned and wholly devoted subjects of King Edward, spending our lives in the service of his will. It is not that we have revolted from these things, it is not that we have grown askew to them and that patching and amendment will serve our need; it is that we have travelled outside them altogether—almost inadvertently, but quite beyond any chance of return to a simple acceptance again. We are no more disposed to call ourselves Liberals or Conservatives and to be stirred to party passion at the clash of these names, than we are to fight again the battles of the Factio Albata or the Factio Prasina. These current dramas, these current conflicts seem scarcely less factitious. Men without faith may be content to spend their lives for things only half believed in, and for causes that are contrived. But that is not our quality. We want reality because we have faith, we seek the beginning of realism in social and political life, we seek it and we are resolved to find it."

So we attempt to give a general expression to the forces that are new at this time, to render something at least of the spirit of the New Republic in a premature and experimental utterance. It is, at any rate, a spirit that finds itself out of intimacy and co-ordination with all the older movements of the world, that sees all pre-existing formulae and political constitutions and political parties and organizations rather as instruments or obstacles than as guiding lines and precedents for its new developing will, its will which will carry it at last irresistibly to the conscious and deliberate making of the future of man. "We are here to get better births and a better result from the births we get; each one of us is going to set himself immediately to that, using whatever power he finds to his hand," such is the form its will must take. And such being its will and spirit these papers will address themselves comprehensively to the problem, What will the New Republic do? All the rest of this series will be a discussion of the forces that go to the making of man, and how far and how such a New Republic might seek to lay its hands upon them.

It is for the adversary to explain how presumptuous such an enterprise must be. But presumption is ineradically interwoven with every beginning that the world has ever seen. I venture to think that even to a reader who does not accept or sympathize with the conception of this New Republic, a general review of current movements and current interpretations of morality from this new standpoint may be suggestive and interesting. Assuredly it is only by some such general revision, if not on these lines then on others, that a practicable way of escape is to be found for any one, from that base and shifty opportunism in public and social matters, that predominance of fluctuating

H. G. Wells

aims and spiritless conformities, in which so many of us, without any great positive happiness at all to reward us for the sacrifice we are making, bury the solitary talents of our lives.

II

THE PROBLEM OF THE BIRTH SUPPLY

Within the last minute seven new citizens were born into that great English-speaking community which is scattered under various flags and governments throughout the world. And according to the line of thought developed in the previous paper we perceive that the real and ultimate business, so far as this world goes, of every statesman, every social organizer, every philanthropist, every business manager, every man who lifts his head for a moment from the mean pursuit of his immediate personal interests, from the gratification of his private desires, is, as the first and immediate thing, to do his best for these new-comers, to get the very best result, so far as his powers and activities can contribute to it, from their undeveloped possibilities. And in the next place, as a remoter, but perhaps finally more fundamental duty, he has to inquire what may be done individually or collectively to raise the standard and quality of the average birth. All the great concerns of life work out with a very little analysis to that, even our wars, our orgies of destruction, have, at the back of them, a claim, an intention, however futile in its conception and disastrous in its consequences, to establish a wider security, to destroy a standing menace, to open new paths and possibilities, in the interest of the generations still to come. One may present the whole matter in a simplified picture by imagining all our statesmen, our philanthropists and public men, our parties and institutions gathered into one great hall, and into this hall a huge spout, that no man can stop, discharges a baby

H. G. Wells

every eight seconds. That is, I hold, a permissible picture of human life, and whatever is not represented at all in that picture is a divergent and secondary concern. Our success or failure with that unending stream of babies is the measure of our civilization; every institution stands or falls by its contribution to that result, by the improvement of the children born, or by the improvement in the quality of births attained under its influence.

To begin these speculations in logical order we must begin at the birth point, we must begin by asking how much may we hope, now or at a later time, to improve the supply of that raw material which is perpetually dumped upon our hands? Can we raise, and if so, what can we do to raise the quality of the average birth?

This speculation is as old at least as Plato, and as living as the seven or eight babies born into the English-speaking world since the reader began this Paper. The conclusion that if we could prevent or discourage the inferior sorts of people from having children, and if we could stimulate and encourage the superior sorts to increase and multiply, we should raise the general standard of the race, is so simple, so obvious, that in every age I suppose there have been voices asking in amazement, why the thing is not done? It is so usual to answer that it is not done on account of popular ignorance, public stupidity, religious prejudice or superstition, that I shall not apologize for giving some little space here to the suggestion that in reality it is not done for quite a different reason.

We blame the popular mind overmuch. Earnest but imperfect men, with honest and reasonable but imperfect proposals for bettering the world, are all too apt to raise this bitter cry of popular stupidity, of the sheep-like quality of common men. An unjustifiable persuasion of moral and intellectual superiority is one of the last infirmities of innovating minds. We may be right, but we must be provably, demonstrably and overpoweringly right before we are justified in calling the dissentient a fool. I am one of those who believe firmly in the invincible nature of truth, but a truth that is badly put is not a truth, but an infertile hybrid lie. Before we men of the study blame the general body of people for remaining unaffected by reforming proposals of an almost obvious advantage, it would be well if we were to change our standpoint and examine our machinery at the point of application. A rock-drilling machine may be excellently invented and in the most perfect order except for a want of hardness in the drill, and yet there will remain an unpierced rock as obdurate as the general public to so many of our innovations.

I believe that if a canvass of the entire civilized world were put to the vote in this matter, the proposition that it is desirable that the better sort of people should intermarry and have plentiful children, and that the inferior sort of people should abstain from multiplication, would be carried by an overwhelming majority. They might disagree with Plato's methods, [Footnote: *The Republic*, Bk. V.] but they would certainly agree to his principle. And that this is not a popular error Mr. Francis Galton has shown. He has devoted a very large amount of energy and capacity to the vivid and convincing presentation of this idea, and to its courageous propagation. His Huxley Lecture to the Anthropological Institute in 1901 [Footnote: *Nature*, vol. lxiv. p. 659.] puts the whole matter as vividly as it ever can be put. He classifies humanity about their average in classes which he indicates by the letters R S T U V rising above the average and r s t u v falling below, and he saturates the whole business in quantitative colour. Indeed, Mr. Galton has drawn up certain definite proposals. He has suggested that "noble families" should collect "fine specimens of humanity" around them, employing these fine specimens in menial occupations of a light and comfortable sort, that will leave a sufficient portion of their energies free for the multiplication of their superior type. "Promising young couples" might be given "healthy and convenient houses at low rentals," he suggests, and no doubt it could be contrived that they should pay their rent partly or entirely per stone of family annually produced. And he has also proposed that "diplomas" should be granted to young men and women of high class—big S and upward—and that they should be encouraged to intermarry young. A scheme of "dowries" for diploma holders would obviously be the simplest thing in the world. And only the rules for identifying your great S T U and V in adolescence, are wanting from the symmetrical completeness of his really very noble-spirited and high-class scheme.

At a more popular level Mrs. Victoria Woodhull Martin has battled bravely in the cause of the same foregone conclusion. The work of telling the world what it knows to be true will never want self-sacrificing workers. The *Humanitarian* was her monthly organ of propaganda. Within its cover, which presented a luminiferous stark ideal of exemplary muscularity, popular preachers, popular bishops, and popular anthropologists vied with titled ladies of liberal outlook in the service of this conception. There was much therein about the Rapid Multiplication of the Unfit, a phrase never properly explained, and I must confess that the transitory presence of this instructive little magazine in my house, month after month (it is now, unhappily, dead), did much to direct my attention to the gaps and difficulties that intervene between the general proposition and its practical application by sober and honest men. One took it up and asked time after time, "Why should there be this queer flavour of absurdity and pretentiousness about the thing?" Before the *Humanitarian* period I was entirely in agreement with the *Humanitarian's* cause. It seemed to me then that to prevent the multiplication of people below a certain standard, and to encourage the multiplication of exceptionally superior people, was the only real and permanent way of mending the ills of the world. I think that still. In that way man has risen from the beasts, and in that way men will rise to be over-men. In those days I asked in amazement why this thing was not done, and talked the usual nonsense about the obduracy and stupidity of the world. It is only after a considerable amount of thought and inquiry that I am beginning to understand why for many generations, perhaps, nothing of the sort can possibly be done except in the most marginal and tentative manner.

If to-morrow the whole world were to sign an unanimous round-robin to Mr. Francis Galton and Mrs. Victoria Woodhull Martin, admitting absolutely their leading argument that it *is* absurd to breed our horses and sheep and improve the stock of our pigs and fowls, while we leave humanity to mate in the most heedless manner, and if, further, the whole world, promising obedience, were to ask these two to gather together a consultative committee, draw up a scheme of rules, and start forthwith upon the great work of improving the human stock as fast as it can be done, if it undertook that marriages should no longer be made in heaven or earth, but only under licence from that committee, I venture to think that, after a very brief epoch of fluctuating legislation, this committee, except for an extremely short list of absolute prohibitions, would decide to leave matters almost exactly as they are now; it would restore love and private preference to their ancient authority and freedom, at the utmost it would offer some greatly qualified advice, and so released, it would turn its attention to those flaws and gaps in our knowledge that at present render these regulations no more than a theory and a dream.

The first difficulty these theorists ignore is this: we are, as a matter of fact, not a bit clear what points to breed for and what points to breed out.

The analogy with the breeder of cattle is a very misleading one. He has a very simple ideal, to which he directs the entire pairing of his stock. He breeds for beef, he breeds for calves and milk, he breeds for a homogeneous docile herd. Towards that ideal he goes simply and directly, slaughtering and sparing, regardless entirely of any divergent variation that may arise beneath his control. A young calf with an incipient sense of humour, with a bright and inquiring disposition, with a gift for athleticism or a quaintly-marked hide, has no sort of chance with him at all on that account. He can throw these proffered gifts of nature aside without hesitation. Which is just what our theoretical breeders of humanity cannot venture to do. They do not want a homogeneous race in the future at all. They want a rich interplay of free, strong, and varied personalities, and that alters the nature of the problem absolutely.

This the reader may dispute. He may admit the need of variety, but he may argue that this variety must arise from a basis of common endowment. He may say that in spite of the complication introduced by the consideration that a divergent variation from one ideal may be a divergence towards another ideal, there remain certain definable points, that could be bred for universally, for all that.

What are they?

There will be little doubt he will answer "Health." After that probably he may say "Beauty." In addition the reader of Mr. Galton's *Hereditary Genius* will probably say, "ability," "capacity," "genius," and "energy." The reader of Doctor Nordau will add "sanity." And the reader of Mr. Archdall Reid will round up the list with "immunity" from dipsomania and all contagious diseases. "Let us mark our human beings," the reader of that way of thinking will suggest, "let us give marks for 'health,' for 'ability,' for various sorts of specific immunity and so forth, and let us weed out those who are low in the scale and multiply those who stand high. This will give us a straight way to practical amelioration, and the difficulty you are trying to raise," he urges, "vanishes forthwith."

It would, if these points were really points, if "beauty," "capacity," "health," and "sanity" were simple and uniform things. Unfortunately they are not simple, and with that fact a host of difficulties arise. Let me take first the most simple and obvious case of "beauty." If beauty were a simple thing, it would be possible to arrange human beings in a simple scale, according to whether they had more or less of this simple quality—just as one can do in the case of what are perhaps really simple and breedable qualities—height or weight. This person, one might say, is at eight in the scale of beauty, and this at ten, and this at twenty-seven. But it complicates the case beyond the possibilities of such a scale altogether when one begins to consider that there are varieties and types of beauty having very wide divergences and made up of a varying number of elements in dissimilar proportions. There is, for example, the flaxen, kindly beauty of the Dutch type, the dusky Jewess, the tall, fair Scandinavian, the dark and brilliant south Italian, the noble Roman, the dainty Japanese—to name no others. Each of these types has its peculiar and incommensurable points, and within the limits of each type you will find a hundred divergent, almost unanalyzable, styles, a beauty of expression, a beauty of carriage, a beauty of reflection, a beauty of repose, arising each from a quite peculiar proportion of parts and qualities, and having no definable relation at all to any of the others. If we were to imagine a human appearance as made up of certain elements, a, b, c, d, e, f, etc., then we might suppose that beauty in one case was attained by a certain high development of a and f, in another by a certain fineness of c and d, in another by a delightfully subtle ratio of f and b.

$$A, b, c, d, e, F, \text{etc.}$$
$$a, b, c, d, e, f, \text{etc.}$$
$$a, b, c, d, e, F, \text{etc.,}$$

might all, for example, represent different types of beauty. Beauty is neither a simple nor a constant thing; it is attainable through a variety of combinations, just as the number 500 can be got by adding or multiplying together a great variety of numerical arrangements. Two long numerical formulae might both simplify out to 500, but half the length of one truncated and put end on to the truncated end of the other, might give a very different result. It is quite conceivable that you might select and wed together all the most beautiful people in the world and find that in nine cases out of ten you had simply produced mediocre offspring or offspring below mediocrity. Out of the remaining tenth a great majority would be beautiful simply by "taking after" one or other parent, simply through the predominance, the *prepotency,* of one parent over the other, a thing that might have happened equally well if the other parent was plain. The first sort of beauty (in my three formulae) wedding the third sort of beauty, might simply result in a rather ugly excess of F, and again the first sort might result from a combination of

$$a, b, c, d, e, F, \text{etc.,}$$
$$\text{and}$$
$$A, b, c, d, e, f, \text{etc.,}$$

neither of which arrangements, very conceivably, may be beautiful at all when it is taken alone. In this respect, at any rate, personal value and reproductive value may be two entirely different things.

Now what the elements of personal aspect really are, what these elements a, b, c, d, e, f, etc., may be, we do not know with any sort of exactness. Possibly height, weight, presence of dark pigment in the hair, whiteness of skin, presence of hair upon the body, are simple elements in inheritance that will follow Galton's arithmetical treatment of heredity with some exactness. But we are not even sure of that. The height of one particular person may be due to an exceptional length of leg and neck, of another to an abnormal length of the vertebral bodies of the backbone; the former may have a rather less than ordinary backbone, the latter a stunted type of limb, and an intermarriage may just as conceivably (so far as our present knowledge goes) give the backbone of the first and the legs of the second as it may a very tall person.

The fact is that in this matter of beauty and breeding for beauty we are groping in a corner where science has not been established. No doubt the corner is marked out as a part of the "sphere of influence" of anthropology, but there is not the slightest indication of an effective occupation among these raiding considerations and uncertain facts. Until anthropology produces her Daltons and Davys we must fumble in this corner, just as the old alchemists fumbled for centuries before the dawn of chemistry. Our utmost practice here must be empirical. We do not know the elements of what we have, the human characteristics we are working upon to get that end.

The sentimentalized affinities of young persons in their spring are just as likely to result in the improvement of the race in this respect as the whole science of anthropology in its present state of evolution.

I have suggested that "beauty" is a term applied to a miscellany of synthetic results compounded of diverse elements in diverse proportions; and I have suggested that one can no more generalize about it in relation to inheritance with any hope of effective application than one can generalize about, say, "lumpy substances" in relation to chemical combination. By reasoning upon quite parallel lines nearly every characteristic with which Mr. Galton deals in his interesting and suggestive but quite inconclusive works, can be demonstrated to consist in a similar miscellany. He speaks of "eminence," of "success," of "ability," of "zeal," and "energy," for example, and except for the last two items I would submit that these qualities, though of enormous personal value, are of no practical value in inheritance whatever; that to wed "ability" to "ability" may breed something less than mediocrity, and that "ability" is just as likely or just as unlikely to be prepotent and to assert itself in descent with the most casually selected partner as it is with one picked with all the knowledge, or rather pseudo-knowledge, anthropology in its present state can give us.

When, however, we turn to "zeal" or "energy" or "go," we do seem to be dealing with a simpler and more transmissible thing. Let us assume that in this matter there is a wide range of difference that may be arranged in a direct and simple scale in quantitative relation to the gross output of action of different human beings. One passes from the incessant employment of such a being as Gladstone at the one extreme, a loquacious torrent of interests and achievements, to the extreme of phlegmatic lethargy on the other. Call the former a high energetic and the latter low. Quite possibly it might be found that we could breed "high energetics." But before we did so we should have to consider very gravely that the "go" and "energy" of a man have no ascertainable relation to many other extremely important considerations. Your energetic person

H. G. Wells

may be moral or immoral, an unqualified egotist or as public spirited as an ant, sane, or a raving lunatic. Your phlegmatic person may ripen resolves and bring out truths, with the incomparable clearness of a long-exposed, slowly developed, slowly printed photograph. A man who would exchange the slow gigantic toil of that sluggish and deliberate person, Charles Darwin, for the tumultuous inconsequence and (as some people think it) the net mischief of a Gladstone, would no doubt be prepared to substitute a Catherine-wheel in active eruption for the watch of less adventurous men. But before we could induce the community as a whole to make a similar exchange, he would have to carry on a prolonged and vigorous propaganda.

For my own part—and I write as an ignorant man in a realm where ignorance prevails—I am inclined to doubt the simplicity and homogeneity even of this quality of "energy" or "go." A person without restraint, without intellectual conscience, without critical faculty, may write and jabber and go to and fro and be here and there, simply because every impulse is obeyed so soon as it arises. Another person may be built upon an altogether larger scale of energy, but may be deliberate, concentrated, and fastidious, bent rather upon truth and permanence than upon any immediate quantitative result, and may appear to any one but an extremely penetrating critic, as inferior in energy to the former. So far as our knowledge goes at present, what is popularly known as "energy" or "go" is just as likely to be a certain net preponderance of a varied miscellany of impulsive qualities over a varied miscellany of restraints and inhibitions, as it is to prove a simple indivisible quality transmissible intact. We are so profoundly ignorant in these matters, so far from anything worthy of the name of science, that one view is just as permissible and just as untrustworthy as the other.

Even the qualification of "health" is not sufficient. A thoughtless person may say with the most invincible air, "Parents should, at any rate, be healthy," but that alone is only a misleading vague formula for good intentions. In the first place, there is every reason to believe that transitory ill-health in the parent is of no consequence at all to the offspring. Neither does acquired constitutional ill-health necessarily transmit to a child; it may or it may not react upon the child's nutrition and training, but that is a question to consider later. It is quite conceivable, it is highly probable, that there are hereditary forms of ill-health, and that they may be eliminated from the human lot by discreet and restrained pairing, but what they are and what are the specific conditions of their control we do not know. And furthermore, we are scarcely more certain that the condition of "perfect health" in one human being is the same as the similarly named condition in another, than we are that the beauty of one type is made up of the same essential elements as the beauty of another. Health is a balance, a balance of blood against nerve, of digestion against secretion, of heart against brain. A heart of perfect health and vigour put into the body of a perfectly healthy man who is built upon a slighter scale than that heart, will swiftly disorganize the entire fabric, and burst its way to a haemorrhage in lung perhaps, or brain, or wherever the slightest relative weakening permits. The "perfect" health of a negro may be a quite dissimilar system of reactions to the "perfect health" of a vigorous white; you may blend them only to create an ailing mass of physiological discords. "Health," just as much as these other things, is, for this purpose of marriage diplomas and the like, a vague, unserviceable synthetic quality. It serves each one of us for our private and conversational needs, but in this question it is not hard enough and sharp—enough for the thing we want it to do. Brought to the service of this fine and complicated issue it breaks down altogether. We do not know enough. We have not analyzed enough nor penetrated enough. There is no science yet, worthy of the name, in any of these things. [Footnote: This idea of attempting to define the elements in inheritance, although it is absent from much contemporary discussion, was pretty evidently in mind in the very striking researches of the Abbé Mendel to which Mr. Bateson—with a certain intemperance of manner—has recently called attention. (Bateson, *Mendel's Principles of Heredity*, Cambridge University Press, 1902.)]

H. G. Wells

These considerations should at least suffice to demonstrate the entire impracticability of Mr. Galton's two suggestions. Moreover, this idea of picking out high-scale individuals in any particular quality or group of qualities and breeding them, is not the way of nature at all. Nature is not a breeder; she is a reckless coupler and—she slays. It was a popular misconception of the theory of the Survival of the Fittest, a misconception Lord Salisbury was at great pains to display to the British Association in 1894, that the average of a species in any respect is raised by the selective inter-breeding of the individuals above the average. Lord Salisbury was no doubt misled, as most people who share his mistake have been misled, by the grammatical error of employing the Survival of the Fittest for the Survival of the Fitter, in order to escape a scarcely ambiguous ambiguity. But the use of the word "Survival" should have sufficed to indicate that the real point of application of the force by which Nature modifies species and raises the average in any quality, lies not in selective breeding, but in the disproportionately numerous deaths of the individuals below the average. And even the methods of the breeder of cattle, if they are to produce a permanent alteration in the species of cattle, must consist not only in breeding the desirable but in either killing the undesirable, or at least—what is the quintessence, the inner reality of death—in preventing them from breeding.

The general trend of thought in Mrs. Martin's *Humanitarian* was certainly more in accordance with this reading of biological science than were Mr. Galton's proposals. There was a much greater insistence upon the need of "elimination," upon the evil of the "Rapid Multiplication of the Unfit," a word that, however, was never defined and, I believe, really did not mean anything in particular in this connection. And directly one does attempt to define it, directly one sits down in a businesslike way to apply the method of elimination instead of the method of selection, one is immediately confronted by almost as complex an entanglement of difficulties in defining points to breed out as one is by defining points to breed for. Almost, I say, but not quite. For here there does seem to be, if not certainties, at least a few plausible probabilities that a vigorous and systematic criticism may perhaps hammer into generalizations of sufficient certainty to go upon.

I believe that long before humanity has hammered out the question of what is pre-eminently desirable in inheritance, a certain number of things will have been isolated and defined as pre-eminently undesirable. But before these are considered, let us sweep out of our present regard a number of cruel and mischievous ideas that are altogether too ascendant at the present time.

Anthropology has been compared to a great region, marked out indeed as within the sphere of influence of science, but unsettled and for the most part unsubdued. Like all such hinterland sciences, it is a happy hunting-ground for adventurers. Just as in the early days of British Somaliland, rascals would descend from nowhere in particular upon unfortunate villages, levy taxes and administer atrocity in the name of the Empire, and even, I am told, outface for a time the modest heralds of the government, so in this department of anthropology the public mind suffers from the imposition of theories and assertions claiming to be "scientific," which have no more relation to that organized system of criticism which is science, than a brigand at large on a mountain has to the machinery of law and police, by which finally he will be hanged. Among such raiding theorists none at present are in quite such urgent need of polemical suppression as those who would persuade the heedless general reader that every social failure is necessarily a "degenerate," and who claim boldly that they can trace a distinctly evil and mischievous strain in that unfortunate miscellany which constitutes "the criminal class." They invoke the name of "science" with just as much confidence and just as much claim as the early Victorian phrenologists. They speak and write with ineffable profundity about the "criminal" ear, the "criminal" thumb, the "criminal" glance. They gain access to gaols and pester unfortunate prisoners with callipers and cameras, and quite unforgivable prying into personal and private matters, and they hold out

H. G. Wells

great hopes that by these expedients they will evolve at last a "scientific" revival of the Kaffir's witch-smelling. We shall catch our criminals by anthropometry ere ever a criminal thought has entered their brains. "Prevention is better than cure." These mattoid scientists make a direct and disastrous attack upon the latent self-respect of criminals. And not only upon that tender plant, but also upon the springs of human charity towards the criminal class. For the complex and varied chapter of accidents that carries men into that net of precautions, expedients, prohibitions, and vindictive reprisals, the net of the law, they would have us believe there is a fatal necessity inherent in their being. Criminals are born, not made, they allege. No longer are we to say, "There, but for the grace of God, go I"—when the convict tramps past us—but, "There goes another sort of animal that is differentiating from my species and which I would gladly see exterminated."

Now every man who has searched his heart knows that this formulation of "criminality" as a specific quality is a stupidity, he knows himself to be a criminal, just as most men know themselves to be sexually rogues. No man is born with an instinctive respect for the rights of any property but his own, and few with a passion for monogamy. No man who is not an outrageously vain and foolish creature but will confess to himself that but for advantages and accidents, but for a chance hesitation or a lucky timidity, he, too, had been there, under the ridiculous callipers of witless anthropology. A criminal is no doubt of less personal value to the community than a law-abiding citizen of the same general calibre, but *it does not follow for one moment that he is of less value as a parent.* His personal disaster may be due to the possession of a bold and enterprising character, of a degree of pride and energy above the needs of the position his social surroundings have forced upon him. Another citizen may have all this man's desires and impulses, checked and sterilized by a lack of nervous energy, by an abject fear of the policeman and of the consequences of the disapproval of his more prosperous fellow-citizens. I will frankly confess that for my own part I prefer the wicked to the mean, and that I would rather trust the future to the former strain than to the latter. Whatever preference the reader may entertain, there remains this unmistakable objection to its application to breeding, that "criminality" is not a specific simple quality, but a complex that may interfuse with other complexes to give quite incalculable results in the offspring it produces. So that here again, on the negative side, we find a general expression unserviceable for our use. [Footnote: No doubt the home of the criminal and social failure is generally disastrous to the children born into it. That is a question that will be fully dealt; with in a subsequent paper, and I note it here only to point out that it is outside our present discussion, which is concerned not with the fate of children born into the world, but with the prior question whether we may hope to improve the quality of the average birth by encouraging some sorts of people to have children and discouraging or forbidding others. It is of vital importance to keep these two questions distinct, if we are to get at last to a basis for effective action.]

But it will be alleged that although criminality as a whole means nothing definite enough for our purpose, there can be picked out and defined certain criminal (or at any rate disastrous) tendencies that are simple, specific and transmissible. Those who have read Mr. Archdall Reid's *Alcoholism*, for example, will know that he deals constantly with what is called the "drink craving" as if it were such a specific simple inheritance. He makes a very strong case for this belief, but strong as it is, I do not think it is going to stand the pressure of a rigorously critical examination. He points out that races which have been in possession of alcoholic drinks the longest are the least drunken, and this he ascribes to the "elimination" of all those whose "drink craving" is too strong for them. Nations unused to alcoholic drink are most terribly ravaged at its first coming to them, may even be destroyed by it, in precisely the same way that new diseases coming to peoples unused to them are far more malignant than among peoples who have suffered from them generation after generation. Such instances as the terrible ravages of measles in Polynesia and the ruin worked by fire-water among the Red Indians, he gives in great abundance. He infers from this that interference with the sale of drink to a people may in the long run do more harm than good, by preserving those who would otherwise be eliminated, permitting them to multiply and so, generation by generation, lowering the resisting power of the race. And he proposes to divert temperance legislation from the persecution of drink makers and sellers, to such remedies as the punishment of declared and indisputable drunkards if they incur parentage, and the extension of the grounds of divorce to include this ugly and disastrous habit.

I am not averse to Mr. Reid's remedies because I think of the wife and the home, but I would not go so far with him as to consider this "drink craving" specific and simple, and I retain an open mind about the sale of drink. He has not convinced me that there is an inherited "drink craving" any more than there is an inherited tea craving or an inherited morphia craving.

In the first place I would propound a certain view of the general question of habits. My own private observations in psychology incline me to believe that people vary very much in their power of acquiring habits and in the strength and fixity of the habits they acquire. My most immediate subject of psychological study, for example, is a man of untrustworthy memory who is nearly incapable of a really deep-rooted habit. Nothing is automatic with him. He crams and forgets languages with an equal ease, gives up smoking after fifteen years of constant practice; shaves with a conscious effort every morning and is capable of forgetting to do so if intent upon anything else. He is generally self-indulgent, capable of keen enjoyment and quite capable of intemperance, but he has no invariable delights and no besetting sin. Such a man will not become an habitual drunkard; he will not become anything "habitual." But with another type of man habit is indeed second nature. Instead of the permanent fluidity of my particular case, such people are continually tending to solidify and harden. Their memories set, their opinions set, their methods of expression set, their delights recur and recur, they convert initiative into mechanical habit day by day. Let them taste any pleasure and each time they taste it they deepen a need. At last their habits become imperative needs. With such a disposition, external circumstances and suggestions, I venture to believe, may make a man either into an habitual church-goer or an habitual drunkard, an habitual toiler or an habitual rake. A self-indulgent rather unsocial habit-forming man may very easily become what is called a dipsomaniac, no doubt, but that is not the same thing as an inherited specific craving. With drink inaccessible and other vices offering his lapse may take another line. An aggressive, proud and greatly mortified man may fall upon the same courses. An unwary youth of the plastic type may be taken unawares and pass from free indulgence to excess before he perceives that a habit is taking hold of him.

I believe that many causes and many temperaments go to the making of drunkards. I have read a story by the late Sir Walter Besant, in which he presents the specific craving as if it were a specific magic curse. The story was supposed to be morally edifying, but I can imagine this ugly superstition of the "hereditary craving"—it is really nothing more—acting with absolutely paralyzing effect upon some credulous youngster struggling in the grip of a developing habit. "It's no good trying,"—that quite infernal phrase!

It may be urged that this attempt to whittle down the "inherited craving" to a habit does not meet Mr. Reid's argument from the gradual increase of resisting power in races subjected to alcoholic temptation, an increase due to the elimination of all the more susceptible individuals. There can be no denying that those nations that have had fermented drinks longest are the soberest, but that, after all, may be only one aspect of much more extensive operations. The nations that have had fermented drinks the longest are also those that have been civilized the longest. The passage of a people from a condition of agricultural dispersal to a more organized civilization means a very extreme change in the conditions of survival, of which the increasing intensity of temptation to alcoholic excess is only one aspect. Gluttony, for example, becomes a much more possible habit, and many other vices tender death for the first time to the men who are gathering in and about towns. The city demands more persistent, more intellectualized and less intense physical desires than the countryside. Moral qualities that were a disadvantage in the dispersed stage become advantageous in the city, and conversely. Rugged independence ceases to be helpful, and an intelligent turn for give and take, for collaboration and bargaining, makes increasingly for survival. Moreover, there grows very slowly an indefinable fabric of traditional home training in restraint that is very hard to separate in analysis from mental heredity. People who have dwelt for many generations in towns are not only more temperate and less explosive in the grosser indulgences, but more *urbane* altogether. The drunken people are also the "uncivil" peoples and the individualistic peoples. The great prevalence of drunkenness among the upper classes two centuries ago can hardly have been bred out in the intervening six or seven generations, and it is also a difficult fact for Mr. Reid that drunkenness has increased in France. In most of the cases cited by Mr. Reid a complex of operating forces could be stated in which the appearance of fermented liquors is only one factor, and a tangle of consequent changes in which a gradually increasing insensibility to the charms of intoxication was only one thread. Drunkenness has no doubt played a large part in eliminating certain types of people from the world, but that it specifically eliminates one specific definable type is an altogether different matter.

Even if we admit Mr. Reid's conception, this by no means solves the problem. It is quite conceivable that the world could purchase certain sorts of immunity too dearly. If it was a common thing to adorn the parapets of houses in towns with piles of loose bricks, it is certain that a large number of persons not immune to fracture of the skull by falling bricks would be eliminated. A time would no doubt come when those with a specific liability to skull fracture would all be eliminated, and the human cranium would have developed a practical immunity to damage from all sorts of falling substances. But there would have been far more extensive suppressions than would appear in the letter of the agreement.

This no doubt is a caricature of the case, but it will serve to illustrate my contention that until we possess a far more subtle and thorough analysis of the drunkard's physique and mind— if it really is a distinctive type of mind and physique—than we have at present, we have no justification whatever in artificial intervention to increase whatever eliminatory process may at present be going on in this respect. Even if there is such a specific weakness, it is possible it has a period of maximum intensity, and if that should be only a brief phase in development—let us say at adolescence—it might turn out to be much more to the advantage of humanity to contrive protective legislation over the dangerous years. I argue to establish no view in these matters beyond a view that at present we know very little.

Not only do ignorance and doubt bar our way to anything more than a pious wish to eliminate criminality and drunkenness in a systematic manner, but even the popular belief in ruthless suppression whenever there is "madness in the family" will not stand an intelligent scrutiny. The man in the street thinks madness is a fixed and definite thing, as distinct from sanity as black is from white. He is always exasperated at the hesitation of doctors when in a judicial capacity he demands: "Is this man mad or isn't he?" But a very little reading of alienists will dissolve this clear assurance. Here again it seems possible that we have a number of states that we are led to believe are simple because they are gathered together under the generic word "madness," but which may represent a considerable variety of induced and curable and non-inheritable states on the one hand and of innate and incurable and heritable mental disproportions on the other.

The less gifted portion of the educated public was greatly delighted some years ago by a work by Dr. Nordau called *Degeneration*, in which a great number of abnormal people were studied in a pseudo-scientific manner and shown to be abnormal beyond any possibility of dispute. Mostly the samples selected were men of exceptional artistic and literary power. The book was pretentious and inconsistent—the late Lord Tennyson was quoted, I remember, as a typically "sane" poet in spite of the scope afforded by his melodramatic personal appearance and his morbid passion for seclusion—but it did at least serve to show that if we cannot call a man stupid we may almost invariably call him mad with some show of reason. The public read the book for the sake of its abuse, applied the intended conclusion to every success that awakened its envy, and failed altogether to see how absolutely the definition of madness was destroyed. But if madness is indeed simply genius out of hand and genius only madness under adequate control; if imagination is a snare only to the unreasonable and a disordered mind only an excess of intellectual enterprise—and really none of these things can be positively disproved—then just as reasonable as the idea of suppressing the reproduction of madness, is the idea of breeding it! Let us take all these dull, stagnant, respectable people, one might say, who do nothing but conform to whatever rule is established about them and obstruct whatever change is proposed to them, whose chief quality is a sheer incapacity to imagine anything beyond their petty experiences, and let us tell them plainly, "It is time a lunatic married into your family." Let no one run away from this with the statement that I propose such a thing should be done, but it is, at any rate in the present state of our knowledge, as reasonable a proposal, to make as its quite frequently reiterated converse.

If in any case we are in a position to intervene and definitely forbid increase, it is in the case of certain specific diseases, which I am told are painful and disastrous and inevitably transmitted to the offspring of the person suffering from these diseases. If there are such diseases—and that is a question the medical profession should be able to decide—it is evident that to incur parentage while one suffers from one of them or to transmit them in any avoidable way, is a cruel, disastrous and abominable act. If such a thing is possible it seems to me that in view of the guiding principle laid down in these papers it might well be put at the nadir of crime, and I doubt if any step the State might take to deter and punish the offender, short of torture, would meet with opposition from sane and reasonable men. For my own part I am inclined at times almost to doubt if there are such diseases. If there are, the remedy is so simple and obvious, that I cannot but blame the medical profession for very discreditable silences. I am no believer in the final wisdom of the mass of mankind, but I do believe enough in the sanity of the English-speaking peoples to be certain that any clear statement and instruction they received from the medical profession, as a whole, in these matters, would be faithfully observed. In the face of the collective silence of this great body of specialists, there is nothing for it but to doubt such diseases exist.

Such a systematic suppression of a specific disease or so is really the utmost that could be done with any confidence at present, so far as the State and collective action go. [Footnote: Since the above was written, a correspondent in Honolulu has called my attention to a short but most suggestive essay by Doctor Harry Campbell in the *Lancet*, 1898, ii., p. 678. He uses, of course, the common medical euphemism of "should not marry" for "should not procreate," and he gives the following as a list of "bars to marriage": pulmonary consumption, organic heart disease, epilepsy, insanity, diabetes, chronic Bright's disease, and rheumatic fever. I wish I had sufficient medical knowledge to analyze that proposal. He mentions inherited defective eyesight and hearing also, and the "neurotic" quality, with which I have dealt in my text. He adds two other suggestions that appeal to me very strongly. He proposes to bar all "cases of non-accidental disease in which life is saved by the surgeon's knife," and he instances particularly, strangulated hernia and ovarian cyst. And he also calls attention to apoplectic breakdown and premature senility. All these are suggestions of great value for individual conduct, but none of them have that quality of certainty that justifies collective action.] Until great advances are made in anthropology—and at present there are neither men nor endowments to justify the hope that any such advances will soon be made—that is as much as can be done hopefully for many years in the selective breeding of individuals by the community as a whole. [Footnote: If at any time certainties should replace speculations in the field of inheritance, then I fancy the common-sense of humanity will be found to be in favour of the immediate application of that knowledge to life.] At present almost every citizen in the civilized State respects the rules of the laws of consanguinity, so far as they affect brothers and sisters, with an absolute respect—an enormous triumph of training over instinct, as Dr. Beattie Crozier has pointed out—and if in the future it should be found possible to divide up humanity into groups, some of which could pair with one another only to the disadvantage of the offspring, and some of which had better have no offspring, I believe there would be remarkably little difficulty in enforcing a system of taboos in accordance with such knowledge. Only it would have to be absolutely certain knowledge proved and proved again up to the hilt. If a truth is worth application it is worth hammering home, and we have no right to expect common men to obey conclusions upon which specialists are as yet not lucidly agreed. [Footnote: It has been pointed out to me by my friend, Mr. Graham Wallas, that although the State may not undertake any positive schemes for selective breeding in the present state of our knowledge, it can no more evade a certain reaction upon these things than the individual can evade a practical solution. Although we cannot say of any specific individual that he or she is, or is not, of exceptional reproductive value to the State, we may still be able, he thinks, to point out classes which are very probably, as a whole, *good* reproductive classes, and we may be able to promote, or at least to avoid hindering, their increase. He instances the female elementary teacher as being probably, as a type, a more intelligent and more energetic and capable girl than the average of the stratum from which she arises, and he concludes she has a higher reproductive value—a view contrary to my argument in the text that reproductive and personal value are perhaps independent. He tells me that it is the practice of many large school boards in this country to dismiss women teachers on marriage, or to refuse promotion to these when they become mothers, which is, of course, bad for the race if personal and reproductive value are identical. He would have them retain their positions regardless of the check to their efficiency maternity entails. This is a curiously indirect way towards what one might call Galtonism. Practically he proposes to endow mothers in the name of education. For my own part I do not agree with him that this class, any more than any other class, can be shown to have a high reproductive value—which is the matter under analysis in this paper—though I will admit that an ex-teacher will probably do infinitely more for her children than if she were an illiterate or untrained woman. I can only reiterate my conviction that nothing really effective can be organized in these matters until we are much clearer than we are at present in our ideas about them, and that a public body devoted to education has no business either to impose celibacy, or subsidize families, or experiment at all in these affairs. Not only in the case of elementary teachers, but in the case of soldiers, sailors, and so on, the State may do much to promote or discourage marriage and offspring, and no doubt it is also true, as Mr. Wallas insists, that the problems of the foreign immigrant and of racial intermarriage, loom upon us. But since we have no applicable science whatever here, since there is no certainty in any direction that any collective course may not be collectively evil rather than good, there is nothing for it, I hold, but to leave these things to individual experiment, and to concentrate our efforts where there is a clearer hope of effective consequence. Leave things to individual initiative and some of us will, by luck or inspiration, go right; take public action on an insufficient basis of knowledge and there is a clear prospect of collective error. The imminence of these questions argues for nothing except prompt and vigorous research.]

That, however, is only one aspect of this question. There are others from which the New Republican may also approach this problem of the quality of the birth supply.

In relation to personal conduct all these things assume another colour altogether. Let us be clear upon that point. The state, the community, may only act upon certainties, but the essential fact in individual life is experiment. Individuality is experiment. While in matters of public regulation and control it is wiser not to act at all than to act upon theories and uncertainties; while the State may very well wait for a generation or half a dozen generations until knowledge comes up to these—at present—insoluble problems, the private life *must* go on now, and go upon probabilities where certainties fail. When we do not know what is indisputably right, then we have to use our judgments to the utmost to do each what seems to him probably right. The New Republican in his private life and in the exercise of his private influence, must do what seems to him best for the race; [Footnote: He would certainly try to discourage this sort of thing. The paragraph is from the *Morning Post* (Sept., 1902):—

"*Wedded in Silence.*—A deaf and dumb wedding was celebrated at Saffron Walden yesterday, when Frederick James Baish and Emily Lettige King, both deaf and dumb, were married. The bride was attended by deaf and dumb bridesmaids, and upwards of thirty deaf and dumb friends were present. The ceremony was performed by the Rev. A. Payne, of the Deaf and Dumb Church, London."] he must not beget children heedlessly and unwittingly because of his incomplete assurance. It is pretty obviously his duty to examine himself patiently and thoroughly, and if he feels that he is, on the whole, an average or rather more than an average man, then upon the cardinal principle laid down in our first paper, it is his most immediate duty to have children and to equip them fully for the affairs of life. Moreover he will, I think, lose no opportunity of speaking and acting in such a manner as to restore to marriage something of the solemnity and gravity the Victorian era—that age of nasty sentiment, sham delicacy and giggles—has to so large an extent refused to give it.

And though the New Republicans, in the existing lack of real guiding knowledge, will not dare to intervene in specific cases, there is another method of influencing parentage that men of good intent may well bear in mind. To attack a specific type is one thing, to attack a specific quality is another. It may be impossible to set aside selected persons from the population and say to them, "You are cowardly, weak, silly, mischievous people, and if we tolerate you in this world it is on condition that you do not found families." But it may be quite possible to bear in mind that the law and social arrangements may foster and protect the cowardly and the mean, may guard stupidity against the competition of enterprise, and may secure honour, power and authority in the hands of the silly and the base; and, by the guiding principle we have set before ourselves, to seek every conceivable alteration of such laws and such social arrangements is no more than the New Republican's duty. It may be impossible to select and intermarry the selected best of our race, but at any rate we can do a thousand things to equalize the chances and make good and desirable qualities lead swiftly and clearly to ease and honourable increase.

At present it is a shameful and embittering fact that a gifted man from the poorer strata of society must too often buy his personal development at the cost of his posterity; he must either die childless and successful for the children of the stupid to reap what he has sown, or sacrifice his gift—a wretched choice and an evil thing for the world at large. [Footnote: This aspect of New Republican possibilities comes in again at another stage, and at that stage its treatment will be resumed. The method and possibility of binding up discredit and failure with mean and undesirable qualities, and of setting a premium upon the nobler attributes, is a matter that touches not only upon the quality of births, but upon the general educational quality of the State in which a young citizen develops. It is convenient to hold over any detailed expansions of this, therefore, until we come to the general question, how the laws, institutions and customs of to-day go to make or unmake the men of to-morrow.]

So far at least we may go, towards improving the quality of the average birth now, but it is manifestly only a very slow and fractional advance that we shall get by these expedients. The obstacle to any ampler enterprise is ignorance and ignorance alone—not the ignorance of a majority in relation to a minority, but an absolute want of knowledge. If we knew more we could do more.

Our main attack in this enterprise of improving the birth supply must lie, therefore, through research. If we cannot act ourselves, we may yet hold a light for our children to see. At present, if there is a man specially gifted and specially disposed for such intricate and laborious inquiry, such criticism and experiment as this question demands, the world offers him neither food nor shelter, neither attention nor help; he cannot hope for a tithe of such honours as are thrust in profusion upon pork-butchers and brewers, he will be heartily despised by ninety-nine per cent. of the people he encounters, and unless he has some irrelevant income, he will die childless and his line will perish with him, for all the service he may give to the future of mankind. And as great mental endowments do not, unhappily, necessarily involve a passion for obscurity, contempt and extinction, it is probable that under existing conditions such a man will give his mind to some pursuit less bitterly unremunerative and shameful. It is a stupid superstition that "genius will out" in spite of all discouragement. The fact that great men have risen against crushing disadvantages in the past proves nothing of the sort; this roll-call of survivors does no more than give the measure of the enormous waste of human possibility human stupidity has achieved. Men of exceptional gifts have the same broad needs as common men, food, clothing, honour, attention, and the help of their fellows in self-respect; they may not need them as ends, but they need them by the way, and at present the earnest study of heredity produces none of these bye-products. It lies before the New Republican to tilt the balance in this direction.

There are, no doubt, already a number of unselfish and fortunately placed men who are able to do a certain amount of work in this direction; Professor Cossar Ewart, for example, one of those fine, subtle, unhonoured workers who are the glory of British science and the condemnation of our social order, has done much to clarify the discussion of telegony and prepotency, and there are many such medical men as Mr. Reid who broaden their daily practice by attention to these great issues. One thinks of certain other names. Professors Karl Pearson, Weldon, Lloyd Morgan, J. A. Thomson and Meldola, Dr. Benthall and Messrs. Bateson, Cunningham, Pocock, Havelock Ellis, E. A. Fay and Stuart Menteath occur to me, only to remind me how divided their attention has had to be. As many others, perhaps, have slipped my memory now. Not half a hundred altogether in all this wide world of English-speaking men! For one such worker we need fifty if this science of heredity is to grow to practicable proportions. We need a literature, we need a special public and an atmosphere of attention and discussion. Every man who grasps the New Republican idea brings these needs nearer satisfaction, but if only some day the New Republic could catch the ear of a prince, a little weary of being the costumed doll of grown-up children, the decoy dummy of fashionable tradesmen, or if it could invade and capture the mind of a multi-millionaire, these things might come almost at a stride. This missing science of heredity, this unworked mine of knowledge on the borderland of biology and anthropology, which for all practical purposes is as unworked now as it was in the days of Plato, is, in simple truth, ten times more important to humanity than all the chemistry and physics, all the technical and industrial science that ever has been or ever will be discovered.

So much for the existing possibilities of making the race better by breeding. For the rest of these papers we shall take the births into the world, for the most part, as we find them.

[Mr. Stuart Menteath remarks *apropos* of this question of the reproduction of exceptional people that it is undesirable to suggest voluntary extinction in any case. If a man, thinking that his family is "tainted," displays so much foresighted patriotism, humility, and lifelong self-denial as to have no children, the presumption is that the loss to humanity by the discontinuance of such a type is greater than the gain.

H. G. Wells

"Conceit in smallest bodies strongest works," and it does not follow that a sense of one's own excellence justifies one's utmost fecundity or the reverse. Mr. Vrooman, who, with Mrs. Vrooman, founded Ruskin Hall at Oxford, writes to much the same effect. He argues that people intelligent enough and moral enough to form such resolutions are just the sort of people who ought not to form them. Mr. Stuart Menteath also makes a most admirable suggestion with regard to male and female geniuses who are absorbed in their careers. Although the genius may not have or rear a large family, something might be done to preserve the stock by assisting his or her brothers and sisters to support and educate their children.]

III

CERTAIN WHOLESALE ASPECTS
OF MAN-MAKING

§ 1

With a skin of infinite delicacy that life will harden very speedily, with a discomforted writhing little body, with a weak and wailing outcry that stirs the heart, the creature comes protesting into the world, and unless death win a victory, we and chance and the forces of life in it, make out of that soft helplessness a man. Certain things there are inevitable in that man and unalterable, stamped upon his being long before the moment of his birth, the inherited things, the inherent things, his final and fundamental self. This is his "heredity," his incurable reality, the thing that out of all his being, stands the test of survival and passes on to his children. Certain things he must be, certain things he may be, and certain things are for ever beyond his scope. That much his parentage defines for him, that is the natural man.

But, in addition, there is much else to make up the whole adult man as we know him. There is all that he has learnt since his birth, all that he has been taught to do and trained to do, his language, the circle of ideas he has taken to himself, the disproportions that come from unequal exercise and the bias due to circumambient suggestion. There are a thousand habits and a thousand prejudices, powers undeveloped and skill laboriously acquired. There are scars upon his body, and scars upon his mind. All these are secondary things, things capable of modification and avoidance; they constitute the manufactured man, the artificial man. And it is chiefly with all this superposed and adherent and artificial portion of a man that this and the following paper will deal. The question of improving the breed, of raising the average human heredity we have discussed and set aside. We are going to draw together now as many things as possible that bear upon the artificial constituent, the made and controllable constituent in the mature and fully-developed man. We are going to consider how it is built up and how it may be built up, we are going to attempt a rough analysis of the whole complex process by which the civilized citizen is evolved from that raw and wailing little creature.

Before his birth, at the very moment when his being becomes possible, the inherent qualities and limitations of a man are settled for good and all, whether he will be a negro or a white man, whether he will be free or not of inherited disease, whether he will be passionate or phlegmatic or imaginative or six-fingered or with a snub or aquiline nose. And not only that, but even before his birth the qualities that are not strictly and inevitably inherited are also beginning to be made. The artificial, the avoidable handicap also, may have commenced in the worrying, the overworking or the starving of his mother. In the first few months of his life very slight differences in treatment may have life-long consequences. No doubt there is an extraordinary recuperative power in very young children; if they do not die under neglect or ill-treatment they recover to an extent incomparably greater than any adult could do, but there remains still a wide marginal difference between what they become and what they might have been. With every year of life the recuperative quality diminishes, the initial handicap becomes more irrevocable, the effects of ill-feeding, of unwholesome surroundings, of mental and moral infections, become more inextricably a part of the growing individuality. And so we may well begin our study by considering the circumstances under which the opening phase, the first five years of life, are most safely and securely passed.

Food, warmth, cleanliness and abundant fresh air there must be from the first, and unremitting attention, such attention as only love can sustain. And in addition there must be knowledge. It is a pleasant superstition that Nature (who in such connections becomes feminine and assumes a capital N) is to be trusted in these matters. It is a pleasant superstition to which, some of us, under the agreeable counsels of sentimental novelists, of thoughtless mercenary preachers, and ignorant and indolent doctors, have offered up a child or so. We are persuaded to believe that a mother has an instinctive knowledge of whatever is necessary for a child's welfare, and the child, until it reaches the knuckle-rapping age at least, an instinctive knowledge of its own requirements. Whatever proceedings are most suggestive of an ideal naked savage leading a "natural" life, are supposed to be not only more advantageous to the child but in some mystical way more moral. The spectacle of an undersized porter-fed mother, for example, nursing a spotted and distressful baby, is exalted at the expense of the clean and simple artificial feeding that is often advisable to-day. Yet the mortality of first-born children should indicate that a modern woman carries no instinctive system of baby management about with her in her brain, even if her savage ancestress had anything of the sort, and both the birth rate and the infantile death rate of such noble savages as our civilization has any chance of observing, suggest a certain generous carelessness, a certain spacious indifference to individual misery, rather than a trustworthy precision of individual guidance about Nature's way.

This cant of Nature's trustworthiness is partly a survival of the day of Rousseau and Sturm (of the Reflections), when untravelled men, orthodox and unorthodox alike, in artificial wigs, spouted in unison in this regard; partly it is the half instinctive tactics of the lax and lazy-minded to evade trouble and austerities. The incompetent medical practitioner, incapable of regimen, repeats this cant even to-day, though he knows full well that, left to Nature, men over-eat themselves almost as readily as dogs, contract a thousand diseases and exhaust their last vitality at fifty, and that half the white women in the world would die with their first children still unborn. He knows, too, that to the details of such precautionary measures as vaccination, for example, instinct is strongly opposed, and that drainage and filterage and the use of soap in washing are manifestly unnatural things. That large, naked, virtuous, pink, Natural Man, drinking pure spring water, eating the fruits of the earth, and living to ninety in the open air is a fantasy; he never was nor will be. The real savage is a nest of parasites within and without, he smells, he rots, he starves. Forty is a great age for him. He is as full of artifice as his civilized brother, only not so wise. As for his moral integrity, let the curious inquirer seek an account of the Tasmanian, or the Australian, or the Polynesian before "sophistication" came.

The very existence and nature of man is an interference with Nature and Nature's ways, using Nature in this sense of the repudiation of expedients. Man is the tool-using animal, the word-using animal, the animal of artifice and reason, and the only possible "return to Nature" for him—if we scrutinize the phrase—would be a return to the scratching, promiscuous, arboreal simian. To rebel against instinct, to rebel against limitation, to evade, to trip up, and at last to close with and grapple and conquer the forces that dominate him, is the fundamental being of man. And from the very outset of his existence, from the instant of his birth, if the best possible thing is to be made of him, wise contrivance must surround him. The soft, new, living thing must be watched for every sign of discomfort, it must be weighed and measured, it must be thought about, it must be talked to and sung to, skilfully and properly, and presently it must be given things to see and handle that the stirring germ of its mind may not go unsatisfied. From the very beginning, if we are to do our best for a child, there must be forethought and knowledge quite beyond the limit of instinct's poor equipment.

Now, for a child to have all these needs supplied implies certain other conditions. The constant loving attention is to be got only from a mother or from some well-affected girl or woman. It is not a thing to be hired for money, nor contrivable on any wholesale plan. Possibly there may be ways of cherishing and nursing infants by wholesale that will keep them alive, but at best these are second best ways, and we are seeking the best possible. A very noble, exceptionally loving and quite indefatigable woman might conceivably direct the development of three or four little children from their birth onward, or, with very good assistance, even of six or seven at a time, as well as a good mother could do for one, but it would be a very rare and wonderful thing. We must put that aside as an exceptional thing, quite impossible to provide when it is most needed, and we must fall back upon the fact that the child must have a mother or nurse—and it must have that attendant exclusively to itself for the first year or so of life. The mother or nurse must be in health, physically and morally, well fed and contented, and able to give her attention mainly, if not entirely, to the little child. The child must lie warmly in a well-ventilated room, with some one availably in hearing day and night, there must be plentiful warm water to wash it, plenty of wrappings and towellings and so forth for it; it is best to take it often into the open air, and for this, under urban or suburban conditions at any rate, a perambulator is almost necessary. The room must be clean and brightly lit, and prettily and interestingly coloured if we are to get the best results. These things imply a certain standard of prosperity in the circumstances of the child's birth. Either the child must be fed in the best way from a mother in health and abundance, or if it is to be bottle fed, there must be the most elaborate provision for sterilizing and warming the milk, and adjusting its composition to the changing powers of the child's assimilation. These conditions imply a house of a certain standard of comfort and equipment, and it is manifest the mother cannot be earning her own living before and about the time of the child's birth, nor, unless she is going to employ a highly skilled, trustworthy, and probably expensive person as nurse, for some year or so after it. She or the nurse must be of a certain standard of intelligence and education, trained to be observant and keep her temper, and she must speak her language with a good, clear accent. Moreover, behind the

H. G. Wells

mother and readily available, must be a highly-skilled medical man.

Not to have these things means a handicap. Not to have that very watchful feeding and attention at first means a loss of nutrition, a retarding of growth, that will either never be recovered or will be recovered later at the expense of mental development or physical strength. The early handicap may also involve a derangement of the digestion, a liability to stomachic and other troubles, that may last throughout life. Not to have the singing and talking, and the varied interest of coloured objects and toys, means a falling away from the best mental development, and a taciturn nurse, or a nurse with a base accent, means backwardness and needless difficulty with the beginning of speech. Not to be born within reach of abundant changes of clothing and abundant water, means—however industrious and cleanly the instincts of nurse and mother—a lack of the highest possible cleanliness and a lack of health and vitality. And the absence of highly-skilled medical advice, or the attentions of over-worked and under-qualified practitioners, may convert a transitory crisis or a passing ailment into permanent injury or fatal disorder.

It is very doubtful if these most favourable conditions fall to the lot of more than a quarter of the children born to-day even in England, where infant mortality is at its lowest. The rest start handicapped. They start handicapped, and fail to reach their highest possible development. They are born of mothers preoccupied by the necessity of earning a living or by vain occupations, or already battered and exhausted by immoderate child-bearing; they are born into insanity and ugly or inconvenient homes, their mothers or nurses are ignorant and incapable, there is insufficient food or incompetent advice, there is, if they are town children, nothing for their lungs but vitiated air, and there is not enough sunlight for them. And accordingly they fall away at the very outset from what they might be, and for the most part they never recover their lost start.

Just what this handicap amounts to, so far as it works out in physical consequences, is to be gauged by certain almost classical figures, which I have here ventured to present again in graphic form. These figures do not present our total failure, they merely show how far the less fortunate section of the community falls short of the more fortunate. They are taken from Clifford Allbutt's *System of Medicine* (art. "Hygiene of Youth," Dr. Clement Dukes). 15,564 boys and young men were measured and weighed to get these figures. The black columns indicate the weight (+9 lbs. of clothes) and height respectively of youths of the town artisan population, for the various ages from ten to twenty-five indicated at the heads of the columns. The white additions to these columns indicate the additional weight and height of the more favoured classes at the same ages. Public school-boys, naval and military cadets, medical and university students, were taken to represent the more favoured classes. It will be noted that while the growth in height of the lower class boy falls short from the very earliest years, the strain of the adolescent period tells upon his weight, and no doubt upon his general stamina, most conspicuously. These figures, it must be borne in mind, deal with the living members of each class at the ages given. The mortality, however, in the black or lower class is probably far higher than in the upper class year by year, and if this could be allowed for it would greatly increase the apparent failure of the lower class. And these matters of height and weight are only coarse material deficiencies. They serve to suggest, but they do not serve to gauge, the far graver and sadder loss, the invisible and immeasurable loss through mental and moral qualities undeveloped, through activities warped and crippled and vitality and courage lowered.

Moreover, defective as are these urban artisans, they are, after all, much more "picked" than the youth of the upper classes. They are survivors of a much more stringent process of selection than goes on amidst the more hygienic upper and middle-class conditions. The opposite three columns represent the mortality of children under five in Rutlandshire, where it is lowest, in the year 1900, in Dorsetshire, a reasonably good

H. G. Wells

county, and in Lancashire, the worst in England, for the same year. Each entire column represents 1,000 births, and the blackened portion represents the proportion of that 1,000 dead before the fifth birthday. Now, unless we are going to assume that the children born in Lancashire are inherently weaker than the children born in Rutland or Dorset—and there is not the shadow of a reason why we should believe that—we must suppose that at least 161 children out of every 1,000 in Lancashire were killed by the conditions into which they were born. That excess of blackness in the third column over that in the first represents a holocaust of children, that goes on year by year, a perennial massacre of the innocents, out of which no political capital can be made, and which is accordingly outside the sphere of practical politics altogether as things are at present. The same men who spouted infinite mischief because a totally unforeseen and unavoidable epidemic of measles killed some thousands of children in South Africa, who, for some idiotic or wicked vote-catching purpose, attempted to turn that epidemic to the permanent embitterment of Dutch and English, these same men allow thousands and thousands of avoidable deaths of English children close at hand to pass absolutely unnoticed. The fact that more than 21,000 little children died needlessly in Lancashire in that very same year means nothing to them at all. It cannot be used to embitter race against race, and to hamper that process of world unification which it is their pious purpose to delay.

It does not at all follow that even the Rutland 103 represents the possible minimum of infant mortality. One learns from the Register-General's returns for 1891 that among the causes of death specified in the three counties of Dorset, Wiltshire, and Hereford, where infant mortality is scarcely half what it is in the three vilest towns in England in this respect, Preston, Leicester, and Blackburn, the number of children killed by injury at birth is three times as great as it is in these same towns. Unclassified "violence" also accounts for more infant deaths in the country than in towns. This suggests pretty clearly a delayed and uncertain medical attendance and rough conditions, and it points us to still better possibilities. These diagrams and these facts justify together a reasonable hope that the mortality of infants under five throughout England might be brought to less than one-third what it is in child-destroying Lancashire at the present time, to a figure that is well under ninety in the thousand.

A portion of infant and child mortality represents no doubt the lingering and wasteful removal from this world of beings with inherent defects, beings who, for the most part, ought never to have been born, and need not have been born under conditions of greater foresight. These, however, are the merest small fraction of our infant mortality. It leaves untouched the fact that a vast multitude of children of untainted blood and good mental and moral possibilities, as many, perhaps, as 100 in each 1,000 born, die yearly through insufficient food, insufficient good air, and insufficient attention. The plain and simple truth is that they are born needlessly. There are still too many births for our civilisation to look after, we are still unfit to be trusted with a rising birth-rate. [Footnote: It is a digression from the argument of this Paper, but I would like to point out here a very popular misconception about the birth-rate which needs exposure. It is known that the birth-rate is falling in all European countries—a fall which has a very direct relation to a rise in the mean standard of comfort and the average age at marriage—and alarmists foretell a time when nations will be extinguished through this decline. They ascribe it to a certain decay in religious faith, to the advance of science and scepticism, and so forth; it is a part, they say, of a general demoralization. The thing is a popular cant and quite unsupported by facts. The decline in the birth-rate is—so far as England and Wales goes—partly a real decline due to a decline in gross immorality, partly to a real decline due to the later age at which women marry, and partly a statistical decline due to an increased proportion of people too old or too young for child-bearing. Wherever the infant mortality is falling there is an apparent misleading fall in the birth-rate due to the "loading" of the population with children. Here are the sort of figures that are generally given. They are the figures for England and Wales for two typical periods.

H. G. Wells

Period 1846-1850 — 33 8 births per 1000
Period 1896-1900 — 28 0 births per 1000

5.8 fall in the birth-rate.

This as it stands is very striking. But if we take the death-rates of these two periods we find that they have fallen also.

Period 1846-1850 — 23 3 deaths per 1000
Period 1896-1900 — 17 7 deaths per 1000

5.6 fall in the death-rate.

Let us subtract death-rate from birth-rate and that will give the effective rate of increase of the population.

Period 1846-1850 — 10 5 effective rate of increase
Period 1896-1900 — 10 3 effective rate of increase

.2 fall in the rate of increase.

But now comes a curious thing that those who praise the good old pre-Board School days—the golden age of virtuous innocence—ignore. The *Illegitimate births* in 1846-1850 numbered 2.2 per 1000, in 1896- 1900 they numbered 1.2 per 1000. So that if it were not for this fall in illegitimate births the period 1896-1900 would show a positive rise in the effective rate of increase of .8 per thousand. The eminent persons therefore who ascribe our falling birth-rate to irreligion and so forth, either speak without knowledge or with some sort of knowledge beyond my ken. England is, as a matter of fact, becoming not only more hygienic and rational, but more moral and more temperate. The highly moral, healthy, prolific, pious England of the past is just another poetical delusion of the healthy savage type.]

These poor little souls are born, amidst tears and suffering they gain such love as they may, they learn to feel and suffer, they struggle and cry for food, for air, for the right to develop; and our civilisation at present has neither the courage to kill them outright quickly, cleanly, and painlessly, nor the heart and courage and ability to give them what they need. They are overlooked and misused, they go short of food and air, they fight their pitiful little battle for life against the cruellest odds; and they are beaten. Battered, emaciated, pitiful, they are thrust out of life, borne out of our regardless world, stiff little life-soiled sacrifices to the spirit of disorder against which it is man's preeminent duty to battle. There has been all the pain in their lives, there has been the radiated pain of their misery, there has been the waste of their grudged and insufficient food, and all the pain and labour of their mothers, and all the world is the sadder for them because they have lived in vain.

§ 2

Now, since our imaginary New Republic, which is to set itself to the making of a better generation of men, will find the possibility of improving the race by selective breeding too remote for anything but further organised inquiry, it is evident that its first point of attack will have to be the wastage of such births as the world gets to-day. Throughout the world the New Republic will address itself to this problem, and when a working solution has been obtained, then the New Republican on press and platform, the New Republican in pulpit and theatre, the New Republican upon electoral committee and in the ballot box, will press weightily to see that solution realised. Upon the theory of New Republicanism as it was discussed in our first paper an effective solution (effective enough, let us say, to abolish seventy or eighty per cent.) of this scandal of infantile suffering would have precedence over almost every existing political consideration.

The problem of securing the maximum chance of life and health for every baby born into the world is an extremely complicated one, and the reader must not too hastily assume that a pithy, complete recipe is attempted here. Yet, complicated though the problem is, there does not occur any demonstrable impossibility such as there is in the question of selective breeding. I believe that a solution is possible, that its broad lines may be already stated, and that it could very easily be worked out to an immediate practical application.

Let us glance first at a solution that is now widely understood to be incorrect. Philanthropic people in the past have attempted, and many are still striving, to meet the birth waste by the very obvious expedients of lying-in hospitals, orphanages and foundling institutions, waifs' homes, Barnardo institutions and the like, and within certain narrow limits these things no doubt serve a useful purpose in individual cases. But nowadays there is an increasing indisposition to meet the general problem by such methods, because nowadays people are alive to certain ulterior consequences that were at first overlooked.

Any extensive relief of parental responsibility we now know pretty certainly will serve to encourage and stimulate births in just those strata of society where it would seem to be highly reasonable to believe they are least desirable. It is just where the chances for a child are least that passions are grossest, basest, and most heedless, and stand in the greatest need of a sense of the gravity of possible consequences to control their play, and to render it socially innocuous. If we were to take over or assist all the children born below a certain level of comfort, or, rather, if we were to take over their mothers before the birth occurred, and bring up that great mass of children under the best conditions for them—supposing this to be possible—it would only leave our successors in the next generation a heavier task of the same sort. The assisted population would grow generation by generation relatively to the assisting until the Sinbad of Charity broke down. And quite early in the history of Charities it was found that a very grave impediment to their beneficial action lay in one of the most commendable qualities to be found in poor and poorish people, and that is pride. While Charities, perhaps, catch the quite hopeless cases, they leave untouched the far more extensive mass of births in non-pauper, not very prosperous homes—the lower middle-class homes in towns, for example, which supply a large proportion of poorly developed adults to our community. Mr. Seebohm Rowntree, in his "Poverty" (that noble, able, valuable book), has shown that nearly thirty per cent. at least of a typical English town population goes short of the physical necessities of life. These people are fiercely defensive in such matters as this, and one may no more usurp and share their parental responsibility, badly though they discharge it, than one may handle the litter of a she-wolf.

These considerations alone would suffice to make us very suspicious of the philanthropic method of direct assistance, so far as the remedial aspect goes. But there is another more sweeping and comprehensive objection to this method. Philanthropic institutions, as a matter of fact, rarely succeed in doing what they profess and intend to do.

H. G. Wells

I do not allude here to the countless swindlers and sham institutions that levy a tremendous tribute upon the heedless good. Quite apart from that wastage altogether, and speaking only of such *bonâ fide* institutions as would satisfy Mr. Labouchere, they do not work. It is one thing for the influential and opulent inactive person of good intentions to provide a magnificent building and a lavish endowment for some specific purpose, and quite another to attain in reality the ostensible end of the display. It is easy to create a general effect of providing comfort and tender care for helpless women who are becoming mothers, and of tending and training and educating their children, but, in cold fact, it is impossible to get enough capable and devoted people to do the work. In cold fact, lying-in hospitals have a tendency to become austere, hard, unsympathetic, wholesale concerns, with a disposition to confuse and substitute moral for physical well-being. In cold fact, orphanages do not present any perplexing resemblance to an earthly paradise. However warm the heart behind the cheque, the human being at the other end of the chain is apt to find the charity no more than a rather inhuman machine. Shining devotees there are, but able, courageous, and vigorous people are rare, and the world urges a thousand better employments upon them than the care of inferior mothers and inferior children. Exceptionally good people owe the world the duty of parentage themselves, and it follows that the rank and file of those in the service of Charity falls far below the standard necessary to give these poor children that chance in the world the cheque-writing philanthropist believes he is giving them. The great proportion of the servants and administrators of Charities are doing that work because they can get nothing better to do—and it is not considered remarkably high-class work. These things have to be reckoned with by every philanthropic person with sufficient faith to believe that an enterprise may not only look well, but do well. One gets a Waugh or a Barnardo now and then, a gleam of efficiency in the waste, and for the rest this spectacle of stinted thought and unstinted giving, this modern Charity, is often no more than a pretentious wholesale substitute for retail misery and disaster. Fourteen million pounds a year, I am told, go to

British Charities, and I doubt if anything like a fair million's worth of palliative amelioration is attained for this expenditure. As for any permanent improvement, I doubt if all these Charities together achieve a net advance that could not be got by the discreet and able expenditure of ten or twelve thousand pounds.

It is one of the grimmest ironies in life, that athwart the memory of sainted founders should be written the most tragic consequences. The Foundling Hospital of London, established by Coram—to save infant lives!—buried, between 1756 and 1760, 10,534 children out of 14,934 received, and the Dublin Foundling Hospital (suppressed in 1835) had a mortality of eighty per cent. The two great Russian institutions are, I gather, about equally deadly with seventy-five per cent., and the Italian institutes run to about ninety per cent. The Florentine boasts a very beautiful and touching series of *putti* by Delia Robbia, that does little or nothing to diminish its death-rate. So far from preventing infant murder these places, with the noblest intentions in the world, have, for all practical purposes, organized it. The London Foundling, be it noted, in the reorganized form it assumed after its first massacres, is not a Foundling Hospital at all. An extremely limited number of children, the illegitimate children of recommended respectable but unfortunate mothers, are converted into admirable bandsmen for the defence of the Empire or trained to be servants for people who feel the need of well-trained servants, at a gross cost that might well fill the mind of many a poor clergyman's son with amazement and envy. And this is probably a particularly well-managed charity. It is doing all that can be expected of it, and stands far above the general Charitable average.

Every Poor Law Authority comes into the tangles of these perplexities. Upon the hands of every one of them come deserted children, the children of convicted criminals, the children of pauper families, a miscellaneous pitiful succession of responsibilities. The enterprises they are forced to undertake to meet these charges rest on taxation, a financial basis far stabler than the fitful good intentions of the rich, but apart from this advantage there is little about them to differentiate them from Charities. The method of treatment varies from a barrack system, in which the children are herded in huge asylums like those places between Sutton and Banstead, to what is perhaps preferable, the system of boarding-out little groups of children with suitable poor people. Provided such boarded-out children are systematically weighed, measured and examined, and at once withdrawn when they drop below average mental and bodily progress, it would seem more likely that a reasonable percentage should grow into ordinary useful citizens under these latter conditions than under the former.

It is well, however, to anticipate a very probable side result if we make the boarding out of pauper children a regular rural industry. There will arise in many rural homes a very strong pecuniary inducement to limit the family. Side by side will be a couple with eight children—of their own, struggling hard to keep them, and another family with, let us say, two children of their own blood and six "boarded-out," living in relative opulence. That side consequence must be anticipated. For my own part and for the reasons given in the second of these papers, I do not see that it is a very serious one so far as the future goes, because I do not think there is much to choose between the "heredity" of the rural and the urban strain. It is nonsense to pretend that we shall get the fine flower of the cottage population to board pauper children; we shall induce respectable inferior people living in healthy conditions to take care of an inferior sort of children rescued from unhealthy disreputable conditions—that is all. The average inherent quality of the resultant adults will be about the same whichever element predominates.

Possibly this indifference may seem undesirable. But we must bear in mind that the whole problem is hard to cope with, it is an aspect of failure, and no sentimental juggling with facts will convert the business into a beautiful or desirable thing. Somehow or other we have to pay. All expedients must be palliatives, all will involve sacrifices; we must, no doubt, adopt some of them for our present necessities, but they are like famine relief works, to adopt them in permanence is a counsel of despair.

Clearly it is not along these lines that the capable men-makers we suppose to be attacking the problem will spend much of their energies. All the experiences of Charities and Poor-Law Authorities simply confirm our postulate of the necessity of a standard of comfort if a child is to have a really good initial chance in the world. The only conceivable solution of this problem is one that will ensure that no child, or only a few accidental and exceptional children, will be born outside these advantages. It is no good trying to sentimentalize the issue away. This is the end we must attain, to attain any effectual permanent improvement in the conditions of childhood. A certain number of people have to be discouraged and prevented from parentage, and a great number of homes have to be improved. How can we ensure these ends, or how far can we go towards ensuring them?

The first step to ensuring them is certainly to do all we can to discourage reckless parentage, and to render it improbable and difficult. We must make sure that whatever we do for the children, the burden of parental responsibility must not be lightened a feather-weight. All the experience of two hundred years of charity and poor law legislation sustains that. But to accept that as a first principle is one thing, and to apply it by using a wretched little child as our instrument in the exemplary punishment of its parent is another. At present that is our hideous practice. So long as the parents are not convicted criminals, so long as they do not practise indictable cruelty upon their offspring, so long as the children themselves fall short of criminality, we insist upon the parent "keeping" the child. It may be manifest the child is ill-fed, harshly treated, insufficiently clothed, dirty and living among surroundings harmful to body and soul alike, but we merely take the quivering damaged victim and point the moral to the parent. "This is what comes of your recklessness," we say. "Aren't you ashamed of it?" And after inscrutable meditations

H. G. Wells

the fond parent usually answers us by sending out the child to beg or sell matches or by some equally effective retort. Now a great number of excellent people pretend that this is a dilemma. "Take the child away," it is argued, "and you remove one of the chief obstacles to the reckless reproduction of the unfit. Leave it in the parents' hands and you must have the cruelty." But really this is not a dilemma at all. There is a quite excellent middle way. It may not be within the sphere of practical politics at present—if not, it is work for the New Republic to get it there—but it would practically settle all this problem of neglected children. This way is simply to make the parent the debtor to society on account of the child for adequate food, clothing, and care for at least the first twelve or thirteen years of life, and in the event of parental default to invest the local authority with exceptional powers of recovery in this matter. It would be quite easy to set up a minimum standard of clothing, cleanliness, growth, nutrition and education, and provide, that if that standard was not maintained by a child, or if the child was found to be bruised or maimed without the parents being able to account for these injuries, the child should be at once removed from the parental care, and the parents charged with the cost of a suitable maintenance—which need not be excessively cheap. If the parents failed in the payments they could be put into celibate labour establishments to work off as much of the debt as they could, and they would not be released until their debt was fully discharged. Legislation of this type would not only secure all and more of the advantages children of the least desirable sort now get from charities and public institutions, but it would certainly invest parentage with a quite unprecedented gravity for the reckless, and it would enormously reduce the number of births of the least desirable sort. Into this net, for example, every habitual drunkard who was a parent would, for his own good and the world's, be almost certain to fall. [Footnote: Mr. C. G. Stuart Menteath has favored me with some valuable comments upon this point. He writes: "I agree that calling such persons as have shown themselves incapable of parental duties debtors to the State, would help to reconcile popular ideas of the 'liberty of the subject' with the enforcement as well as the passing of such laws. But the notions of drastically enforcing parental duties, and of discouraging and even prohibiting the marriages of those unable to show their ability to perform these duties, has long prevailed. See Nicholl's *History of the Poor Law* (1898, New Edition), i. 229, and ii. 140, 278, where you will find chargeable bastardy has been punishable in the first offence by one year's imprisonment, and in the second, by imprisonment until sureties are given, which thus might amount to imprisonment for life. See also, J. S. Mill, *Political Economy*, Bk. II., ch. ii., for extreme legislation on the Continent against the marriage of people unable to support a family. In Denmark there seem to be very severe laws impeding the marriage of those who have been paupers. The English law was sufficiently effective to produce infanticide, so that a law was passed making concealment of birth almost infanticide."]

So much for the worst fringe of this question, the maltreated children, the children of the slum, the children of drunkards and criminals, and the illegitimate. But the bulk of the children of deficient growth, the bulk of the excessive mortality, lies above the level of such intervention, and the method of attack of the New Republican must be less direct. Happily there already exists a complicated mass of legislation that without any essential change of principle could be applied to this object.

The first of the expedients which would lead to a permanent improvement in these matters is the establishment of a minimum of soundness and sanitary convenience in houses, below which standard it shall be illegal to inhabit a house at all. There should be a certain relation between the size of rooms and their ventilating appliances, a certain minimum of lighting, certain conditions of open space about the house and sane rules about foundations and materials. These regulations would vary with the local density of population—many things are permissible in Romney marsh, for example, which the south-west wind sweeps everlastingly, that would be deadly in Rotherhithe. At present in England there are local building regulations, for the most part vexatious and stupid to an almost incredible degree, and compiled without either imagination or understanding, but it should be possible to substitute for these a national minimum of habitability without any violent revolution. A house that failed to come up to this minimum—which might begin very low and be raised at intervals of years—would, after due notice, be pulled down. It might be pulled down and the site taken over and managed by the local authority—allowing its owner a portion of its value in compensation—if it was evident his failure to keep up to the standard had an adequate excuse. In time it might be possible to level up the minimum standard of all tenements in towns and urban districts at any rate to the possession of a properly equipped bathroom for example, without which, for hardworking people, regular cleanliness is a practical impossibility. This process of levelling-up the minimum tenement would be enormously aided by a philanthropic society which would devote itself to the study of building methods and materials, to the evolution of conveniences, and the direction of invention to lessening the cost and complication of building wholesome dwellings.

The state of repair of inhabited buildings is also already a matter of public concern. All that is needed is a slow, persistent tightening-up of the standard. This would ensure, at any rate, that the outer shell of the child's surroundings gave it a fair chance in life. In the next place comes legislation against overcrowding. There must be a maximum number of inhabitants to any tenement, and a really sane law will be far more stringent to secure space and air for young children than for adults. There is little reason, except the possible harbouring of parasites and infectious disease, why five or six adults should not share a cask on a dust heap as a domicile—if it pleases them. But directly children come in we touch the future. The minimum permissible tenement for a maximum of two adults and a very young child is one properly ventilated room capable of being heated, with close and easy access to sanitary conveniences, a constant supply of water and easy means of getting warm water. More than one child should mean another room, and it seems only reasonable if we go so far as this, to go further and require a minimum of furniture and equipment, a fire-guard, for instance, and a separate bed or cot for the child. In a civilized community little children should not sleep with adults, and the killing of children by "accidental" overlaying should be a punishable offence. [Footnote: In the returns I have quoted from Blackburn, Leicester, and Preston the number of deaths from suffocation per 100,000 infants born was 232 in the first year of life.]

If a woman does not wish to be dealt with as a half-hearted murderess she should not behave like one. It should also be punishable on the part of a mother to leave children below a certain age alone for longer than a certain interval. It is absurd to punish people as we do, for the injuries inflicted by them upon their children during uncontrollable anger, and not to punish them for the injuries inflicted by uncontrolled carelessness. Such legislation should ensure children space, air and attention. [Footnote: It is less within the range of commonly grasped ideas, it is therefore less within the range of practical expedients, to point out that a graduated scale of building regulation might be contrived for use in different localities. Districts could be classed in grades determined by the position of each district in the scale of infant mortality, and in those in which the rate was highest the hygienic standard could be made most stringent and onerous upon the house owner. This would force up the price of house-room, and that would force up the price of labour, and this would give the proprietors of unwholesome industries a personal interest in hygienic conditions about them. It would also tend to force population out of districts intrinsically unhealthy into districts intrinsically healthy. The statistics of low-grade districts could be examined to discover the distinctive diseases which determine their lowness of grade, and if these were preventable diseases they could be controlled by special regulations. A further extension of these principles might be made. Direct inducements to attract the high birth-rates towards exceptionally healthy districts could be contrived by a differential rating of sound families with children in such districts, the burthen of heavy rates could be thrown upon silly and selfish landowners who attempted to stifle sound populations by using highly habitable areas as golf links, private parks, game preserves, and the like, and public-spirited people could combine to facilitate communications that would render life in such districts compatible with industrial occupation. Such deliberate redistribution of population as this differential treatment of districts involves, is, however, quite beyond the available power and intelligence of our public control at present, and I suggest it here as something that our grandchildren perhaps may begin to consider. But if in the obscurity of this footnote I may let myself go, I would point out that, in the future, a time may come when locomotion will be so swift and convenient and cheap that it will be unnecessary to spread out the homes of our great communities where the industrial and trading centres are gathered together; it will be unnecessary for each district to sustain the renewal and increase of its own population. Certain wide regions will become specifically administrative and central—the home lands, the mother lands, the centres of education and population, and others will become specifically fields of action. Something of this kind is to a slight degree already the case with Scotland, which sends out its hardy and capable sons wherever the world has need of them; the Swiss mountains, too, send their sons far and wide in the world; and on the other hand, with regard to certain elements of population, at any rate, London and the Gold Coast and, I suspect, some regions in the United States of America, receive to consume.]

But it will be urged that these things are likely to bear rather severely on the very poor parent. To which a growing number of people will reply that the parent should not be a parent under circumstances that do not offer a fair prospect of sound child-birth and nurture. It is no good trying to eat our cake and have it; if the parent does not suffer the child will, and of the two, we, of the New Republic, have no doubt that the child is the more important thing.

It may be objected, however, that existing economic

conditions make life very uncertain for many very sound and wholesome kinds of people, and that it is oppressive and likely to rob the State of good citizens to render parentage burthensome, and to surround it with penalties. But that directs our attention to a second scheme of expedients which have crystallized about the expression, the Minimum Wage. The cardinal idea of this group of expedients is this, that it is unjust and cruel in the present and detrimental to the future of the world to let any one be fully employed at a rate of payment at which a wholesome, healthy, and, by the standards of comfort at the time, a reasonable happy life is impossible. *It is better in the long run that people whose character and capacity will not render it worth while to employ them at the Minimum Wage should not be employed at all.* The sweated employment of such people, as Mr. and Mrs. Sidney Webb show most conclusively in their great work, "Industrial Democracy," arrests the development of labour-saving machinery, replaces and throws out of employment superior and socially more valuable labour, enables these half capables to establish base families of inadequately fed and tended children (which presently collapse upon public and private charity), and so lowers and keeps down the national standard of life. As these writers show very clearly, an industry that cannot adequately sustain sound workers is not in reality a source of public wealth at all, but a disease and a parasite upon the public body. It is eating up citizens the State has had the expense of educating, and very often the indirect cost of rearing. Obviously the minimum wage for a civilized adult male should be sufficient to cover the rent of the minimum tenement permissible with three or four children, the maintenance of himself and his wife and children above the minimum standard of comfort, his insurance against premature or accidental death or temporary economic or physical disablement, some minimum provision for old age and a certain margin for the exercise of his individual freedom. [Footnote: An excellent account of experiments already tried in the establishment of a Minimum Wage will be found in W.P. Reeves' *State Experiments in Australia and New Zealand*, vol. ii., p. 47 *et seq.*]

So that while those who are bent on this conception of making economy in life and suffering the guiding principle of their public and social activity, are seeking to brace up the quality of the home on the one hand, they must also do all they can to bring about the realization of this ideal of a minimum wage on the other. In the case of government and public employment and of large, well-organized industries, the way is straight and open, and the outlook very hopeful. Wherever licenses, tariffs, and any sort of registration occurs there are practicable means of bringing in this expedient. But where the employment is shifting and sporadic, or free from regulation, there we have a rent in our social sieve, and the submissive, eager inferior will still come in, the failures of our own race, the immigrant from baser lands, desperately and disastrously underselling our sound citizens. Obviously we must use every contrivance we can to mend these rents, by promoting the organization of employments in any way that will not hamper progress in economic production. And if we can persuade the Trade Unions—and there is every sign that the old mediaeval guild conception of water-tight trade limitations is losing its hold upon those organizations—to facilitate the movement of workers from trade to trade under the shifting stress of changing employment and of changing economy of production, we shall have gone far to bring the possibilities of the rising operative up to the standard of the minimum home permissible for children.

These things—if we could bring them about—would leave us with a sort of clarified Problem of the Unemployed on our hands. Our Minimum Wage would have strained these people out, and, provided there existed what is already growing up, an intelligent system of employment bureaus, we should have much more reason to conclude than we have at present, that they were mainly unemployed because of a real incapacity in character, strength, or intelligence for efficient citizenship. Our raised standards of housing, our persecution of overcrowding, and our obstruction of employment below the minimum wage, would have swept out the rookeries and hiding-places of these people of the Abyss. They would exist, but they would not multiply—and that is our supreme end. They would be tramping on roads where mendicity laws would prevail, there would be no house-room for them, no squatting-places. The casual wards would catch them and register them, and telephone one to the other about them. It is rare that children come into this world without a parent or so being traceable. Everything would converge to convince these people that to bear children into such an unfavourable atmosphere is an extremely inconvenient and undesirable thing. They would not have many children, and such children as they had would fall easily into our organized net and get the protection of the criticised and improved development of the existing charitable institutions. [Footnote: "I wonder whether there is any legal flaw in the second section of the Prevention of Cruelty to Children Act of 1894, which may have been *specially* aimed at beggars with offspring. It is specially punishable to beg having an infant in their arms, quite apart from teaching the infant in question to beg. Or is this law insufficiently enforced through popular apathy?"—C. G. STUART MENTEATH.] This is the best we can do for those poor little creatures. As for that increasing section of the Abyss that will contrive to live childless, these papers have no quarrel with them. A childless wastrel is a terminating evil, and it may be, a picturesque evil. I must confess that a lazy rogue is very much to my taste, provided there is no tragedy of children to smear the joke with misery. And if he or she neither taints nor tempts the children, who are our care, a childless weakling we may freely let our pity and mercy go out to. To go childless is in them a virtue for which they merit our thanks.

These are the first necessities, then, in the Making of Men and the bettering of the world, this courageous interference with what so many people call "Nature's methods" and "Nature's laws," though, indeed, they are no more than the methods and laws of the beasts. By such expedients we may hope to see, first, a certain fall in the birth-rate, a fall chiefly in the birth-rate of improvident, vicious, and feeble types, a continuation, in fact, of that fall that is already so conspicuous in illegitimate births in Great Britain; secondly, a certain, almost certainly more considerable fall in the death-rate of infants and young children, and that fall in the infantile death-rate will serve to indicate, thirdly, a fall no statistics will fully demonstrate in what I may call the partial death-rate, the dwarfing and limiting of that innumerable host of children who do, in an underfed, meagre sort of a way, survive. This raising of the standard of homes will do a work that will not end with the children; the death-line will sag downward for all the first twenty or thirty years of life. Dull-minded, indolent, prosperous people will say that all this is no more than a proposal to make man better by machinery, that you cannot reform the world by Board of Trade Regulations and all the rest of it. They will say that such work as this is a scheme of grim materialism, and that the Soul of Man gains no benefit by this "so-called Progress," that it is not birth-rates that want raising but Ideals. We shall deal later with Ideals in general. Here I will mention only one, and that is, unhappily, only an Ideal Argument. I wish I could get together all these people who are so scornful of materialistic things, out of the excessively comfortable houses they inhabit, and I wish I could concentrate them in a good typical East London slum—five or six together in each room, one lodging with another, and I wish I could leave them there to demonstrate the superiority of high ideals to purely material considerations for the rest of their earthly career while we others went on with our sordid work unencumbered by their ideality.

Think what these dry-looking projects of building and trade regulation, and inspection and sanitation, mean in reality! think of the promise they hold out to us of tears and suffering abolished, of lives invigorated and enlarged!

[Endnote 1

I am greatly obliged to Mr. J. Leaver for a copy of the following notice:

"DEATHS OF CHILDREN FROM BURNING.
"TO PARENTS AND GUARDIANS.

"Attention is drawn to the frequency with which the death of young children is caused owing to their clothing taking fire at unprotected firegrates. During the years 1899 and 1900 inquests were held on the bodies of 1684 YOUNG CHILDREN whose death had resulted from burning, and in 1425 of these cases the fire by which the burning was caused was unprotected by a guard.

"With a view to prevent such deplorable loss of life it is suggested to Parents and Guardians, who have the care of young children, that it is very desirable that efficient fire-guards should be provided, in order to render it impossible for children to obtain access to the fire-grates.

E. R. C. BRADFORD,
"The Commissioner of Police of the Metropolis.
"Metropolitan Police Office,
"New Scotland Yard,
"January 28th, 1902."]

IV

THE BEGINNINGS OF THE MIND
AND LANGUAGE

§ 1

The newborn child is at first no more than an animal. Indeed, it is among the lowest and most helpless of all animals, a mere vegetative lump; assimilation incarnate—wailing. It is for the first day in its life deaf, it squints blindly at the world, its limbs are beyond its control, its hands clutch drowningly at anything whatever that drifts upon this vast sea of being into which it has plunged so amazingly. And imperceptibly, subtly, so subtly that never at any time can we mark with certainty the increment of its coming, there creeps into this soft and claimant little creature a mind, a will, a personality, the beginning of all that is real and spiritual in man. In a little while there are eyes full of interest and clutching hands full of purpose, smiles and frowns, the babbling beginning of expression and affections and aversions. Before the first year is out there is obedience and rebellion, choice and self-control, speech has commenced, and the struggle of the newcomer to stand on his feet in this world of men. The process is unanalyzable; given a certain measure of care and protection, these things come spontaneously; with the merest rough encouragement of things and voices about the child, they are evoked.

But every day the inherent impulse makes a larger demand

upon the surroundings of the child, if it is to do its best and fullest. Obviously, quite apart from physical consequences, the environment of a little child may be good or bad, better or worse for it in a thousand different ways. It may be distracting or over-stimulating, it may evoke and increase fear, it may be drab and dull and depressing, it may be stupefying, it may be misleading and productive of vicious habits of mind. And our business is to find just what is the best possible environment, the one that will give the soundest and fullest growth, not only of body but of intelligence.

Now from the very earliest phase the infant stands in need of a succession of interesting things. At first these are mere vague sense impressions, but in a month or so there is a distinct looking at objects; presently follows reaching and clutching, and soon the little creature is urgent for fresh things to see, handle, hear, fresh experiences of all sorts, fresh combinations of things already known. The newborn mind is soon as hungry as the body. And if a healthy well-fed child cries, it is probably by reason of this unsatisfied hunger, it lacks an interest, it is bored, that dismal vacant suffering that punishes the failure of living things to live fully and completely. As Mr. Charles Booth has pointed out in his *Life and Labour of the People*, it is probable that in this respect the children of the relatively poor are least at a disadvantage. The very poor infant passes its life in the family room, there is a going and coming, and interesting activity of domestic work on the part of its mother, the preparation of meals, the intermittent presence of the father, the whole gamut of its mother's unsophisticated temper. It is carried into crowded and eventful streets at all hours. It participates in pothouse soirées and assists at the business of shopping. It may not lead a very hygienic life, but it does not lead a dull one. Contrast with its lot that of the lonely child of some woman of fashion, leading its beautifully non-bacterial life in a carefully secluded nursery under the control of a virtuous, punctual, invariable, conscientious rather than emotional nurse. The poor little soul wails as often for events as the slum baby does for nourishment. Into its grey nursery there rushes every day, or every other day, a breathless, preoccupied, excessively dressed, cleverish, many-sided, fundamentally silly, and universally incapable woman, vociferates a little conventional affection, slaps a kiss or so upon her offspring, and goes off again to collect that daily meed of admiration and cheap envy which is the gusto of her world. After that gushing, rustling, incomprehensible passage, the child relapses into the boring care of its bored hireling for another day. The nurse writes her letters, mends her clothes, reads and thinks of the natural interests of her own life, and the child is "good" just in proportion to the extent to which it doesn't "worry."

That, of course, is an extreme case. It assumes a particularly bad mother and a particularly ill-chosen nurse, and what is probably only a transitory phase of sexual debasement. The average nurse of the upper-class child is often a woman of highly developed motherly instincts, and it is probable that our upper class and our upper middle-class is passing or has already passed through that phase of thought which has made solitary children so common in the last decade or so. The effective contrast must not take us too far. We must remember that all women do not possess the passion for nursing, and that some of those who are defective in this direction may be, for all that, women of exceptional gifts and capacity, and fully capable of offspring. Civilization is based on the organized subdivision of labour, and, as the able lady who writes as "L'amie Inconnue" in the *County Gentleman* has pointed out in a very helpful criticism of the original version of this paper, it is as absurd to require every woman to be a nursery mother as it is, to require every man to till the soil. We move from homogeneous to heterogeneous conditions, and we must beware of every generalization we make.

For all that, one is inclined to think the ideal average environment should contain the almost constant presence of the mother, for no one is so likely to be continuously various and interesting and untiring as she, and only as an exception, for exceptional mothers and nurses, can we admit the mother-substitute. When we admit her we admit other things. It is entirely on account of such an ideal environment, we must remember, that monogamy finds its practical sanction; it claims to ensure the presiding mother the maximum of security and self-respect. A woman who enjoys the full rights of a wife to maintenance and exclusive attention, without a complete discharge of the duties of motherhood, profits by the imputation of things she has failed to perform. She may be justified by other things, by an effectual co-operation with her husband in joint labours for example, but she has altered her footing none the less. To secure an ideal environment for children in as many cases as possible is the second of the two great practical ends—the first being sound births, for which the restrictions of sexual morality exist. In addition there is the third almost equally important matter of adult efficiency; we have to adjust affairs, if we can, to secure the maximum of health, sane happiness and vigorous mental and physical activity, and to abolish, as far as possible, passionate broodings, over-stimulated appetites, disease, and destructive indulgence. Apart from these aspects, sexual morality is outside the scope of the New Republican altogether. . . . Do not let this passage be misunderstood. I do not mean that a New Republican ignores sexual morality except on these grounds, but so far as his New Republicanism goes he does, just as a member of the Aeronautical Society, so far as his aeronautical interests go, or as an ecclesiastical architect, so far as his architecture goes.

The ideal environment should, without any doubt at all, centre about a nursery—a clean, airy, brightly lit, brilliantly adorned room, into which there should be a frequent coming and going of things and people; but from the time the child begins to recognize objects and individuals it should be taken for little spells into other rooms and different surroundings. In the homely, convenient, servantless abode over which the able-bodied, capable, skilful, civilized women of the ordinary sort will preside in the future, the child will naturally follow its mother's morning activities from room to room. Its mother will talk to it, chance visitors will sign to it. There should be a public or private garden available where its perambulator could stand in fine weather; and its promenades should not be too

H. G. Wells

much a matter of routine. To go along a road with some traffic is better for a child than to go along a secluded path between hedges; a street corner is better than a laurel plantation as a pitch for perambulators.

When a child is five or six months old it will have got a certain use and grip with its hands, and it will want to handle and examine and test the properties of as many objects as it can. Gifts begin. There seems scope for a wiser selection in these early gifts. At present it is chiefly woolly animals with bells inside them, woolly balls, and so forth, that reach the baby's hands. There is no reason at all why a child's attention should be so predominantly fixed on wool. These toys are coloured very tastefully, but as Preyer has advanced strong reasons for supposing that the child's discrimination of colours is extremely rudimentary until the second year has begun, these tasteful arrangements are simply an appeal to the parent. Light, dark, yellow, perhaps red and "other colours" seem to constitute the colour system of a very young infant. It is to the parent, too, that the humorous and realistic quality of the animal forms appeal. The parent does the shopping and has to be amused. The parent who ought to have a doll instead of a child is sufficiently abundant in our world to dominate the shops, and there is a vast traffic in facetious baby toys, facetious nursery furniture, "art" cushions and "quaint" baby clothing, all amazingly delightful things for grown-up people. These things are bought and grouped about the child, the child is taught tricks to complete the picture, and parentage becomes a very amusing afternoon employment. So long as convenience is not sacrificed to the æsthetic needs of the nursery, and so long as common may compete with "art" toys, there is no great harm done, but it is well to understand how irrelevant these things are to the real needs of a child's development.

A child of a year or less has neither knowledge nor imagination to see the point of these animal resemblances—much less to appreciate either quaintness or prettiness. That comes only in the second year. He is much more interested in the crumpling and tearing of paper, in the crumpling of chintz, and in the taking off and replacing of the lid of a little box. I think it would be possible to devise a much more entertaining set of toys for an infant than is at present procurable, but, unhappily, they would not appeal to the intelligence of the average parent. There would be, for example, one or two little boxes of different shapes and substances, with lids to take off and on, one or two rubber things that would bend and twist about and admit of chewing, a ball and a box made of china, a fluffy, flexible thing like a rabbit's tail, with the vertebræ replaced by cane, a velvet-covered ball, a powder puff, and so on. They could all be plainly and vividly coloured with some non-soluble inodorous colour. They would be about on the cot and on the rug where the child was put to kick and crawl. They would have to be too large to swallow, and they would all get pulled and mauled about until they were more or less destroyed. Some would probably survive for many years as precious treasures, as beloved objects, as powers and symbols in the mysterious secret fetichism of childhood—confidants and sympathetic friends.

§ 2

While the child is engaged with its first toys, and with the collection of rudimentary sense impressions, it is also developing a remarkable variety of noises and babblements from which it will presently disentangle speech. Day by day it will show a stronger and stronger bias to associate definite sounds with definite objects and ideas, a bias so comparatively powerful in the mind of man as to distinguish him from all other living creatures. Other creatures may think, may, in a sort of concrete way, come almost indefinably near reason (as Professor Lloyd Morgan in his very delightful *Animal Life and Intelligence* has shown); but man alone has in speech the apparatus, the possibility, at any rate, of being a reasoning and reasonable creature. It is, of course, not his only apparatus. Men may think out things with drawings, with little models, with signs and symbols upon paper, but speech is the common way, the high road, the current coin of thought.

With speech humanity begins. With the dawn of speech the child ceases to be an animal we cherish, and crosses the boundary into distinctly human intercourse. There begins in its mind the development of the most wonderful of all conceivable apparatus, a subtle and intricate keyboard, that will end at last with thirty or forty or fifty thousand keys. This queer, staring, soft little being in its mother's arms is organizing something within itself, beside which the most wonderful orchestra one can imagine is a lump of rude clumsiness. There will come a time when, at the merest touch upon those keys, image will follow image and emotion develop into emotion, when the whole creation, the deeps of space, the minutest beauties of the microscope, cities, armies, passions, splendours, sorrows, will leap out of darkness into the conscious being of thought, when this interwoven net of brief, small sounds will form the centre of a web that will hold together in its threads the universe, the All, visible and invisible, material and immaterial, real and imagined, of a human mind. And if we are to make the best of a child, it is in no way secondary to its physical health and growth that it should acquire a great and thorough command over speech, not merely that it should speak, but, what is far more vital, that it should understand swiftly and subtly things written and said. Indeed, this is more than any physical need. The body is the substance and the implement; the mind, built and compact of language, is the man. All that has gone before, all that we have discussed of sound birth and physical growth and care, is no more than the making ready of the soil for the mind that is to grow therein. As we come to this matter of language, we come a step nearer to the intimate realities of our subject—we come to the mental plant that is to bear the flower and the ripe fruit of the individual life. The next phase of our inquiry, therefore, is to examine how we can get this mental plant, this foundation substance, this abundant mastered language best developed in the individual, and how far we may go to ensure this best development for all children born into the world.

From the ninth month onward the child begins serious attempts to talk. In order that it may learn to do this as easily as possible, it requires to be surrounded by people speaking one language, and speaking it with a uniform accent. Those who are most in the child's hearing should endeavour to speak—even when they are not addressing the child—deliberately and clearly. All authorities are agreed upon the mischievous effect of what is called "baby talk," the use of an extensive sham vocabulary, a sort of deciduous milk vocabulary that will presently have to be shed again. Froebel and Preyer join hands on this. The child's funny little perversions of speech are really genuine attempts to say the right word, and we simply cause trouble and hamper development if we give back to the seeking mind its own blunders again. When a child wants to indicate milk, it wants to say milk, and not "mooka" or "mik," and when it wants to indicate bed, the needed word is not "bedder" or "bye-bye," but "bed." But we give the little thing no chance to get on in this way until suddenly one day we discover it is "time the child spoke plainly." Preyer has pointed out very instructively the way in which the quite sufficiently difficult matter of the use of I, mine, me, my, you, yours, and your is made still more difficult by those about the child adopting irregularly the experimental idioms it produces. When a child says to its mother, "Me go mome," it is doing its best to speak English, and its remark should be received without worrying comment; but when a mother says to her child, "Me go mome," she is simply wasting an opportunity of teaching her child its mother-tongue. One sympathizes with her all too readily, one understands the sweetness to her of these soft, infantile mispronunciations; but, indeed, she ought to understand; it is her primary business to know better than her feelings in this affair.

In learning to speak, the children of the more prosperous classes are probably at a considerable advantage when compared with their poorer fellow children. They hear a clearer and more uniform intonation than the blurred, uncertain speech of our commonalty, that has resulted from the reaction of the great synthetic process, of the past century upon dialects. But this natural advantage of the richer child is discounted in one of two ways: in the first place by the mother, in the second by the nurse. The mother in the more prosperous classes is often much more vain and trivial than the lower-class woman; she looks to her children for amusement, and makes them contributors to her "effect," and, by taking up their quaint and pretty mispronunciations, and devising humorous additions to their natural baby talk, she teaches them to be much greater babies than they could ever possibly be themselves. They specialise as charming babies until their mother tires of the pose, and then they are thrust back into the nursery to recover leeway, if they can, under the care of governess or nurse.

The second disadvantage of the upper-class child is the foreign nurse or nursery governess. There is a widely diffused idea that a child is particularly apt to master and retain languages, and people try and inoculate with French and German as Lord Herbert of Cherbury would have inoculated children with antidotes, for all the ills their flesh was heir to—even, poor little wretches, to an anticipatory *regimen* for gout. The root error of these attempts to form infantile polyglots is embodied in an unverified quotation from Byron's *Beppo,* dear to pedagogic writers—

"Wax to receive and marble to retain"

runs the line—which the curious may discover to be a description of the faithful lover, though it has become as firmly associated with the child-mind as has Sterne's "tempering the wind to the shorn lamb" with Holy Writ. And this idea of infantile receptivity and retentiveness is held by an unthinking world, in spite of the universally accessible fact that hardly one of us can remember anything that happened before the age of five, and very little that happened before seven or eight, and that children of five or six, removed into foreign surroundings, will in a year or so—if special measures are not taken— reconstruct their idiom, and absolutely forget every word of their mother-tongue. This foreign nurse comes into the child's world, bringing with her quite weird errors in the quantities, the accent and idiom of the mother-tongue, and greatly increasing the difficulty and delay on the road to thought and speech. And this attempt to acquire a foreign language prematurely at the expense of the mother-tongue, to pick it up cheaply by making the nurse an informal teacher of languages, entirely ignores a fact upon which I would lay the utmost stress in this paper—which, indeed, is the gist of this paper—that only a very small minority of English or American people have more than half mastered the splendid heritage of their native speech. To this neglected and most significant limitation the amount of public attention given at present is quite surprisingly small. [Footnote: My friend, Mr. L. Cope Cornford, writes *apropos* of this, and I think I cannot do better than print what he says as a corrective to my own assertions: "All you say on the importance of letting a child hear good English cleanly accented is admirable; but we think you have perhaps overlooked the importance of ear-training as such, which should begin by the time the child can utter its first attempts at speech. By ear-training I mean the differentiation of sounds—articulate, inarticulate, and musical—fixing the child's attention and causing it to *imitate*. As every sound

H. G. Wells

requires a particular movement of the vocal apparatus, the child will soon be able to adapt its apparatus unconsciously and to distinguish accurately. And if it does not so learn before the age of five or six, it probably will never do so. By the age of two—or less—the child should be able to *imitate* exactly any speech-sound. Our youngsters can do so; and, consequently, the fact that they had a nurse with a Sussex accent ceased to matter, because they learned to distinguish her talk from correct English. So in the case of a foreign nurse; the result of a foreigner's influence would be good in this way, that it would train a child to a *new series of speech-sounds*, thus enlarging its ear capacity. Nor need it necessarily adopt these speech-sounds as those which it should use; it merely knows them; and if the foreigner have a good accent, and speaks her own tongue well, the child's ear is trained for life, *irrespective of expression*. Experience shows that a child can keep separate in its mind two or three languages—at first the speech-sounds, later the expression. *Modes of expression* need not begin till after five, or later. With regard to music, every child should begin to undergo a simple course of ear-training on the sol-fa system as elaborated and taught by McNaught, because the faculty of so learning is lost—atrophied—by the age of twelve or fourteen. But, beginning early—as early as possible—every child, 'musical' or not, can be trained, just as every child, 'artistic' or not, may be taught to draw accurately up to a certain point."]

There can be little or no dispute that the English language in its completeness presents a range too ample and appliances too subtle for the needs of the great majority of those who profess to speak it. I do not refer to the half-civilized and altogether barbaric races who are coming under its sway, but to the people we are breeding of our own race—the barbarians of our streets, our suburban "white niggers," with a thousand a year and the conceit of Imperial destinies. They live in our mother-tongue as some half-civilized invaders might live in a gigantic and splendidly equipped palace. They misuse this, they waste that, they leave whole corridors and wings unexplored, to fall into disuse and decay. I doubt if the ordinary member of the prosperous classes in England has much more than a third of the English language in use, and more than a half in knowledge, and as we go down the social scale we may come at last to strata having but a tenth part of our full vocabulary, and much of that blurred and vaguely understood. The speech of the Colonist is even poorer than the speech of the home-staying English. In America, just as in Great Britain and her Colonies, there is the same limitation and the same disuse. Partly, of course, this is due to the pettiness of our thought and experience, and so far it can only be remedied by a general intellectual amplification; but partly it is due to the general ignorance of English prevailing throughout the world. It is atrociously taught, and taught by ignorant men. It is atrociously and meanly written. So far as this second cause of sheer ignorance goes, the gaps in knowledge are continually resulting in slang and the addition of needless neologisms to the language. People come upon ideas that they know no English to express, and strike out the new phrase in a fine burst of ignorant discovery. There are Americans in particular who are amazingly apt at this sort of thing. They take an enormous pride in the jargon they are perpetually increasing—they boast of it, they give exhibition performances in it, they seem to regard it as the culminating flower of their continental Republic—as though the Old World had never heard of shoddy. But, indeed, they are in no better case than that unfortunate lady at Earlswood who esteems newspapers stitched with unravelled carpet and trimmed with orange peel, the extreme of human splendour. In truth, their pride is baseless, and this slang of theirs no sort of distinction whatever. Let me assure them that in our heavier way we in this island are just as busy defiling our common inheritance. We can send a team of linguists to America who will murder and misunderstand the language against any eleven the Americans may select.

Of course there is a natural and necessary growth and development in a living language, a growth that no one may arrest. In appliances, in politics, in science, in philosophical interpretation, there is a perpetual necessity for new words, words to express new ideas and new relationships, words free

H. G. Wells

from ambiguity and encumbering associations. But the neologisms of the street and the saloon rarely supply any occasion of this kind. For the most part they are just the stupid efforts of ignorant men to supply the unnecessary. And side by side with the invention of inferior cheap substitutes for existing words and phrases, and infinitely more serious than that invention, goes on a perpetual misuse and distortion of those that are insufficiently known. These are processes not of growth but of decay—they distort, they render obsolete, and they destroy. The obsolescence and destruction of words and phrases cuts us off from the nobility of our past, from the severed masses of our race overseas, far more effectually than any growth of neologisms. A language may grow—our language must grow—it may be clarified and refined and strengthened, but it need not suffer the fate of an algal filament, and pass constantly into rottenness and decay whenever growth is no longer in progress. That has been the fate of languages in the past because of the feebler organization, the slenderer, slower intercommunication, and, above all, the insufficient records of human communities; but the time has come now—or, at the worst, is rapidly coming—when this will cease to be a fated thing. We may have a far more copious and varied tongue than had Addison or Spenser—that is no disaster—but there is no reason why we should not keep fast hold of all they had. There is no reason why the whole fine tongue of Elizabethan England should not be at our disposal still. Conceivably Addison would find the rich, allusive English of George Meredith obscure; conceivably we might find a thousand words and phrases of the year 2000 strange and perplexing; but there is no reason why a time should ever come when what has been written well in English since Elizabethan days should no longer be understandable and fine.

The prevailing ignorance of English in the English-speaking communities, enormously hampers the development of the racial consciousness. Except for those who wish to bawl the crudest thoughts, there is no means of reaching the whole mass of these communities to-day. So far as material requirements go it would be possible to fling a thought broadcast like seed over the whole world to-day, it would be possible to get a book into the hands of half the adults of our race. But at the hands and eyes one stops—there is a gap in the brains. Only thoughts that can be expressed in the meanest commonplaces will ever reach the minds of the majority of the English-speaking peoples under present conditions.

A writer who aims to be widely read to-day must perpetually halt, must perpetually hesitate at the words that arise in his mind; he must ask himself how many people will stick at this word altogether or miss the meaning it should carry; he must ransack his memory for a commonplace periphrase, an ingenious rearrangement of the familiar; he must omit or overaccentuate at every turn. Such simple and necessary words as "obsolescent," "deliquescent," "segregation," for example, must be abandoned by the man who would write down to the general reader; he must use "impertinent" as if it were a synonym for "impudent" and "indecent" as the equivalent of "obscene." And in the face of this wide ignorance of English, seeing how few people can either read or write English with any subtlety, and how disastrously this reacts upon the general development of thought and understanding amidst the English-speaking peoples, it would be preposterous even if the attempt were successful, to complicate the first linguistic struggles of the infant with the beginnings of a second language. But people deal thus lightly with the mother-tongue because they know so little of it that they do not even suspect their own ignorance of its burthen and its powers. They speak a little set of ready-made phrases, they write it scarcely at all, and all they read is the weak and shallow prose of popular fiction and the daily press. That is knowing a language within the meaning of their minds, and such a knowledge a child may very well be left to "pick up" as it may. Side by side with this they will presently set themselves to erect a similar "knowledge" of two or three other languages. One is constantly meeting not only women but men who will solemnly profess to "know" English and Latin, French, German and Italian, perhaps Greek, who are in fact—beyond

H. G. Wells

the limited range of food, clothing, shelter, trade, crude nationalism, social conventions and personal vanity—no better than the deaf and dumb. In spite of the fact that they will sit with books in their hands, visibly reading, turning pages, pencilling comments, in spite of the fact that they will discuss authors and repeat criticisms, it is as hopeless to express new thoughts to them as it would be to seek for appreciation in the ear of a hippopotamus. Their linguistic instruments are no more capable of contemporary thought than a tin whistle, a xylophone, and a drum are capable of rendering the Eroica Symphony.

In being also ignorant of itself, this wide ignorance of English partakes of all that is most hopeless in ignorance. Except among a few writers and critics, there is little sense of defect in this matter. The common man does not know that his limited vocabulary limits his thoughts. He knows that there are "long words" and rare words in the tongue, but he does not know that this implies the existence of definite meanings beyond his mental range. His poor collection of everyday words, worn-out phrases and battered tropes, constitute what he calls "plain English," and speech beyond these limits he seriously believes to be no more than the back-slang of the educated class, a mere elaboration and darkening of intercourse to secure privacy and distinction. No doubt there is justification enough for his suspicion in the exploits of pretentious and garrulous souls. But it is the superficial justification of a profound and disastrous error. A gap in a man's vocabulary is a hole and tatter in his mind; words he has may indeed be weakly connected or wrongly connected—one may find the whole keyboard jerry-built, for example, in the English-speaking Baboo—but words he has not signify ideas that he has no means of clearly apprehending, they are patches of imperfect mental existence, factors in the total amount of his personal failure to live.

This world-wide ignorance of English, this darkest cloud almost upon the fair future of our confederated peoples, is something more than a passive ignorance. It is active, it is aggressive. In England at any rate, if one talks beyond the range of white-nigger English, one commits a social breach. There are countless "book words" well-bred people never use. A writer with any tenderness for half-forgotten phrases, any disposition to sublimate the mingling of unaccustomed words, runs as grave a risk of organized disregard as if he tampered with the improper. The leaden censures of the *Times,* for example, await any excursion beyond its own battered circumlocutions. Even nowadays, and when they are veterans, Mr. George Meredith and Mr. Henley get ever and again a screed of abuse from some hot champion of Lower Division Civil Service prose. "Plain English" such a one will call his desideratum, as one might call the viands on a New Cut barrow "plain food." The hostility to the complete language is everywhere. I wonder just how many homes may not be witnessing the self-same scene as I write. Some little child is struggling with the unmanageable treasure of a new-found word, has produced it at last, a nice long word, forthwith to be "laughed out" of such foolish ambitions by its anxious parent. People train their children not to speak English beyond a threadbare minimum, they resent it upon platform and in pulpit, and they avoid it in books. Schoolmasters as a class know little of the language. In none of our schools, not even in the more efficient of our elementary schools, is English adequately taught. And these people expect the South African Dutch to take over their neglected tongue! As though the poor partial King's English of the British Colonist was one whit better than the Taal! To give them the reality of what English might be: that were a different matter altogether.

These things it is the clear business of our New Republicans to alter. It follows, indeed, but it is in no way secondary to the work of securing sound births and healthy childhoods, that we should secure a vigorous, ample mental basis for the minds born with these bodies. We have to save, to revive this scattered, warped, tarnished and neglected language of ours, if we wish to save the future of our world. We should save not only the world of those who at present speak English, but the world of many kindred and associated peoples who would

H. G. Wells

willingly enter into our synthesis, could we make it wide enough and sane enough and noble enough for their honour.

To expect that so ample a cause as this should find any support among the festering confusion of the old politics is to expect too much. There is no party for the English language anywhere in the world. We have to take this problem as we took our former problem and deal with it as though the old politics, which slough so slowly, were already happily excised. To begin with, we may give our attention to the foundation of this foundation, to the growth of speech in the developing child.

From the first the child should hear a clear and uniform pronunciation about it, a precise and careful idiom and words definitely used. Since language is to bring people together and not to keep them apart, it would be well if throughout the English-speaking world there could be one accent, one idiom, and one intonation. This there never has been yet, but there is no reason at all why it should not be. There is arising even now a standard of good English to which many dialects and many influences are contributing. From the Highlanders and the Irish, for example, the English of the South are learning the possibilities of the aspirate *h* and *wh*, which latter had entirely and the former very largely dropped out of use among them a hundred years ago. The drawling speech of Wessex and New England—for the main features of what people call Yankee intonation are to be found in perfection in the cottages of Hampshire and West Sussex—are being quickened, perhaps from the same sources. The Scotch are acquiring the English use of *shall* and *will,* and the confusion of reconstruction is world-wide among our vowels. The German *w* of Mr. Samuel Weller has been obliterated within the space of a generation or so. There is no reason at all why this natural development of the uniform English of the coming age should not be greatly forwarded by our deliberate efforts, why it should not be possible within a little while to define a standard pronunciation of our tongue. It is a less important issue by far than that of a uniform vocabulary and phraseology, but it is still a very notable need.

We have available now for the first time, in the more highly evolved forms of phonograph and telephone, a means of storing, analyzing, transmitting, and referring to sounds, that should be of very considerable value in the attempt to render a good and beautiful pronunciation of English uniform throughout the world. It would not be unreasonable to require from all those who are qualifying for the work of education, the reading aloud of long passages in the standard accent. At present there is no requirement of this sort in England, and too often our elementary teachers at any rate, instead of being missionaries of linguistic purity, are centres of diffusion for blurred and vicious perversions of our speech. They must read and recite aloud in their qualifying examinations, it is true, but under no specific prohibition of provincial intonations. In the pulpit and the stage, moreover, we have ready to hand most potent instruments of dissemination, that need nothing but a little sharpening to help greatly towards this end. At the entrance of almost all professions nowadays stands an examination that includes English, and there would be nothing revolutionary in adding to that written paper an oral test in the standard pronunciation. By active exertion to bring these things about the New Republic could do much to secure that every child of our English-speaking people throughout the world would hear in school and church and entertainment the same clear and definite accent. The child's mother and nurse would be helped to acquire almost insensibly a sound and confident pronunciation. No observant man who has lived at all broadly, meeting and talking with people of diverse culture and tradition, but knows how much our intercourse is cumbered by hesitations about quantity and accent, and petty differences of phrase and idiom, and how greatly intonation and accent may warp and limit our sympathy.

And while they are doing this for the general linguistic atmosphere, the New Republicans could also attempt something to reach the children in detail.

By instinct nearly every mother wants to teach. Some teach by instinct, but for the most part there is a need of guidance in their teaching. At present these first and very important phases in education are guided almost entirely by tradition. The necessary singing and talking to very young children is done in imitation of similar singing and talking; it is probably done no better, it may possibly be done much worse, than it was done two hundred years ago. A very great amount of permanent improvement in human affairs might be secured in this direction by the expenditure of a few thousand pounds in the systematic study of the most educational method of dealing with children in the first two or three years of life, and in the intelligent propagation of the knowledge obtained. There exist already, it is true, a number of Child Study Associations, Parents' Unions, and the like, but for the most part these are quite ineffectual talking societies, akin to Browning Societies, Literary and Natural History Societies: they attain a trifling amount of mutual improvement at their best, the members read papers to one another, and a few medical men and schools secure a needed advertisement. They have no organization, no concentration of their energy, and their chief effect seems to be to present an interest in education as if it were a harmless, pointless fad. But if a few men of means and capacity were to organize a committee with adequate funds, secure the services of specially endowed men for the exhaustive study of developing speech, publish a digested report, and, with the assistance of a good writer or so, produce very cheaply, advertise vigorously, and disseminate widely a small, clearly printed, clearly written book of pithy instructions for mothers and nurses in this matter of early speech they would quite certainly effect a great improvement in the mental foundations of the coming generation. We do not yet appreciate the fact that for the first time in the history of the world there exists a state of society in which almost every nurse and mother reads. It is no longer necessary to rely wholly upon instinct and tradition, therefore, for the early stages of a child's instruction. We can reinforce and organize these things through the printed word.

For example, an important factor in the early stage of speech-teaching is the nursery rhyme. A little child, towards the end of the first year, having accumulated a really very comprehensive selection of sounds and noises by that time, begins to imitate first the associated motions, and then the sounds of various nursery rhymes—"Pat-a-cake," for example. In the book I imagine, there would be, among many other things, a series of little versicles, old and new, in which, to the accompaniment of simple gestures, all the elementary sounds of the language could be easily and agreeably made familiar to the child's ears. [Footnote: Messrs. Heath of Boston, U.S.A., have sent me a book of Nursery Rhymes, arranged by Mr. Charles Welsh, which is certainly the best thing I have seen in this way. It is worthy of note that the neglect of pedagogic study in Great Britain is forcing the intelligent British parent and teacher to rely more and more upon American publishers for children's books. The work of English writers is often very tasteful and pretty, but of the smallest educational value.]

And the same book I think might well contain a list of foundation things and words and certain elementary forms of expression which the child should become perfectly familiar with in the first three or four years of life. Much of each little child's vocabulary is its personal adventure, and Heaven save us all from system in excess! But I think it would be possible for a subtle psychologist to trace through the easy natural tangle of the personal briar-rose of speech certain necessary strands, that hold the whole growth together and render its later expansion easy and swift and strong. Whatever else the child gets, it must get these fundamental strands well and early if it is to do its best. If they do not develop now their imperfection will cause delay and difficulty later. There are, for example, among these fundamental necessities, idioms to express comparison, to express position in space and time, elementary conceptions of form and colour, of tense and mood, the pronouns and the like. No doubt, in one way or another, most of these forms are acquired by every child, but there is no reason why their acquisition should not be watched with the help of a wisely framed list, and any deficiency deliberately and carefully supplied. It would have to be a wisely framed list, it would demand the utmost effort of the best intelligence, and that is why something more than the tradesman enterprise of publishers is needed in this work. The publisher's ideal of an author of an educational work is a clever girl in her teens working for pocket-money. What is wanted is a little quintessential book better and cheaper than any publisher, publishing for gain, could possibly produce, a book so good that imitation would be difficult, and so cheap and universally sold that no imitation would be profitable.

Upon this foundation of a sound accent and a basic vocabulary must be built the general fabric of the language. For the most part this must be done in the school. At present in Great Britain a considerable proportion of schoolmasters and school-mistresses—more particularly those in secondary and private schools—are too ill-educated to do this properly; there is excellent reason for supposing things are very little better in America; and, to begin with, it must be the care of every good New Republican to bring about a better state of things in this most lamentable profession. Until the teacher can read and write, in the fullest sense of these words, it is idle to expect him or her to teach the pupil to do these things. As matters are at present, the attempt is scarcely made. In the elementary and lower secondary schools ill-chosen reading-books are scampered through and abandoned all too soon in favour of more pretentious "subjects," and a certain preposterous nonsense called English Grammar is passed through the pupil —stuff which happily no mind can retain. Little girls and boys of twelve or thirteen, who cannot understand, and never will understand anything but the vulgarest English, and who will never in their lives achieve a properly punctuated letter, are taught such mysteries as that there are eight—I believe it is eight—sorts of nominative, and that there is (or is not) a gerundive in English, and trained month after month and year after year to perform the oddest operations, a non-analytical analysis, and a ritual called parsing that must be seen to be believed. It is no good mincing the truth about all this sort of thing. These devices are resorted to by the school teachers of the present just as the Rules of Double and Single Alligation and Double Rule of Three, and all the rest of that solemn tomfoolery, were "taught" by the arithmetic teachers in the academies of the eighteenth century, because they are utterly ignorant, and know themselves to be utterly ignorant, of the reality of the subject, and because, therefore, they have to humbug the parent and pass the time by unreal inventions. The case is not a bit better in the higher grade schools. They do not do so much of the bogus teaching of English, but they do nothing whatever in its place.

Now it is little use to goad the members of an ill-trained, ill-treated, ill-organized, poorly respected and much-abused [Footnote: *Peccavi.*] profession with reproaches for doing what they cannot do, or to clamour for legislation that will give more school time or heavier subsidies to the pretence of teaching what very few people are able to teach. We all know how atrociously English is taught, but proclaiming that will not mend matters a bit, it will only render matters worse by making schoolmasters and schoolmistresses shameless and effortless, unless we also show how well English may be taught. The sane course is to begin by establishing the proper way to do the thing, to develop a proper method and demonstrate what can be done by that method in a few selected schools, to prepare and render acceptable the necessary class-books, and then to use examination and inspector, grant in aid, training college, lecture, book and pamphlet to spread the sound expedients. We want an English Language Society, of affluent and vigorous people, that will undertake this work. And one chief duty of that society will be to devise, to arrange and select, to print handsomely, to illustrate beautifully and to sell cheaply and vigorously *everywhere,* a series of reading books, and perhaps of teachers' companions to these reading books, that shall serve as the basis of instruction in Standard English throughout the whole world. These books, as I conceive them, would begin as reading primers, they would progress through a long series of subtly graded stories, passages and extracts until they had given the complete range of our tongue. They would be read from, recited from, quoted in exemplification and imitated by the pupils. Such splendid matter as Henley and Whibley's collection of Elizabethan Prose, for example, might

　　　　　　　H. G. Wells

well find a place toward the end of that series of books. There would be an anthology of English lyrics, of all the best short stories in our language, of all the best episodes. From these readers the pupil would pass, still often reading and reciting aloud, to such a series of masterpieces as an efficient English Language Society could force upon every school. At present in English schools a library is an exception rather than a rule, and your clerical head-master on public occasions will cheerfully denounce the "trash" reading, "snippet" reading habits of the age, with that defect lying like a feather on his expert conscience. A school without an easily accessible library of at least a thousand volumes is really scarcely a school at all—it is a dispensary without bottles, a kitchen without a pantry. For all that, if the inquiring New Republican find two hundred linen-covered volumes of the *Eric, or Little by Little* type, mean goody-goody thought dressed in its appropriate language, stored away in some damp cupboard of his son's school, and accessible once a week, he may feel assured things are above the average there. My imaginary English Language Society would make it a fundamental duty, firstly to render that library of at least a thousand volumes or so specially cheap and easily procurable, and secondly, by pamphlets and agitation, to render it a compulsory minimum requirement for every grade of school. It is far more important, and it would be far less costly even as things are, than the cheapest sort of chemical laboratory a school could have, and it should cost scarcely more than a school piano.

I know very little of the practical teaching of English, my own very fragmentary knowledge of the more familiar clichés of our tongue was acquired in a haphazard fashion, but I am inclined to think that in addition to much reading aloud and recitation from memory the work of instruction might consist very largely of continually more extensive efforts towards original composition. Paraphrasing is a good exercise, provided that it does not consist in turning good and beautiful English into bad. I do not see why it should not follow the reverse direction. Selected passages of mean, stereotyped, garrulous or inexact prose might very well be rewritten, under the direction of an intelligent master. Retelling a story that has just been read and discussed, with a change of incident perhaps, would also not be a bad sort of exercise, writing passages in imitation of set passages and the like. Written descriptions of things displayed to a class should also be instructive. Caught at the right age, most little girls, and many little boys I believe, would learn very pleasantly to write simple verse. This they should be encouraged to read aloud. At a later stage the more settled poetic forms, the ballade, the sonnet, the rondeau, for example, should afford a good practice in handling language. Pupils should be encouraged to import fresh words into their work—even if the effect is a little startling at times—they should hunt the dictionary for material. A good book for the upper forms in schools dealing in a really intelligent and instructive way with Latin and Greek, so far as it is necessary to know these languages in order to use and manipulate technical English freely, would, I conceive, be of very great service. It must be a good exercise to write precise definitions of words. Logic also is an integral portion of the study of the mother-tongue.

But to throw out suggestions in this way is an easy task. The educational papers are full of this sort of thing, educational conferences resound with it. What the world is not full of is the capacity to organize these things, to drag them, struggling and clinging to a thousand unanticipated difficulties, from the region of the counsel of perfection to the region of manifest practicability. For that there is needed attention, industry, and an intelligent use of a fair sum of money. We want an industrious committee, and we want one or two rich men. A series of books, a model course of instruction, has to be planned and made, tried over, criticised, revised and altered. When the right way is no longer indicated by prophetic persons pointing in a mist, but marked out, levelled, mapped and fenced, then the scholastic profession, wherever the English language is spoken, has to be lured and driven along it. The New Republican must make his course cheap, attractive, easy for the teacher and good for the teacher's pocket and reputation. Just as there are plays that, as actors say, "act themselves," so, with a profession that is rarely at its best and often at its worst, and which at its worst consists of remarkably dull young men and remarkably dreary young women, those who want English well taught must see to it that they provide a series of books and instructors that will teach by themselves, whatever the teacher does to prevent them.

Surely this enterprise of text-books and teachers, of standard phonographs and cheaply published classics, is no fantastic impossible dream! So far as money goes—if only money were the one thing needful—a hundred thousand pounds would be a sufficient fund from first to last for all of it. Yet modest as its proportions are, its consequences, were it done by able men throwing their hearts into it, might be of incalculable greatness. By such expedients and efforts as these we might enormously forward the establishment of that foundation of a world-wide spacious language, the foundation upon which there will arise for our children subtler understandings, ampler imaginations, sounder judgments and clearer resolutions, and all that makes at last a nobler world of men.

But in this discussion of school libraries and the like, we wander a little from our immediate topic of mental beginnings.

§ 3

At the end of the fifth year, as the natural outcome of its instinctive effort to experiment and learn, acting amidst wisely ordered surroundings, the little child should have acquired a certain definite foundation for the educational structure. It should have a vast variety of perceptions stored in its mind, and a vocabulary of three or four thousand words, and among these, and holding them together, there should be certain structural and cardinal ideas. They are ideas that will have been gradually and imperceptibly instilled, and they are necessary as the basis of a sound mental existence. There must be, to begin with, a developing sense and feeling for truth and for duty as something distinct and occasionally conflicting with immediate impulse and desire, and there must be certain clear intellectual elements established already almost impregnably in the mind, certain primary distinctions and classifications. Many children are called stupid, and begin their educational career with needless difficulty through an unsoundness of these fundamental intellectual elements, an unsoundness in no way inherent, but the result of accident and neglect. And a starting handicap of this sort may go on increasing right through the whole life.

The child at five, unless it is colour blind, should know the range of colours by name, and distinguish them easily, blue and green not excepted; it should be able to distinguish pink from pale red and crimson from scarlet. [Footnote: There could be a set of colour bands in the book that the English Language Society might publish.] Many children through the neglect of those about them do not distinguish these colours until a very much later age. I think also—in spite of the fact that many adults go vague and ignorant on these points—that a child of five may have been taught to distinguish between a square, a circle, an oval, a triangle and an oblong, and to use these words. It is easier to keep hold of ideas with words than without them, and none of these words should be impossible by five. The child should also know familiarly by means of toys, wood blocks and so on, many elementary solid forms. It

H. G. Wells

is matter of regret that in common language we have no easy, convenient words for many of these forms, and instead of being learnt easily and naturally in play, they are left undistinguished, and have to be studied later under circumstances of forbidding technicality. It would be quite easy to teach the child in an incidental way to distinguish cube, cylinder, cone, sphere (or ball), prolate spheroid (which might be called "egg"), oblate spheroid (which might be called "squatty ball"), the pyramid, and various parallelepipeds, as, for example, the square slab, the oblong slab, the brick, and post. He could have these things added to his box of bricks by degrees, he would build with them and combine them and play with them over and over again, and absorb an intimate knowledge of their properties, just at the age when such knowledge is almost instinctively sought and is most pleasant and easy in its acquisition. These things need not be specially forced upon him. In no way should he be led to emphasize them or give a priggish importance to his knowledge of them. They will come into his toys and play mingled with a thousand other interests, the fortifying powder of clear general ideas, amidst the jam of play.

In addition the child should be able to count, [Footnote: There can be little doubt that many of us were taught to count very badly, and that we were hampered in our arithmetic throughout life by this defect. Counting should be taught be means of small cubes, which the child can arrange and rearrange in groups. It should have at least over a hundred of these cubes—if possible a thousand; they will be useful as toy bricks, and for innumerable purposes. Our civilization is now wedded to a decimal system of counting, and, to begin with, it will be well to teach the child to count up to ten and to stop there for a time. It is suggested by Mrs. Mary Everest Boole that it is very confusing to have distinctive names for eleven and twelve, which the child is apt to class with the single numbers and contrast with the teens, and she proposes at the beginning (*The Cultivation of the Mathematical Imagination*, Colchester: Benham & Co.) to use the words "one-ten," "two-ten," thirteen, fourteen, etc., for the second decade in counting. Her proposal is entirely in harmony with the general drift of the admirably suggestive diagrams of number order collected by Mr. Francis Gallon. Diagram after diagram displays the same hitch at twelve, the predominance in the mind of an individualized series over quantitatively equal spaces until the twenties are attained. Many diagrams also display the mental scar of the clock face, the early counting is overmuch associated with a dial. One might perhaps head off the establishment of that image, and supply a more serviceable foundation for memories by equipping the nursery with a vertical scale of numbers divided into equal parts up to two or three hundred, with each decade tinted. When the child has learnt to count up to a hundred with cubes, it should be given an abacus, and it should also be encouraged to count and check quantities with all sorts of things, marbles, apples, bricks in a wall, pebbles, spots on dominoes, and so on; taught to play guessing games with marbles in a hand, and the like. The abacus, the hundred square and the thousand cube, will then in all probability become its cardinal numerical memories. Playing cards (without corner indices) and dominoes supply good recognizable arrangements of numbers, and train a child to grasp a number at a glance. The child should not be taught the Arabic numerals until it has counted for a year or more. Experience speaks here. I know one case only too well of a man who learnt his Arabic numerals prematurely, before he had acquired any sound experimental knowledge of numerical quantity, and, as a consequence, his numerical ideas are incurably associated with the peculiarities of the figures. When he hears the word seven he does not really think of seven or seven-ness at all, even now, he thinks of a number rather like four and very unlike six. Then again, six and nine are mysteriously and unreasonably linked in his mind, and so are three and five. He confuses numbers like sixty-three and sixty-five, and finds it hard to keep seventy-four distinct from forty-seven. Consequently, when it came to the multiplication table, he learnt each table as an arbitrary arrangement of relationships, and with an extraordinary amount of needless labour and punishment. But obviously with cubes or abacus at hand, it would be the easiest thing in the world for a child to construct and learn its own multiplication table whenever the need arose.] it should be capable of some mental and experimental arithmetic, and I am told that a child of five should be able to give the *sol-fa* names to notes, and sing these names at their proper pitch. Possibly in social intercourse the child will have picked up names for some of the letters of the alphabet, but there is no great hurry for that before five certainly, or even later. There is still a vast amount of things immediately about the child that need to be thoroughly learnt, and a premature attack on letters divides attention from these more appropriate and educational objects. It should, for the reason given in the footnote, be still ignorant of the Arabic numerals. It should be able to handle a pencil and amuse itself with freehand of this sort:—and its mind should be quite uncontaminated by that imbecile drawing upon squared paper by means of which ignorant teachers destroy both the desire and the capacity to sketch in so many little children. Such sketching could be enormously benefited by a really intelligent teacher who would watch the child's efforts, and draw with the child just a little above its level. For example, the teacher might stimulate effort by rejoining to such a sketch as the above, something in this vein:—

The child will already be a great student of picture-books at five, something of a critic (after the manner of the realistic school), and it will be easy to egg it almost imperceptibly to a level where copying from simple outline illustrations will become possible. About five, a present of some one of the plastic substitutes for modelling clay now sold by educational dealers, *plasticine* for example, will be a discreet and acceptable present to the child—if not to its nurse.

The child's imagination will also be awake and active at five. He will look out on the world with anthropomorphic (or rather with pædomorphic) eyes. He will be living on a great flat earth—unless some officious person has tried to muddle his wits by telling him the earth is round; amidst trees, animals, men, houses, engines, utensils, that are all capable of being good or naughty, all fond of nice things and hostile to nasty ones, all thumpable and perishable, and all conceivably esurient. And the child should know of Fairy Land. The beautiful fancy of the "Little People," even if you do not give it to him, he will very probably get for himself; they will lurk always just out of reach of his desiring curious eyes, amidst the grass and flowers and behind the wainscot and in the shadows of the bedroom. He will come upon their traces; they will do him little kindnesses. Their affairs should interweave with the affairs of the child's dolls and brick castles and toy furniture. At first the child will scarcely be in a world of sustained stories, but very eager for anecdotes and simple short tales.

This is the hopeful foundation upon which at or about the fifth year the formal education of every child in a really civilized community ought to begin. [Footnote: One may note here, perhaps, the desirability too often disregarded by over-solicitous parents, and particularly by the parents of the solitary children who are now so common, of keeping the child a little out of focus, letting it play by itself whenever it will, never calling attention to it in a manner that awakens it to the fact of an audience, never talking about it in its presence. Solitary children commonly get too much control, they are forced and beguiled upward rather than allowed to grow, their egotism is over-stimulated, and they miss many of the benefits of play and competition. It seems a pity, too, in the case of so many well-to-do people, that having equipped nurseries they should not put them to a fuller use—if in no other way than by admitting foster children. None of this has been very fully analyzed, of course (there are enormous areas of valuable research in these matters waiting for people of intelligence and leisure, or of intelligence and means), but the opinion that solitary children are handicapped by their loneliness is very strong. It is nearly certain that as a rule they make less agreeable boys and girls, but to me at any rate it is not nearly so certain that they make adult failures. It would be interesting to learn just what proportion of solitary children there is on the roll of those who have become great in our world. One thinks of John Ruskin, a particularly fine specimen of the highly focussed single son. Prig perhaps he was, but this world has a certain need of such prigs. A correspondent (a schoolmistress of experience) who has collected statistics in her own neighbourhood, is strongly of opinion not only that solitary children are below the average, but that all elder children are inferior in quality. I do not believe this, but it would be interesting and valuable if some one could find time for a wide and thorough investigation of this question.]

V

THE MAN-MAKING FORCES OF
THE MODERN STATE

So far we have concerned ourselves with the introductory and foundation matter of the New Republican project, with the measures and methods that may be resorted to, firstly, if we would raise the general quality of the children out of whom we have to make the next generation, and, secondly, if we would replace divergent dialects and partial and confused expression by a uniform, ample and thorough knowledge of English throughout the English-speaking world. These two things are necessary preliminaries to the complete attainment of the more essential nucleus in the New Republican idea. So much has been discussed. This essential nucleus, thus stripped, reveals itself as the systematic direction of the moulding forces that play upon the developing citizen, towards his improvement, with a view to a new generation of individuals, a new social state, at a higher level than that at which we live to-day, a new generation which will apply the greater power, ampler knowledge and more definite will our endeavours will give it, to raise its successor still higher in the scale of life. Or we may put the thing in another and more concrete and vivid way. On the one hand imagine an average little child let us say in its second year. We have discussed all that can be done to secure that this average little child shall be well born, well fed, well cared for, and we will imagine all that can be done has been done. Accordingly, we have a sturdy, beautiful healthy little creature to go upon, just beginning to walk, just beginning to

H. G. Wells

clutch at things with its hands, to reach out to and apprehend things with its eyes, with its ears, with the hopeful commencement of speech. We want to arrange matters so that this little being shall develop into its best possible adult form. That is our remaining problem.

Is our contemporary average citizen the best that could have been made out of the vague extensive possibilities that resided in him when he was a child of two? It has been shown already that in height and weight he, demonstrably, is not, and it has been suggested, I hope almost as convincingly, that in that complex apparatus of acquisition and expression, language, he is also needlessly deficient. And even upon this defective foundation, it is submitted, he still fails, morally, mentally, socially, aesthetically, to be as much as he might be. "As much as he might be," is far too ironically mild. The average citizen of our great state to-day is, I would respectfully submit, scarcely more than a dirty clout about his own buried talents.

I do not say he might not be infinitely worse, but can any one believe that, given better conditions, he might not have been infinitely better? Is it necessary to argue for a thing so obvious to all clear-sighted men? Is it necessary, even if it were possible, that I should borrow the mantle of Mr. George Gissing or the force of Mr. Arthur Morrison, and set myself in cold blood to measure the enormous defect of myself and my fellows by the standards of a remote perfection, to gauge the extent of this complex muddle of artificial and avoidable shortcomings through which we struggle? Must one, indeed, pass in review once more, bucolic stupidity, commercial cunning, urban vulgarity, religious hypocrisy, political clap-trap, and all the raw disorder of our incipient civilization before the point will be conceded? What benefit is there in any such revision? rather it may overwhelm us with the magnitude of what we seek to do. Let us not dwell on it, on all the average civilized man still fails to achieve; admit his imperfection, and for the rest let us keep steadfastly before us that fair, alluring and reasonable conception of all that, even now, the average man might be.

Yet one is tempted by the effective contrast to put against that clean and beautiful child some vivid presentation of the average thing, to sketch in a few simple lines the mean and graceless creature of our modern life, his ill-made clothes, his clumsy, half-fearful, half-brutal bearing, his coarse defective speech, his dreary unintelligent work, his shabby, impossible, bathless, artless, comfortless home; one is provoked to suggest him in some phase of typical activity, "enjoying himself" on a Bank Holiday, or rejoicing, peacock feather in hand, hat askew, and voice completely gone, on some occasion of public festivity—on the defeat of a numerically inferior enemy for example, or the decision of some great international issue at baseball or cricket. This, one would say, we have made out of that, and so point the New Republican question, "Cannot we do better?" But the thing has been done so often without ever the breath of a remedy. Our business is with remedies. We mean to do better, we live to do better, and with no more than a glance at our present failures we will set ourselves to that.

To do better we must begin with a careful analysis of the process of this man's making, of the great complex of circumstances which mould the vague possibilities of the average child into the reality of the citizen of the modern state.

We may begin upon this complex most hopefully by picking out a few of the conspicuous and typical elements and using them as a basis for an exhaustive classification. To begin with, of course, there is the home. For our present purpose it will be convenient to use "home" as a general expression for that limited group of human beings who share the board and lodging of the growing imperial citizen, and whose personalities are in constant, close contact with his until he reaches fifteen or sixteen. Typically, the chief figures of this group are mother, brothers and sisters, and father, to which are often added nursemaid, governess, and other servants. Beyond these are playmates again. Beyond these acquaintances figure. Home has indeed nowadays, in our world, no very definite boundaries—no such boundaries as it has, for example, on the veldt. In the case of a growing number of English upper

H. G. Wells

middle-class children, moreover, and of the children of a growing element in the life of the eastern United States, the home functions are delegated in a very large degree to the preparatory school. It is a distinction that needs to be emphasized that many so-called schools are really homes, often very excellent homes, with which schools, often very inefficient schools, are united. All this we must lump together—it is, indeed, woven together almost inextricably—when we speak of home as a formative factor. The home, so far as its hygienic conditions go, we have already dealt with, and we have dealt, too, with the great neglected necessity, the absolute necessity if our peoples are to keep together, of making and keeping the language of the home uniform throughout our world-wide community. Purely intellectual development beyond the matter of language we may leave for a space. There remains the distinctive mental and moral function of the home, the determination by precept, example, and implication of the cardinal habits of the developing citizen, his general demeanour, his fundamental beliefs about all the common and essential things of life.

This group of people, who constitute the home, will be in constant reaction upon him. If as a whole they bear themselves with grace and serenity, say and do kindly things, control rage, and occupy themselves constantly, they will do much to impose these qualities upon the new-comer. If they quarrel one with another, behave coarsely and spitefully, loiter and lounge abundantly, these things will also stamp the child. A raging father, a scared deceitful mother, vulgarly acting, vulgarly thinking friends, all leave an almost indelible impress. Precept may play a part in the home, but it is a small part, unless it is endorsed by conduct. What these people do, on the whole, believe in and act upon, the child will tend to believe in and act upon; what they believe they believe, but do not act upon, the child will acquire also as a non-operative belief; their practices, habits, and prejudices will be enormously prepotent in his life. If, for example, the parent talks constantly of the contemptible dirtiness of Boers and foreigners, and of the extreme beauty of cleanliness and—even obviously—rarely washes, the child will grow to the same professions and the same practical denial. This home circle it is that will describe what, in modified Herbartian phraseology, one may call the child's initial circle of thought; it is a circle many things will subsequently enlarge and modify, but of which they have the centering at least and the establishment of the radial trends, almost beyond redemption. The effect of home influence, indeed, constitutes with most of us a sort of secondary heredity, interweaving with, and sometimes almost indistinguishable from, the real unalterable primary heredity, a moral shaping by suggestion, example, and influence, that is a sort of spiritual parallel to physical procreation.

It is not simply personalities that are operative in the home influence. There is also the implications of the various relations between one member of the home circle and another. I am inclined to think that the social conceptions, for example, that are accepted in a child's home world are very rarely shaken in afterlife. People who have been brought up in households where there is an organized under-world of servants are incurably different in their social outlook from those who have passed a servantless childhood. They never quite emancipate themselves from the conception of an essential class difference, of a class of beings inferior to themselves. They may theorise about equality—but theory is not belief. They will do a hundred things to servants that between equals would be, for various reasons, impossible. The Englishwoman and the Anglicised American woman of the more pretentious classes honestly regards a servant as physically, morally, and intellectually different from herself, capable of things that would be incredibly arduous to a lady, capable of things that would be incredibly disgraceful, under obligations of conduct no lady observes, incapable of the refinement to which every lady pretends. It is one of the most amazing aspects of contemporary life, to converse with some smart, affected, profoundly uneducated, flirtatious woman about her housemaid's followers. There is such an identity; there is such an abyss. But at present that contrast is not our concern. Our concern at present is with the fact that the social constitution of the home almost invariably shapes the fundamental social conceptions for life, just as its average temperament shapes manners and bearing and its moral tone begets moral predisposition. If the average sensual man of our civilization is noisy and undignified in his bearing, disposed to insult and despise those he believes to be his social inferiors, competitive and disobliging to his equals; abject, servile, and dishonest to those he regards as his betters; if his wife is a silly, shallow, gossiping spendthrift, unfit to rear the children she occasionally bears, perpetually snubbing social inferiors and perpetually cringing to social superiors, it is probable that we have to blame the home, not particularly any specific class of homes, but our general home atmosphere, for the great part of these characteristics. If we would make the average man of the coming years gentler in manner, more deliberate in judgment, steadier in purpose, upright, considerate, and free, we must look first to the possibility of improving the tone and quality of the average home.

Now the substance and constitution of the home, the relations and order of its various members, have been, and are, traditional. But it is a tradition that has always been capable of modification in each generation. In the unlettered, untravelling past, the factor of tradition was altogether dominant. Sons and daughters married and set up homes, morally, intellectually, economically, like those of their parents. Over great areas homogeneous traditions held, and it needed wars and conquests, or it needed missionaries and persecutors and conflicts, or it needed many generations of intercourse and filtration before a new tradition could replace or graft itself upon the old. But in the past hundred years or so the home conditions of the children of our English-speaking population have shown a disposition to break from tradition under influences that are increasing, and to become much more heterogeneous than were any home conditions before. The ways in which these modifications of the old home tradition have arisen will indicate the means and methods by which further modifications may be expected and attempted in the future.

Modification has come to the average home tradition through two distinct, though no doubt finally interdependent channels. The first of these channels is the channel of changing economic necessities, using the phrase to cover everything from domestic conveniences at the one extreme to the financial foundation of the home at the other, and the next is the influx of new systems of thought, of feeling, and of interpretation about the general issues of life.

There are in Great Britain three main interdependent systems of home tradition undergoing modification and readjustment. They date from the days before mechanism and science began their revolutionary intervention in human affairs, and they derive from the three main classes of the old aristocratic, agricultural, and trading state, namely, the aristocratic, the middle, and the labour class. There are local, there are even racial modifications, there are minor classes and subspecies, but the rough triple classification will serve. In America the dominant home tradition is that of the transplanted English middle class. The English aristocratic tradition has flourished and faded in the Southern States; the British servile and peasant tradition has never found any growth in America, and has, in the persons of the Irish chiefly, been imported in an imperfect condition, only to fade. The various home traditions of the nineteenth century immigrants have either, if widely different, succumbed, or if not very different assimilated themselves to the ruling tradition. The most marked non-British influence has been the intermixture of Teutonic Protestantism. In both countries now the old home traditions have been and are being adjusted to and modified by the new classes, with new relationships and new necessities, that the revolution in industrial organization and domestic conveniences has created.

The interplay of old tradition and new necessities becomes at times very curious. Consider, for example, the home influences of the child of a shopman in a large store, or those of the child of a skilled operative—an engineer of some sort let us say—in England. Both these are new types in the English social body;

the former derives from the old middle class, the class that was shopkeeping in the towns and farming in the country, the class of the Puritans, the Quakers, the first manufacturers, the class whose mentally active members become the dissenters, the old Liberals, and the original New Englanders. The growth of large businesses has raised a portion of this class to the position of Sir John Blundell Maple, Sir Thomas Lipton, the intimate friend of our King, and our brewer peers; it has raised a rather more numerous section to the red plush glories of Wagon-Lit trains and their social and domestic equivalents, and it has reduced the bulk of the class to the status of employees for life. But the tradition that our English shopman is in the same class as his master, that he has been apprentice and improver, and is now assistant, with a view to presently being a master himself, still throws its glamour over his life and his home, and his child's upbringing. They belong to the middle class, the black coat and silk-hat class, and the silk hat crowns the adolescence of their boys as inevitably as the toga made men in ancient Rome. Their house is built, not for convenience primarily, but to realize whatever convenience is possible after the rigid traditional requirements have been met; it is the extreme and final reduction of the plan of a better class house, and the very type of its owner. As one sees it in the London suburbs devoted to clerks and shopmen, it stands back a yard or so from the road, with a gate and a railing, and a patch, perhaps two feet wide, of gravel between its front and the pavement. This is the last pathetic vestige of the preliminary privacies of its original type, the gates, the drive-up, the front lawn, the shady trees, that gave a great impressive margin to the door. The door has a knocker (with an appeal to realities, "ring also") and it opens into a narrow passage, perhaps four feet wide, which still retains the title of "hall." Oak staining on the woodwork and marbled paper accentuate the lordly memory. People of this class would rather die than live in a house with a front door, even had it a draught-stopping inner door, that gave upon the street. Instead of an ample kitchen in which meals can be taken and one other room in which the rest of life goes on, these two covering the house site, the social distinction from the servant invades the house space first by necessitating a passage to a side-door, and secondly by cutting up the interior into a "dining-room" and a "drawing-room." Economy of fuel throughout the winter and economy of the best furniture always, keeps the family in the dining-room pretty constantly, but there you have the drawing-room as a concrete fact. Though the drawing-room is inevitable, the family will manage without a bath-room well enough. They may, or they may not, occasionally wash all over. There are probably not fifty books in the house, but a daily paper comes and *Tit Bits* or *Pearson's Weekly*, or, perhaps, *M.A.P.*, *Modern Society*, or some such illuminant of the upper circles, and a cheap fashion paper, appear at irregular intervals to supplement this literature.

The wife lives to realize the ideal of the "ladylike"—lady she resigns to the patrician—and she insists upon a servant, however small. This poor wretch of a servant, often a mere child of fourteen or fifteen, lives by herself in a minute kitchen, and sleeps in a fireless attic. To escape vulgar associates, the children of the house avoid the elementary schools—the schools called in America public schools—where there are trained, efficient teachers, good apparatus, and an atmosphere of industry, and go to one of those wretched dens of disorderly imposture, a middle-class school, where an absolute failure to train or educate is seasoned with religious cant, lessons in piano-playing, lessons in French "made in England," mortarboard caps for the boys, and a high social tone. And to emphasize the fact of its social position, this bookless, bathless family tips! The plumber touches his hat for a tip, the man who moves the furniture, the butcher-boy at Christmas, the dustman; these things also, the respect and the tip, at their minimum dimensions. Everything is at its minimum dimensions, it is the last chipped, dwarfed, enfeebled state of a tradition that has, in its time, played a fine part in the world. This much of honour still clings to it, it will endure no tip, no charity, no upper-class control of its privacy. This is the sort of home in which the minds of thousands of young Englishmen and Englishwomen receive their first indelible impressions. Can one expect them to escape the contagion of its cramped pretentiousness, its dingy narrowness, its shy privacy of social degradation, its essential sordidness and inefficiency?

Our skilled operative, on the other hand, will pocket his tip. He is on the other side of the boundary. He presents a rising element coming from the servile mass. Probably his net income equals or exceeds the shopman's, but there is no servant, no black coat and silk hat, no middle-class school in his scheme of things. He calls the shopman "Sir," and makes no struggle against his native accent. In his heart he despises the middle class, the mean tip-givers, and he is inclined to overrate the gentry or big tippers. He is much more sociable, much noisier, relatively shameless, more intelligent, more capable, less restrained. He is rising against his tradition, and almost against his will. The serf still bulks large in him. The whole trend of circumstance is to substitute science for mere rote skill in him, to demand initiative and an intelligent self-adaptation to new discoveries and new methods, to make him a professional man and a job and pieceworker after the fashion of the great majority of professional men. Against all these things the serf element in him fights. He resists education and clings to apprenticeship, he fights for time-work, he obstructs new inventions, he clings to the ideal of short hours, high pay, shirk and let the master worry. His wife is a far more actual creature than the clerk's; she does the house herself in a rough, effectual fashion, his children get far more food for mind and body, and far less restraint. You can tell the age of the skilled operative within a decade by the quantity of books in his home; the younger he is the more numerous these are likely to be. And the younger he is the more likely he is to be alive to certain general views about his rights and his place in the social scale, the less readily will his finger go to his cap at the sight of broad-cloth, or his hand to the proffered half-crown. He will have listened to Trade Union organizers and Socialist speakers; he will have read the special papers of his class. The whole of this home is, in comparison with the shopman's, wide open to new influences. The children go to a Board School, and very probably afterwards to evening classes—or music-halls. Here again is a new type of home, in which the English of 1920 are being made in thousands, and which is forced a little way up the intellectual and moral scale every year, a little further from its original conception of labour, dependence, irresponsibility, and servility.

Compare, again, the home conditions of the child of a well-connected British shareholder inheriting, let us say, seven or eight hundred a year, with the home of exactly the same sort of person deriving from the middle class. On the one hand, one will find the old aristocratic British tradition in an instructively distorted state. All the assumptions of an essential lordliness remain—and none of the duties. All the pride is there still, but it is cramped, querulous, and undignified. That lordliness is so ample that for even a small family the income I have named will be no more than biting poverty, there will be a pervading quality of struggle in this home to avoid work, to frame arrangements, to discover cheap, loyal servants of the old type, to discover six per cent. investments without risk, to interest influential connections in the prospects of the children. The tradition of the ruling class, which sees in the public service a pension scheme for poor relations, will glow with all the colours of hope. Great sacrifices will be made to get the boys to public schools, where they can revive and expand the family connections. They will look forward as a matter of course to positions and appointments, for the want of which men of gifts and capacity from other social strata will break their hearts, and they will fill these coveted places with a languid, discontented incapacity. Great difficulty will be experienced in finding schools for the girls from which the offspring of tradesmen are excluded. Vulgarity has to be jealously anticipated. In a period when Smartness (as distinguished from Vulgarity) is becoming an ideal, this demands at times extremely subtle discrimination. The art of credit will be developed to a high level.

Now in the other family economically indistinguishable from this, a family with seven or eight hundred a year from investments, which derives from the middle class, the tradition is one that, in spite of the essential irresponsibility of the economic position, will urge this family towards exertion as a duty. As a rule the resultant lies in the direction of pleasant, not too arduous exertion, the arts are attacked with great earnestness of intention, literature, "movements" of many sorts are ingredients in these homes. Many things that are imperative to the aristocratic home are regarded as needless, and in their place appear other things that the aristocrat would despise, books, instruction, travel in incorrect parts of the world, *games*, that most seductive development of modern life, played to the pitch of distinction. Into both these homes comes literature, comes the Press, comes the talk of alien minds, comes the observation of things without, sometimes reinforcing the tradition, sometimes insidiously glossing upon it or undermining it, sometimes "letting daylight through it"; but much more into the latter type than into the former. And slowly the two fundamentally identical things tend to assimilate their superficial difference, to homologize their traditions, each generation sees a relaxation of the aristocratic prohibitions, a "gentleman" may tout for wines nowadays— among gentlemen—he may be a journalist, a fashionable artist, a schoolmaster, his sisters may "act," while, on the other hand, each generation of the ex-commercial shareholder reaches out more earnestly towards refinement, towards tone and quality, towards etiquette, and away from what is "common" in life.

So in these typical cases one follows the strands of tradition into the new conditions, the new homes of our modern state. In America one finds exactly the same new elements shaped by quite parallel economic developments, shopmen in a large store, skilled operatives, and independent shareholders developing homes not out of a triple strand of tradition, but out of the predominant home tradition of an emancipated middle class, and in a widely different atmosphere of thought and suggestion. As a consequence, one finds, I am told, a skilled operative already with no eye (or only an angry eye) for tips, sociable shopmen, and shareholding families, frankly common, frankly intelligent, frankly hedonistic, or only with the most naïve and superficial imitation of the haughty incapacity, the mean pride, the parasitic lordliness of the just-independent, well-connected English.

These rough indications of four social types will illustrate the quality of our proposition, that home influence in the making of men resolves itself into an interplay of one substantial and two modifying elements, namely:—

(1) Tradition.

(2) Economic conditions.

(3) New ideas, suggestions, interpretations, changes in the general atmosphere of thought in which a man lives and which he mentally breathes.

The net sum of which three factors becomes the tradition for the next generation.

Both the modifying elements admit of control. How the economic conditions of homes may be controlled to accomplish New Republican ends has already been discussed with a view to a hygienic minimum, and obviously the same, or similar, methods may be employed to secure less materialistic benefits. You can make a people dirty by denying them water, you can make a people cleaner by cheapening and enforcing bath-rooms. Man is indeed so spiritual a being that he will turn every materialistic development you force upon him into spiritual growth. You can aerate his house, not only with air, but with ideas. Build, cheapen, render alluring a simpler, more spacious type of house for the clerk, fill it with labour-saving conveniences, and leave no excuse and no spare corners for the "slavey," and the slavey—and all that she means in mental and moral consequence—will vanish out of being. You will beat tradition. Make it easy for Trade Unions to press for shorter hours of work, but make it difficult for them to obstruct the arrival of labour-saving appliances, put the means of education easily within the reach of every workman, make promotion from the ranks, in the Army, in the Navy, in all business concerns, practicable and natural, and the lingering discolouration of the serf taint will vanish from the workman's mind. The days of mystic individualism have passed, few people nowadays will agree to that strange creed that we must deal with economic conditions as though they were inflexible laws. Economic conditions are made and compact of the human will, and by tariffs, by trade regulation and organization, fresh strands of will may be woven into the complex. The thing may be extraordinarily intricate and difficult, abounding in unknown possibilities and unsuspected dangers, but that is a plea for science and not for despair.

Controllable, too, is the influx of modifying suggestions into our homes, however vast and subtle the enterprise may seem. But here we touch for the first time a question that we shall now continue to touch upon at other points, until at last we shall clear it and display it as the necessarily central question of the whole matter of man-making so far as the human will is concerned, and that is the preservation and expansion of the body of human thought and imagination, of which all conscious human will and act is but the imperfect expression and realization, of which all human institutions and contrivances, from the steam-engine to the ploughed field, and from the blue pill to the printing press, are no more than the imperfect symbols, the rude mnemonics and memoranda.

But this analysis of the modifying factors in the home influence, this formulation of its controllable elements, has now gone as far as the purpose of this paper requires. It has worked out to this, that the home, so far as it is not traditional organization, is really only on the one hand an aspect of the general economic condition of the state, and on the other of that still more fundamental thing, its general atmosphere of thought. Our analysis refers back the man-maker to these two questions. The home, one gathers, is not to be dealt with separately or simply. Nor, on the other hand, are these questions to be dealt with merely in relation to their home application. As the citizen grows up, he presently emerges from his home influences to a more direct and general contact with these two things, with the Fact of the modern state and with the Thought of the modern state, and we must consider each of these in relation to his development as a whole.

The next group of elements in the man-making complex that occurs to one after the home, is the school. Let me repeat a distinction already drawn between the home element in boarding-schools and the school proper. While the child is out of the school-room, playing—except when it is drilling or playing under direction—when it is talking with its playmates, walking, sleeping, eating, it is under those influences that it has been convenient for me to speak of as the home influence. The schoolmaster who takes boarders is, I hold, merely a substitute for the parent, the household of boarders merely a substitute for the family. What is meant by school here, is that which is possessed in common by day school and boarding-school—the schoolroom and the recess playground part. It is something which the savage and the barbarian distinctively do not possess as a phase in their making, and scarcely even its rudimentary suggestion. It is a new element correlated with the establishment of a wider political order and with the use of written speech.

Now I think it will be generally conceded that whatever systematic intellectual training the developing citizen gets, as distinguished from his natural, accidental, and incidental development, is got in school or in its subsequent development of college, and with that I will put aside the question of intellectual development altogether for a later, fuller discussion. My point here is simply to note the school as a factor in the making of almost every citizen in the modern state, and to point out, what is sometimes disregarded, that it is only one of many factors in that making. The tendency of the present time is enormously to exaggerate the importance of school in development, to ascribe to it powers quite beyond its utmost possibilities, and to blame it for evils in which it has no share. And in the most preposterous invasions of the duties of parent, clergyman, statesman, author, journalist, of duties which are in truth scarcely more within the province of a schoolmaster than they are within the province of a butcher, the real and necessary work of the school is too often marred, crippled, and lost sight of altogether. We treat the complex, difficult and honourable task of intellectual development as if it were within the capacity of any earnest but muddle-headed young lady, or any half-educated gentleman in orders; we take that for granted, and we demand in addition from them the "formation of character," moral and ethical training and supervision, aesthetic guidance, the implanting of a taste for the Best in literature, for the Best in art, for the finest conduct; we demand the clue to success in commerce and the seeds of a fine passionate patriotism from these necessarily very ordinary persons.

One might think schoolmasters and schoolmistresses were inaccessible to general observation in the face of these stupendous demands. If we exacted such things from our butcher over and above good service in his trade, if we insisted that his meat should not only build up honest nerve and muscle, but that it should compensate for all that was slovenly in our homes, dishonest in our economic conditions, and slack and vulgar in our public life, he would very probably say that it took him all his time to supply sound meat, that it was a difficult and honourable thing to supply sound meat, that the slackness of business-men and statesmen in the country, the condition of the arts and sciences, wasn't his business, that however lamentable the disorders of the state, there was no reasonable prospect of improving it by upsetting the distribution of meat, and, in short, that he was a butcher and not a Cosmos-healing quack. "You must have meat," he would say, "anyhow." But the average schoolmaster and school-mistress does not do things in that way.

What a school may do for the developing citizen, the original and the developed function of the school, and how its true work may best be accomplished, we shall discuss later. But it may be well to expand a little more fully here the account of what the school has no business to attempt, and what the scholastic profession is, as a whole, quite incapable of doing, and to point to the really responsible agencies in each case.

Now, firstly, with regard to all that the schoolmaster and schoolmistress means by the "formation of character." A large proportion of the scholastic profession will profess, and a still larger proportion of the public believes, that it is possible by talk and specially designed instruction, to give a boy or girl a definite bias towards "truth," towards acts called "healthy" (a word it would puzzle the ordinary schoolmaster or schoolmistress extremely to define, glib as they are with it), towards honour, towards generosity, enterprise, self-reliance, and the like. The masters in our public schools are far from blameless in this respect, and you may gauge the quality of many of these gentlemen pretty precisely by their disposition towards the "school pulpit" line of business. Half an hour's "straight talk to the boys," impromptu vague sentimentality about Earnestness, Thoroughness, True Patriotism, and so forth, seems to assuage the conscience as nothing else could do, for weeks of ill-prepared, ill-planned teaching, and years of preoccupation with rowing-boats and cricket. The more extreme examples of this type will say in a tone of manly apology, "It does the boys good to tell them plainly what I think about serious things"— when the simple fact of the case is too often that he does all he can not to think about any things of any sort whatever, except cricket and promotion. Schoolmistresses, again, will sometimes come near boasting to the inquiring parent of our "ethical hour," and if you probe the facts you will find that means no more and no less than an hour of floundering egotism, in which a poor illogical soul, with a sort of naive indecency, talks nonsense about "Ideals," about the Higher and the Better, about Purity, and about many secret and sacred things, things upon which wise men are often profoundly uncertain, to incredulous or imitative children. All that is needed to do this sort of thing abundantly and freely is a certain degree of aggressive egotism, a certain gift of stupidity, good intentions, and a defective sense of educational possibilities and limitations.

In addition to moral discussions, that at the best are very

H. G. Wells

second-rate eloquence, and at the worst are respect destroying, mind destroying gabble, there are various forms of "ethical" teaching, advocated and practised in America and in the elementary schools of this country. For example, a story of an edifying sort is told to the children, and comments are elicited upon the behaviour of the characters. "Would you have done that?" "Oh, *no*, teacher!" "Why not?" "Because it would be mean." The teacher goes into particulars, whittling away at the verdict, and at last the fine point of the lesson stands out. Now it may be indisputable that such lessons can be conducted effectively and successfully by exceptionally brilliant teachers, that children may be given an excellent code of good intentions, and a wonderful skill in the research for good or bad motives for any given course of action they may or may not want to take, but that they can be systematically trained by the average teacher at our disposal in this desirable "subject" is quite another question. It is one of the things that the educational reformer must guard against most earnestly, the persuasion that what an exceptional man can do ever and again for display purposes can be done successfully day by day in schools. This applies to many other things besides the teaching of ethics. Professor Armstrong can give delightfully instructive lessons in chemistry according to the heuristic method, but in the hands of the average teacher by whom teaching *must* be done for the next few years the heuristic system will result in nothing but a pointless fumble. Mr. Mackinder teaches geography—inimitably—just to show how to do it. Mr. David Devant—the brilliant Egyptian Hall conjuror—will show any assembly of parents how to amuse children quite easily, but for some reason he does not present his legerdemain as a new discovery in educational method.

To our argument that this sort of teaching is not within the capacity of such teachers as we have, or are likely to have, we can, fortunately enough, add that whatever is attempted can be done far better through other agencies. More or less unknown to teachers there exists a considerable amount of well-written literature, true stories and fiction, in which, without any clumsy insistence upon moral points, fine actions are displayed in their elementary fineness, and baseness is seen to be base. There are also a few theatres, and there might be more, in which fine action is finely displayed. Now one nobly conceived and nobly rendered play will give a stronger moral impression than the best schoolmaster conceivable, talking ethics for a year on end. One great and stirring book may give an impression less powerful, perhaps, but even more permanent. Practically these things are as good as example—they are example. Surround your growing boy or girl with a generous supply of good books, and leave writer and growing soul to do their business together without any scholastic control of their intercourse. Make your state healthy, your economic life healthy and honest, be honest and truthful in the pulpit, behind the counter, in the office, and your children will need no specific ethical teaching; they will inhale right. And without these things all the ethical teaching in the world will only sour to cant at the first wind of the breath of the world.

Quite without ethical pretension at all the school is of course bound to influence the moral development of the child. That most important matter, the habit and disposition towards industry, should be acquired there, the sense of thoroughness in execution, the profound belief that difficulty is bound to yield to a resolute attack—all these things are the necessary by-products of a good school. A teacher who is punctual, persistent, just, who tells the truth, and insists upon the truth, who is truthful, not merely technically but in a constant search for exact expression, whose own share of the school work is faultlessly done, who is tolerant to effort and a tireless helper, who is obviously more interested in serious work than in puerile games, will beget essential manliness in every boy he teaches. He need not lecture on his virtues. A slack, emotional, unpunctual, inexact, and illogical teacher, a fawning loyalist, an incredible pietist, an energetic snob, a teacher as eager for games, as sensitive to social status, as easy, kindly, and sentimental, and as shy really of hard toil as—as some teachers—is none the better for ethical flatulence. There is a good deal of cant in certain educational circles, there is a certain type of educational writing in which "love" is altogether too strongly present; a reasonably extensive observation of school-children and school-teachers makes one doubt whether there is ever anything more than a very temperate affection and a still more temperate admiration on either side. Children see through their teachers amazingly, and what they do not understand now they will understand later. For a teacher to lay hands on all the virtues, to associate them with his or her personality, to smear characteristic phrases and expressions over them, is as likely as not to give the virtues unpleasant associations. Better far, save through practice, to leave them alone altogether.

And what is here said of this tainting of moral instruction with the personality of the teacher applies still more forcibly to religious instruction. Here, however, I enter upon a field where I am anxious to avoid dispute. To my mind those ideas and emotions that centre about the idea of God appear at once too great and remote, and too intimate and subtle for objective treatment. But there are a great number of people, unfortunately, who regard religion as no more than geography, who believe that it can be got into daily lessons of one hour, and adequately done by any poor soul who has been frightened into conformity by the fear of dismissal. And having this knobby, portable creed, and believing sincerely that lip conformity is alone necessary to salvation, they want to force every teacher they can to acquire and impart its indestructible, inflexible recipes, and they are prepared to enforce this at the price of inefficiency in every other school function. We must all agree—whatever we believe or disbelieve—that religion is the crown of the edifice we build. But it will simply ruin a vital part of the edifice and misuse our religion very greatly if we hand it over to the excavators and bricklayers of the mind, to use as a cheap substitute for the proper intellectual and ethical foundations; for the ethical foundation which is schooling and the ethical foundation which is habit. I must confess that there is only one sort of man whose insistence upon religious teaching in schools by ordinary school teachers I can understand, and that is the downright Atheist, the man who believes sensual pleasure is all that there is of pleasure, and virtue no more than a hood to check the impetuosity of youth until discretion is acquired, the man who believes there is nothing else in the world but hard material fact, and who has as much respect for truth and religion as he has for stable manure. Such a man finds it convenient to profess a lax version of the popular religion, and he usually does so, and invariably he wants his children "taught" religion, because he so utterly disbelieves in God, goodness, and spirituality that he cannot imagine young people doing even enough right to keep healthy and prosperous, unless they are humbugged into it.

Equally unnecessary is the scholastic attempt to take over the relations of the child to "nature," art, and literature. To read the educational journals, to hear the scholastic enthusiast, one would think that no human being would ever discover there was any such thing as "nature" were it not for the schoolmaster—and quotation from Wordsworth. And this nature, as they present it, is really not nature at all, but a factitious admiration for certain isolated aspects of the universe conventionally regarded as "natural." Few schoolmasters have discovered that for every individual there are certain aspects of the universe that especially appeal, and that that appeal is part of the individuality—different from every human being, and quite outside their range. Certain things that have been rather well treated by poets and artists (for the most part dead and of Academic standing) they regard as Nature, and all the rest of the world, most of the world in which we live, as being in some way an intrusion upon this classic. They propound a wanton and illogical canon. Trees, rivers, flowers, birds, stars—are, and have been for many centuries Nature—so are ploughed fields—really the most artificial of all things—and all the apparatus of the agriculturist, cattle, vermin, weeds, weed-fires, and all the rest of it. A grassy old embankment to protect low-lying fields is Nature, and so is all the mass of apparatus about a water-mill; a new embankment to store an urban water supply, though it may be one mass of splendid weeds, is artificial, and ugly. A wooden windmill is Nature and beautiful, a sky-sign atrocious. Mountains have become Nature and beautiful within the last hundred years—volcanoes even.

Vesuvius, for example, is grand and beautiful, its smell of underground railway most impressive, its night effect stupendous, but the glowing cinder heaps of Burslem, the wonders of the Black Country sunset, the wonderful fire-shot nightfall of the Five Towns, these things are horrid and offensive and vulgar beyond the powers of scholastic language. Such a mass of clotted inconsistencies, such a wild confusion of vicious mental practices as this, is the stuff the schoolmaster has in mind when he talks of children acquiring a love of Nature. They are to be trained, against all their mental bias, to observe and quote about the canonical natural objects and not to observe, but instead to shun and contemn everything outside the canon, and so to hand on the orthodox Love of Nature to another generation. One may present the triumph of scholastic nature-teaching, by the figure of a little child hurrying to school along the ways of a busy modern town. She carries a faded cut-flower, got at considerable cost from a botanical garden, and as she goes she counts its petals, its stamens, its bracteoles. Her love of Nature, her "powers of observation," are being trained. About her, all unheeded, is a wonderful life that she would be intent upon but for this precious training of her mind; great electric trains loom wonderfully round corners, go droning by, spitting fire from their overhead wires; great shop windows display a multitudinous variety of objects; men and women come and go about a thousand businesses; a street-organ splashes a spray of notes at her as she passes, a hoarding splashes a spray of colour.

The shape and direction of one's private observation is no more the schoolmaster's business than the shape and direction of one's nose. It is, indeed, possible to certain gifted and exceptional persons that they should not only see acutely, but abstract and express again what they have seen. Such people are artists—a different kind of people from schoolmasters altogether. Into all sorts of places, where people have failed to see, comes the artist like a light. The artist cannot create nor can he determine the observation of other men, but he can, at any rate, help and inspire it. But he and the pedagogue are temperamentally different and apart. They are at opposite poles of human quality. The pedagogue with his canon comes between the child and Nature only to limit and obscure. His business is to leave the whole thing alone.

If the interpretation of nature is a rare and peculiar gift, the interpretation of art and literature is surely an even rarer thing. Hundreds of schoolmasters and schoolmistresses who could not write one tolerable line of criticism, will stand up in front of classes by the hour together and issue judgments on books, pictures, and all that is comprised under the name of art. Think of it! Here is your great artist, your great exceptional mind groping in the darknesses beneath the surface of life, half apprehending strange elusive things in those profundities, and striving—striving sometimes to the utmost verge of human endeavour—to give that strange unsuspected mystery expression, to shape it, to shadow it in form and wonder of colour, in beautiful rhythms, in phantasies of narrative, in gracious and glowing words. So much in its essential and precious degree is art. Think of what the world must be in the wider vision of the great artist. Think, for example, of the dark splendours amidst which the mind of Leonardo clambered; the mirror of tender lights that reflected into our world the iridescent graciousness of Botticelli! Then to the faint and faded intimations these great men have left us of the things beyond our scope, comes the scholastic intelligence, gesticulating instructively, and in too many cases obscuring for ever the naive vision of the child. The scholastic intelligence, succulently appreciative, blind, hopelessly blind to the fact that every great work of art is a strenuous, an almost despairing effort to express and convey, treats the whole thing as some foolish riddle—"explains it to the children." As if every picture was a rebus and every poem a charade! "Little children," he says, "this teaches you"—and out comes the platitude!

Of late years, in Great Britain more particularly, the School has been called upon to conquer still other fields. It has become apparent that in this monarchy of ours, in which honour is heaped high upon money-making, even if it is money-making that adds nothing to the collective wealth or efficiency, and denied to the most splendid public services unless they are also remunerative; where public applause is the meed of cricketers, hostile guerillas, clamorous authors, yacht-racing grocers, and hopelessly incapable generals, and where suspicion and ridicule are the lot of every man working hard and living hard for any end beyond a cabman's understanding; in this world-wide Empire whose Government is entrusted as a matter of course to peers and denied as a matter of course to any man of humble origin; where social pressure of the most urgent kind compels every capable business manager to sell out to a company and become a "gentleman" at the very earliest opportunity, the national energy is falling away. That driving zeal, that practical vigour that once distinguished the English is continually less apparent. Our workmen take no pride in their work any longer, they shirk toil and gamble. And what is worse, the master takes no pride in the works; he, too, shirks toil and gambles. Our middle-class young men, instead of flinging themselves into study, into research, into literature, into widely conceived business enterprises, into so much of the public service as is not preserved for the sons of the well connected, play games, display an almost oriental slackness in the presence of work and duty, and seem to consider it rather good form to do so. And seeking for some reason and some remedy for this remarkable phenomenon, a number of patriotic gentlemen have discovered that the Schools, the Schools are to blame. Something in the nature of Reform has to be waved over our schools.

It would be a wicked deed to write anything that might seem to imply that our Schools were not in need of very extensive reforms, or that their efficiency is not a necessary preliminary condition to general public efficiency, but, indeed, the Schools are only one factor in a great interplay of causes, and the remedy is a much ampler problem than any Education Act will cure. Take a typical young Englishman, for example, one who has recently emerged from one of our public schools, one of the sort of young Englishmen for whom all commissions in the Army are practically reserved, who will own some great business, perhaps, or direct companies, and worm your way through the tough hide of style and restraint he has acquired, get him to talk about women, about his prospects, his intimate self, and see for yourself how much of him, and how little of him, his school has made. Test him on politics, on the national future, on social relationships, and lead him if you can to an utterance or so upon art and literature. You will be astonished how little you can either blame or praise the teaching of his school for him. He is ignorant, profoundly ignorant, and much of his style and reserve is draped over that; he does not clearly understand what he reads, and he can scarcely write a letter; he draws, calculates and thinks no better than an errand boy, and he has no habit of work; for that much perhaps the school must answer. And the school, too, must answer for the fact that although—unless he is one of the small specialized set who "swat" at games—he plays cricket and football quite without distinction, he regards these games as much more important than military training and things of that sort, spends days watching his school matches, and thumbs and muddles over the records of county cricket to an amazing extent. But these things are indeed only symptons, and not essential factors in general inefficiency. There are much wider things for which his school is only mediately or not at all to blame. For example, he is not only ignorant and inefficient and secretly aware of his ignorance and inefficiency, but, what is far more serious, he does not feel any strong desire to alter the fact; he is not only without the habit of regular work, but he does not feel the defect because he has no desire whatever to do anything that requires work in the doing. And you will find that this is so because there is woven into the tissue of his being a profound belief that work and knowledge "do not pay," that they are rather ugly and vulgar characteristics, and that they make neither for happiness nor success.

He did not learn that at school, nor at school was it possible he should unlearn it. He acquired that belief from his home, from the conversation of his equals, from the behaviour of his inferiors; he found it in the books and newspapers he has read, he breathed it in with his native air. He regards it as manifest

Fact in the life about him. And he is perfectly right. He lives in a country where stupidity is, so to speak, crowned and throned, and where honour is a means of exchange; and he draws his simple, straight conclusions. The much-castigated gentleman with the ferule is largely innocent in this account.

If, too, you ransack your young Englishman for religion, you will be amazed to find scarcely a trace of School. In spite of a ceremonial adhesion to the religion of his fathers, you will find nothing but a profound agnosticism. He has not even the faith to disbelieve. It is not so much that he has not developed religion as that the place has been seared. In his time his boyish heart has had its stirrings, he has responded with the others to "Onward, Christian Soldiers," the earnest moments of the school pulpit, and all those first vague things. But limited as his reading is, it has not been so limited that he does not know that very grave things have happened in matters of faith, that the doctrinal schemes of the conventional faith are riddled targets, that creed and Bible do not mean what they appear to mean, but something quite different and indefinable, that the bishops, socially so much in evidence, are intellectually in hiding.

Here again is something the school did not cause, the school cannot cure.

And in matters sexual, in matters political, in matters social, and matters financial you will find that the flabby, narrow-chested, under-trained mind that hides in the excellent-looking body of the typical young Englishman is encumbered with an elaborate duplicity. Under the cloak of a fine tradition of good form and fair appearances you will find some intricate disbeliefs, some odd practices. You will trace his moral code chiefly to his school-fellows, and the intimates of his early manhood, and could you trace it back you would follow an unbroken tradition from the days of the Restoration. So soon as he pierces into the realities of the life about him, he finds enforcement, ample and complete, for the secret code. The schoolmaster has not touched it; the school pulpit has boomed over its development in vain. Nor has the schoolmaster done anything for or against the young man's political views, his ideas of social exclusiveness, the peculiar code of honour that makes it disgraceful to bilk a cabman and permissible to obtain goods on credit from a tradesman without the means to pay. All this much of the artificial element in our young English gentleman was made outside the school, and is to be remedied only by extra-scholastic forces.

School is only one necessary strand in an enormous body of formative influence. At first that mass of formative influence takes the outline of the home, but it broadens out as the citizen grows until it reaches the limits of his world. And his world, just like his home, resolves itself into three main elements. First, there is the traditional element, the creation of the past; secondly, there is the contemporary interplay of economic and material forces; and thirdly, there is literature, using that word for the current thought about the world, which is perpetually tending on the one hand to realize itself and to become in that manner a material force, and on the other to impose fresh interpretations upon things and so become a factor in tradition. Now the first of these elements is a thing established. And it is the possibility of intervening through the remaining two that it is now our business to discuss.

VI

SCHOOLING

We left the child whose development threads through this discussion ripe to begin a little schooling at the age of five. We have cleared the ground since then of a great number of things that have got themselves mixed up in an illegitimate way with the idea of school, and we can now take him on again through his "schooling" phases. Let us begin by asking what we require and then look to existing conditions to see how far we may hope to get our requirements. We will assume the foundation described in the fourth paper has been well and truly laid, that we have a number of other similarly prepared children available to form a school, and that we have also teachers of fair average intelligence, conscience, and aptitude. We will ask what can be done with such children and teachers, and then we may ask why it is not universally done.

Even after our clarifying discussion, in which we have shown that schooling is only a part, and by no means the major part, of the educational process, and in which we have distinguished and separated the home element in the boarding-school from the schooling proper, there still remains something more than a simple theme in schooling. After all these eliminations we remain with a mixed function and mixed traditions, and it is necessary now to look a little into the nature of this mixture.

The modern school is not a thing that has evolved from a simple germ, by a mere process of expansion. It is the coalescence of several things. In different countries and periods you will find schools taking over this function and throwing out that, and changing not only methods but professions and aims in the most remarkable manner. What has either been teachable or has seemed teachable in human development has played a part in some curriculum or other. Beyond the fact that there is class instruction and an initial stage in which the pupil learns to read and write, there is barely anything in common. But that initial stage is to be noted; it is the thing the Hebrew schoolboy, the Tamil schoolboy, the Chinese schoolboy, and the American schoolboy have in common. So much, at any rate, of the school appears wherever there is a written language, and its presence marks a stage in the civilizing process. As I have already pointed out in my book "Anticipations," the presence of a reading and writing class of society and the existence of an organized nation (as distinguished from a tribe) appear together. When tribes coalesce into nations, schools appear. This first and most universal function of the school is to initiate a smaller or greater proportion of the population into the ampler world, the more efficient methods, of the reading and writing man. And with the disappearance of the slave and the mere labourer from the modern conception of what is necessary in the state, there has now come about an extension of this initiation to the whole of our English-speaking population. And in addition to reading and writing the vernacular, there is also almost universally in schools instruction in counting, and wherever there is a coinage, in the values and simpler computation of coins.

In addition to the vernacular teaching, one finds in the schools—at any rate the schools for males—over a large part of the world, a second element, which is always the language of what either is or has been a higher and usually a dominant civilization. Typically, there is a low or imitative vernacular literature or no literature at all, and this second language is the key to all that literature involves—general views, general ideas, science, poetic suggestion and association. Through this language the vernacular citizen escapes from his parochial and national limitations to a wide commonweal of thought. Such was Greek at one time to the Roman, such was Latin to the Bohemian, the German, the Englishman or the Spaniard of the middle ages, and such it is to-day to the Roman Catholic priest; such is Arabic to the Malay, written Chinese to the Cantonese or the Corean, and English to the Zulu or the Hindoo. In Germany and France, to a lesser degree in Great Britain, and to a still lesser degree in the United States, we find, however, an anomalous condition of things. In each of these countries civilization has long since passed into an unprecedented phase, and each of these countries has long since developed a great living mass of literature in which its new problems are, at any rate, approached. There is scarcely a work left in Latin or Greek that has not been translated into and assimilated and more or less completely superseded by English, French, and German works; but the schoolmaster, heedless of these things, still arrests the pupil at the old portal, fumbles with the keys, and partially opens the door into a ransacked treasure-chamber. The language of literature and of civilized ideas is, for the English-speaking world to-day, English—not the weak, spoken dialect of each class and locality, but the rich and splendid language in which and with which our literature and philosophy grow. That, however, is by the way. Our point at present is that the exhaustive teaching of a language so that it may serve as a key to culture is a second function in the school.

We find in a broad survey of schools in general that there has also been a disposition to develop a special training in thought and expression either in the mother tongue (as in the Roman schools of Latin oratory), or in the culture tongue (as in Roman schools of Greek oratory), and we find the same element in the mediaeval trivium. Quintilian's conception of education, the reader will remember, was oratory. This aspect of school work was the traditional and logical development of the culture language-teaching. But as in Europe the culture language has ceased to be really a culture language but merely a reasonless survival, and its teaching has degenerated more and more into elaborate formalities supposed to have in some mystical way "high educational value," and for the most part conducted by men unable either to write or speak the culture language with any freedom or vigour, this crown of cultivated expression has become more and more inaccessible. It is too manifestly stupid—even for our public schoolmasters—to think of carrying the "classical grind" to that pitch, and, in fact, they carry no part of the education to that pitch. There is no deliberate and professed training at all in logical thought—except for the use of Euclid's Elements to that end—nor in expression in any language at all, in the great mass of modern schools. This is a very notable point about the schools of the present period.

But, on the other hand, the schools of the modern period have developed masses of instruction that were not to be found in the schools of the past. The school has reached downward and taken over, systematized, and on the whole, I think, improved that preliminary training of the senses and the observation that was once left to the spontaneous activity of the child among its playmates and at home. The kindergarten department of a school is a thing added to the old conception of schooling, a conversion of the all too ample school hours to complete and rectify the work of the home, to make sure of the foundation of sense impressions and elementary capabilities upon which the edifice of schooling is to rise. In America it has grown, as a wild flower transferred to the unaccustomed richness of garden soil will sometimes do, rankly and in relation to the more essential schooling, aggressively, and become a highly vigorous and picturesque weed. One must bear in mind that Froebel's original thought was rather of the mother than of the schoolmistress, a fact the kindergarten invaders of the school find it convenient to forget. I believe we shall be carrying out his intentions as well as the manifest dictates of common sense if we do all in our power by means of simply and clearly written books for nurses and mothers to shift very much of the kindergarten back to home and playroom and out of the school altogether. Correlated with this development, there has been a very great growth in our schools of what is called manual training and of the teaching of drawing. Neither of these subjects entered into the school idea of any former period, so far as my not very extensive knowledge of educational history goes.

Modern, too, is the development of efficient mathematical teaching; so modern that for too many schools it is still a thing of tomorrow. The arithmetic (without Arabic numerals, be it remembered) and the geometry of the mediaeval quadrivium were astonishingly clumsy and ineffectual instruments in comparison with the apparatus of modern mathematical method. And while the mathematical subjects of the quadrivium were taught as science and for their own sakes, the new mathematics is a sort of supplement to language, affording a means of thought about form and quantity and a means of expression, more exact, compact, and ready than ordinary language. The great body of physical science, a great deal of the essential fact of financial science, and endless social and political problems are only accessible and only thinkable to those who have had a sound training in mathematical analysis, and the time may not be very remote when it will be understood that for complete initiation as an efficient citizen of one of the new great complex world-wide states that are now developing, it is as necessary to be able to compute, to think in averages and maxima and minima, as it is now to be able to read and write. This development of mathematical teaching is only another aspect of the necessity that is bringing the teaching of drawing into schools, the necessity that is so widely, if not always very intelligently perceived, of clearheadedness about quantity, relative quantity, and form, that our highly mechanical, widely extended, and still rapidly extending environments involve.

Arithmetic and geometry were taught in the mediaeval school as sciences, in addition the quadrivium involved the science of astronomy, and now that the necessary fertilizing inundation of our general education by the classical languages and their literatures subsides, science of a new sort reappears in our schools. I must confess that a lot of the science teaching that appears in schools nowadays impresses me as being a very undesirable encumbrance of the curriculum. The schoolman's science came after the training in language and expression, late in the educational scheme, and it aimed, it pretended—whatever its final effect was—to strengthen and enlarge the mind by a noble and spacious sort of knowledge. But the science of the modern school pretends merely to be a teaching of useful knowledge; the vistas, the tremendous implications of modern science are conscientiously disregarded, and it is in effect too often no more than a diversion of school energies to the acquisition of imperfectly analyzed misstatements about entrails, elements, and electricity, with a view—a quite unjustifiable view—to immediate profitable hygienic and commercial application. Whether there is any educational value in the school-teaching of science we may discuss later. For the present we may note it simply as a revived and developing element.

On the other hand, while these things expand in the modern school, there are declining elements, once in older schemes of scholastic work much more evident. In the culture of the mediaeval knight, for example, and of the eighteenth-century young lady, elegant accomplishments, taught disconnected from the general educational scheme and for themselves, played a large part. The eighteenth-century young lady was taught dancing, deportment, several instruments of music, how to pretend to sketch, how to pretend to know Italian, and so on. The dancing still survives—a comical mitigation of high school austerities—and there is also a considerable interruption of school work achieved by the music-master. If there is one thing that I would say with certainty has no business whatever in schools, it is piano-teaching. The elementary justification of the school is its organization for class-teaching and work in unison, and there is probably no subject of instruction that requires individual tuition quite so imperatively as piano-playing; there is no subject so disadvantageously introduced where children are gathered together. But to every preparatory and girls' school in England—I do not know if the same thing happens in America—the music-master comes once or twice a week, and with a fine disregard of the elementary necessities of

H. G. Wells

teaching, children are called one by one, out of whatever class they happen to be attending, to have their music-lesson. Either the whole of the rest of the class must mark time at some unnecessary exercise until the missing member returns, or one child must miss some stage, some explanation that will involve a weakness, a lameness for the rest of the course of instruction. Not only is the actual music-lesson a nuisance in this way, but all day the school air is loaded with the oppressive tinkling of racked and rackety pianos. Nothing, I think, could be more indicative of the real value the English school-proprietor sets on school-teaching than this easy admission of the music-master to hack and riddle the curriculum into rags. [Footnote 1: Piano playing as an accomplishment is a nuisance and encumbrance to the school course and a specialization that surely lies within the private Home province. To learn to play the piano properly demands such an amount of time and toil that I do not see how we can possibly include it in the educational scheme of the honourable citizens of the coming world state. To half learn it, to half learn anything, is a training in failure. But it is probable that a different sort of music teaching altogether—a teaching that would aim, not at instrumentalization, but at intelligent appreciation—might find a place in a complete educational scheme. The general ignorance that pervades, and in part inspires these papers, does, in the matter of music, become special, profound, and distinguished. It seems to me, however, that what the cultivated man or woman requires is the ability to read a score intelligently rather than to play it—to distinguish the threads, the values, of a musical composition, to have a quickened ear rather than a disciplined hand. I owe to my friend, Mr. Graham Wallas, the suggestion that the piano is altogether too exacting an instrument to use as the practical vehicle for such instruction, and that something simpler and cheaper—after the fashion of the old spinet—is required. Possibly some day a teacher of genius will devise and embody in a book a course of class lessons, sustained by simple practice and written work, that would attain this end. But, indeed, after all is said and done, music is the most detached and the purest of arts, the most accessory of attainments.] Apart from the piano work, the special teaching of elegant accomplishments seems just at present on the wane. And on the whole I think what one might call useful or catchpenny accomplishments are also passing their zenith—shorthand lessons, book-keeping lessons, and such-like impostures upon parental credulity.

There is, however, a thing that was once done in schools as a convenient accomplishment, and which has—with that increase in communication which is the salient material fact of the nineteenth century—developed in Western Europe to the dimensions of a political necessity, and that is the teaching of one or more modern foreign languages. The language-teaching of all previous periods has been done with a view to culture, artistic, as in the case of Elizabethan Italian, or intellectual as with English Latin. But the language-teaching of to-day is deliberately, almost conscientiously, not for culture. It would, I am sure, be a very painful and shocking thought indeed to an English parent to think that French was taught in school with a view to reading French books. It is taught as a vulgar necessity for purposes of vulgar communication. The stirring together of the populations that is going on, the fashion and facilities for travel, the production of the radii from the trading foci, are rapidly making a commonplace knowledge of French, German, and Italian a necessity to the merchant and tradesman, and the ever more extensive travelling class. So that so far as Europe goes, one may very well regard this modern modern-language teaching as—with the modern mathematics —an extension of the *trivium*, of the apparatus, that is, of thought and expression. [Footnote: In the United States there is less sense of urgency about modern languages, but sooner or later the American may wake up to the need of Spanish in his educational schemes.] It is an extension and a very doubtful improvement. It is a modern necessity, a rather irksome necessity, of little or no essential educational value, an unavoidable duty the school will have to perform. [Footnote: In one way the foreign language may be made educationally very useful, and that is as an exercise in writing translations into good English.]

There are two subjects in the modern English school that stand by themselves and in contrast with anything one finds in the records of ancient and oriental schools, as a very integral part of what is regarded as our elementary general education. They are of very doubtful value in training the mind, and most of the matter taught is totally forgotten in adult life. These are history and geography. These two subjects constitute, with English grammar and arithmetic, the four obligatory subjects for the very lowest grade of the London College of Preceptors' examinations, for example. The examination papers of this body reveal the history as an affair of dated events, a record of certain wars and battles, and legislative and social matters quite beyond the scope of a child's experience and imagination. Scholastic history ends at 1700 or 1800, always long before it throws the faintest light upon modern political or social conditions. The geography is, for the most part, topography, with a smattering of quantitative facts, heights of mountains, for example, populations of countries, and lists of obsolete manufactures and obsolete trade conditions. Any one who will take the trouble to run through the text-books of these subjects gathered together in the library of the London Teachers' Guild, will find that the history is generally taught without maps, pictures, descriptive passages, or anything to raise it above the level of an arid misuse of memory; and the highest levels to which ordinary school geography has attained are to be found in the little books of the late Professor Meiklejohn. These two subjects are essentially "information" subjects. They differ in prestige rather than in educational quality from school chemistry and natural history, and their development marks the beginning of that great accumulation of mere knowledge which is so distinctive of this present civilization.

There are, no doubt, many minor subjects, but this revision will at least serve to indicate the scope and chief varieties of school work. Out of some such miscellany it is that in most cases the student passes to specialization, to a different and narrower process which aims at a specific end, to the course of the College. In some cases this specialized course may be correlated with a real and present practice, as in the case of the musical, medical, and legal faculties of our universities; it may be correlated with obsolete needs and practices and regardless of modern requirements, as in the case of the student of divinity who takes his orders and comes into a world full of the ironical silences that follow great controversies, nakedly ignorant of geology, biology, psychology, and modern biblical criticism; or it may have no definite relation to special needs, and it may profess to be an upward prolongation of schooling towards a sort of general wisdom and culture, as in the case of the British "Arts" degrees. The ordinary Oxford, Cambridge, or London B.A. has a useless smattering of Greek, he cannot read Latin with any comfort, much less write or speak that tongue; he knows a few unedifying facts round and about the classical literature, he cannot speak or read French with any comfort; he has an imperfect knowledge of the English language, insufficient to write it clearly, and none of German, he has a queer, old-fashioned, and quite useless knowledge of certain rudimentary sections of mathematics, and an odd little bite out of history. He knows practically nothing of the world of thought embodied in English literature, and absolutely nothing of contemporary thought; he is totally ignorant of modern political or social science, and if he knows anything at all about evolutionary science and heredity it is probably matter picked up in a casual way from the magazines. Art is a sealed book to him. Still, the inapplicability of his higher education to any professional or practical need in the world is sufficiently obvious, it seems, to justify the claim that it has put him on a footing of thought and culture above the level of a shopman. It is either that or nothing. And without deciding between these alternatives, we may note here for our present purpose, that the conception of a general upward prolongation of schooling beyond adolescence, as distinguished from a specific upward prolongation into professional training, is necessary to the complete presentation of the school and college scheme in the modern state.

There has always been a tendency to utilize the gathering together of children in schools for purposes irrelevant to schooling proper, but of some real or fancied benefit.

H. G. Wells

Wherever there is a priestly religion, the lower type of religious fanatic will always look to the schools as a means of doctrinal dissemination; will always be seeking to replace efficiency by orthodoxy upon staff and management; and, with an unconquerable, uncompromising persistency, will seek perpetually either to misconduct or undermine; and the struggle to get him out and keep him out of the school, and to hold the school against him, will be one of the most necessary and thankless of New Republican duties. I have, however, already adduced reasons that I think should appeal to every religious mind, for the exclusion of religious teaching from school work. The school gathering also affords opportunity for training in simple unifying political conceptions; the salutation of the flag, for example, or of the idealized effigies of King and Queen. The quality of these conceptions we shall discuss later. The school also gives scope for physical training and athletic exercises that are, under the crowded conditions of a modern town, almost impossible except by its intervention. And it would be the cheapest and easiest way of raising the military efficiency of a country, and an excellent thing for the moral tone and public order of a people, to impose upon the school gathering half an hour a day of vigorous military drill. The school, too, might very easily be linked more closely than it is at present with the public library, and made a means of book distribution; and its corridors may easily be utilized as a loan picture gallery, in which good reproductions of fine pictures might bring the silent influence of the artist mind to bear. But all these things are secondary applications of the school gathering; at their best they are not conducted by the school-teacher at all, and I remark upon them here merely to avoid any confusion their omission might occasion.

Now if we dip into this miscellany of things that figure and have figured in schools, if we turn them over and look at them, and seek to generalize about them, we shall begin to see that the most persistently present, and the living reality of it all, is this: to expand, to add to and organize and supplement that apparatus of understanding and expression the savage possesses in colloquial speech. The pressing business of the school is *to widen the range of intercourse.* [Footnote: This way of putting it may jar a little upon the more or less explicit preconceptions of many readers, who are in reality in harmony with the tone of thought of this paper. They will have decided that the school work is to "train the mind," to "teach the pupil to think," or upon some similar phrase. But I venture to think that most of these phrases are at once too wide and too narrow. They are too wide because they ignore the spontaneous activity of the child and the extra-scholastic forces of mind-training, and they are too narrow because they ignore the fact that we do not progress far with our thoughts unless we throw them out into objective existence by means of words, diagrams, models, trial essays. Even if we do not talk to others we must, silently or vocally or visibly, talk to ourselves at least to get on. To acquire the means of intercourse is to learn to think, so far as learning goes in the matter.] It is only secondarily—so far as schooling goes—or, at any rate, subsequently, that the idea of shaping, or, at least, helping to shape, the expanded natural man into a citizen, comes in. It is only as a subordinate necessity that the school is a vehicle for the inculcation of facts. The facts come into the school not for their own sake, but in relation to intercourse. It is only upon a common foundation of general knowledge that the initiated citizens of an educated community will be able to communicate freely together. With the net of this phrase, "widening the range of intercourse," I think it is possible to gather together all that is essential in the deliberate purpose of schooling. Nothing that remains outside is of sufficient magnitude to be of any importance in the small-scale sketch of human development we are now making:—

If we take this and hold to it as a guide, and explore a scheme of school work, in the direction it takes us, we shall find it shaping itself (for an English-speaking citizen) something after this fashion: —

A. Direct means of understanding and expression.

    1. Reading.

           H. G. Wells

2. Writing.

3. Pronouncing English correctly.

Which studies will expand into—

4. A thorough study of English as a culture language, its origin, development, and vocabulary, and

5. A sound training in English prose composition and versification.

And in addition—

6. Just as much of mathematics as one can get in.

7. Drawing and painting, not as "art," but to train and develop the appreciation of form and colour, and as a collateral means of expression.

8. Music [perhaps] to the same end.

B. To speak the ordinary speech, read with fair intelligence, and write in a passably intelligible manner the foreign language or languages, the social, political, and intellectual necessities of the time require.

And *C.* A division arising out of A and expanding in the later stages of the school course to continue and replace A: the acquisition of the knowledge (and of the art of acquiring further knowledge from books and facts) necessary to participate in contemporary thought and life.

Now this project is at once more modest in form and more ambitious in substance than almost any school scheme or prospectus the reader is likely to encounter. Let us (on the assumption of our opening paragraph) inquire what is needed to carry it into execution. So far as 1 and 2 in this table go, we have to recognize that since the development of elementary schools in England introduced a spirit of endeavour into teaching, there has been a steady progress in the art of education. Reading and writing are taught somehow or other to most people nowadays, they are frequently taught quickly and well, especially well, I think, in view of the raw material, in many urban Board Schools in England, and there is nothing to do here but to inquire if anything can be done to make this teaching, which is so exceptional in attaining its goal, still quicker and easier, and in bringing the average up to the level of the present best. We have already suggested as the work of an imaginary English Language Society, how much might be done in providing everywhere, cheaply and unavoidably, the best possible reading-books, and it is manifest that the standard of copy-books for writing might also be pressed upward by similar methods. In addition, we have to consider —what is to me a most uncongenial subject—the possible rationalization of English spelling. I will frankly confess I know English as much by sight as by sound, and that any extensive or striking alteration, indeed that almost any alteration, in the printed appearance of English, worries me extremely. Even such little things as Mr. Bernard Shaw's weakness for printing "I've" as "Ive," and the American "favor," "thro," and "catalog" catch at my attention as it travels along the lane of meaning, like trailing briars. But I have to admit this habit of the old spelling, which I am sure most people over four-and-twenty share with me, will trouble neither me nor any one else who reads books now, in the year 1990. I have to admit that the thing is an accident of my circumstances. I have learnt to read and write in a certain way, and I am concerned with the thing said and not with the vehicle, and so it is that it distresses me when the medium behaves in an unusual way and distracts my attention from the thing it conveys. But if it is true—and I think it must be true—that the extremely arbitrary spelling of English—and more especially of the more familiar English words—greatly increases the trouble of learning to read and write, I do not think the mental comfort of one or two generations of grown-up people must be allowed to stand in the way of a permanent economy in the educational process. I believe even that such a reader as I might come to be very easy in the new way. But whatever is done must be done widely, simultaneously, all over the English-speaking community, and after the fullest consideration. The local "spelling reform" of a few half-educated faddists here and there, helps not at all, is a mere nuisance. This is a thing to be worked out in a scientific way by the students of phonetics; they must have a complete alphabet settled for good, a dictionary ready, reading-books well tested, the whole system polished and near perfection before the thing passes out of the specialists' hands. The really practical spelling-reformer will devote his guineas to endowing chairs of phonetics and supporting publication in phonetic science, and his time to study and open-minded discussion. Such organisations as the *Association Phonétique Internationale*, may be instanced. Systems concocted in a hurry, in a half-commercial or wholly commercial and in a wholly presumptuous manner, pushed like religious panaceas and advertised like soap—Pitman's System, Barnum's System, Quackbosh the Gifted Postman's System, and all that sort of thing—do nothing but vulgarize, discredit, and retard this work.

Before a system of phonetic spelling can be established, it is advisable that a standard pronunciation of English should exist. With that question also these papers have already dealt. But for the sake of emphasis I would repeat here the astonishment that has grown upon me as I have given my mind to these things, that, save for local exceptions, there should be no pressure even upon those who desire to become teachers in our schools or preachers in our pulpits, to attain a qualifying minimum of correct pronunciation.

Now directly we pass beyond these first three elementary matters, reading, writing, and pronunciation, and come to the fourth and fifth items of our scheme, to the complete mastery of English that is, we come upon a difficulty that is all too completely disregarded in educational discussions—always by those who have had no real scholastic experience, and often by those who ought to know better. It is extremely easy for a political speaker or a city magnate or a military reformer or an irresponsible writer, to proclaim that the schoolmaster must mend his ways forthwith, give up this pointless Latin of his, and teach his pupils the English language "*thoroughly*"—with much emphasis on the "thoroughly," but it is quite another thing for the schoolmaster to obey our magnificent directions. For the plain, simple, insurmountable fact is this, that no one knows how to teach English as in our vague way we critics imagine it taught; that no working schoolmaster alive can possibly give the thing the concentrated attention, the experimental years necessary for its development, that it is worth nobody's while, and that (except in a vein of exalted self-sacrifice) it will probably not be worth any one's while to do so for many years unless some New Republicans conspire to make it so. The teaching of English requires its Sturm, its energetic modern renascence schoolmasters, its set of school books, its branches and grades, before it can become a discipline, even to compare with the only subject taught with any shadow of orderly progressive thoroughness in secondary schools, namely, Latin. At present our method in English is a foolish caricature of the Latin method; we spend a certain amount of time teaching children classificatory bosh about the eight sorts of Nominative Case, a certain amount of time teaching them the "derivation" of words they do not understand, glance shyly at Anglo-Saxon and at Grimm's Law, indulge in a specific reminiscence of the Latin method called parsing, supplement with a more modern development called the analysis of sentences, give a course of exercises in paraphrasing (for the most part the conversion of good English into bad), and wind up with lessons in "Composition" that must be seen to be believed. Essays are produced, and the teacher noses blindly through the product for false concords, prepositions at the end of sentences, and, if a person of peculiarly fine literary quality, for the word "reliable" and the split infinitive. These various exercises are so little parts of an articulate whole that they may be taken in almost any order and any relative quantity. And in the result, if some pupil should, by a happy knack of apprehension, win through this confusion to a sense of literary quality, to the enterprise of even trying to write, the thing is so rare and wonderful that almost inevitably he or she, in a fine outburst of discovered genius, takes to the literary life. For the rest, they will understand nothing but the flattest prose; they will be deaf to everything but the crudest meanings; they will be the easy victims of the boom, and terribly shy of a pen. They will revere the dead Great and respect the new Academic, read the living quack, miss and neglect the living promise, and become just a fresh volume of that atmosphere of *azote*, in which our literature stifles.

Now the schoolmaster is not to blame for this any more than he is to blame for sticking to Latin. It is no more possible for schoolmasters and schoolmistresses, whose lives are encumbered with a voluminous mass of low-grade mental toil and worries and reasonable and unreasonable responsibilities, to find the energy and mental freedom necessary to make any vital changes in the methods that text-books, traditions, and examinations force upon them, than it is for a general medical practitioner to invent and make out of the native ore the steel implements some operation of frequent occurrence in his practice may demand. If they are made, and accessible by purchase and not too expensive, he will get them; if they are not he will have to fumble along with the next best thing; and if nothing that is any good can be got, then there is nothing for it, though he be the noblest character, the finest intelligence that ever lived behind a brass plate, but either to shirk that operation altogether or to run the chance of making a disastrous mess of it.

Scolding the schoolmaster, gibing at the schoolmaster, guying, afflicting and exasperating the schoolmaster in every conceivable way, is an amusement so entirely congenial to my temperament that I do not for one moment propose to abandon it. It is a devil I have, and I admit it. He insults schoolmasters and bishops in particular, and I do not cast him out, but at the same time I would most earnestly insist that all that sort of thing does nothing whatever to advance education, that it is a mere outbreak of personal grace-notes so far as this discussion goes. The real practical needs in the matter are a properly worked-out method, a proper set of school books, and then a progressive alteration of examinations in English, to render that method and that set of school books imperative. These are needs the schoolmaster and schoolmistress can do amazingly little to satisfy. Of course, when these things are ready and the pressure to enforce them begins to tell on the schools, schoolmasters and schoolmistresses, having that almost instinctive dread of any sort of change that all hard-worked and rather worried people acquire, will obstruct and have to be reckoned with, but that is a detail in the struggle and not a question of general objective. And to satisfy those real practical needs, what is wanted is in the first place an organizer, a reasonable sum of money, say ten thousand pounds for ten years, and access for experimental purposes to a variety of schools. This organizer would set himself to secure the whole time and energy and interest of a dozen or so of good men; they would include several expert teachers, a clear-headed pedagogic expert or so, a keen psychologist perhaps with a penetrating mind—for example, one might try and kidnap Professor William James in his next Sabbatical year—one or two industrious young students, a literary critic perhaps, a philologist, a grammarian, and set them all, according to their several gifts and faculties, towards this end. At the end of the first year this organizer would print and publish for the derision of the world in general and the bitter attacks of the men he had omitted from the enterprise in particular, for review in the newspapers and for trial in enterprising schools, a "course" in the English language and composition. His team of collaborators, revised perhaps, probably weeded by a quarrel or so and supplemented by the ablest of the hostile critics, would then, working with all their time and energy, revise the course for the second year. And you would repeat the process for ten years. In the end at the cost of £100,000—really a quite trivial sum for the object in view—there would exist the scheme, the method, the primers and text-books, the School Dictionary, the examination syllabus, and all that is now needed for the proper teaching of English. You would have, moreover, in the copyrights of the course an asset that might go far to recoup those who financed the enterprise.

It is precisely this difficulty about text-books and a general scheme that is the real obstacle to any material improvement in our mathematical teaching. Professor Perry, in his opening address to the Engineering Section of the British Association at Belfast, expressed an opinion that the average boy of fifteen might be got to the infinitesimal calculus. As a matter of fact the average English boy of fifteen has only just looked at elementary algebra. But every one who knows anything of educational science knows, that by the simple expedient of throwing overboard all that non-educational, mind-sickening and complex rubbish about money and weights and measures, practice, interest, "rule of three," and all the rest of the solemn clap-trap invented by the masters of the old Academy for Young Gentlemen to fool the foolish predecessors of those who clamour for commercial education to-day, and by setting aside the pretence in teaching geometry, that algebraic formulae and the decimal notation are not yet invented, little boys of nine may be got to apply quadratic equations to problems, plot endless problems upon squared paper, and master and apply the geometry covered by the earlier books of Euclid with the utmost ease. But to do this with a class of boys at present demands so much special thought, so much private planning, so much sheer toil on the part of the teacher, that it becomes practically impossible. The teacher must arrange the whole course himself, invent his examples, or hunt them laboriously through a dozen books; he must be not only teacher, but text-book. I know of no School Arithmetic which does not groan under a weight of sham practical work, and that does not, with an absurd priggishness, exclude the use of algebraic symbols. Except for one little volume, I know of no sane book which deals with arithmetic and elementary algebra under one cover or gives any helpful exercises or examples in squared paper calculations. Such books, I am told, exist in the seclusion of publishers' stock-rooms, but if I, enjoying as I do much more leisure and opportunity of inquiry than the average mathematical master, cannot get at them, how can we expect him to do so? And the thing to do now is obviously to discover or create these books, and force them kindly but firmly into the teachers' hands.

The problem is much simpler in the case of mathematical teaching than in the case of English, because the educational theory and method have been more thoroughly discussed. There is no need for the ten years of experiment and trial I have suggested for the organization of English teaching. The mathematical reformer may begin now at a point the English language reformer will not reach for some years. Suppose now a suitably authenticated committee were to work out—on the basis of Professor Perry's syllabus perhaps—a syllabus of school mathematics, and then make a thorough review of all the mathematical textbooks on sale throughout the English-speaking world, admitting some perhaps as of real permanent value for teaching of the new type, provisionally recognizing others as endurable, but with clear recommendations for their revision and improvement, and condemning the others specifically *by name*. Let them make it clear that this syllabus and report will be respected by all public examining bodies; let them spend a hundred pounds or so in the intelligent distribution of their report, and the scholastic profession will not be long before it is equipped with the recommended books. Meanwhile, the English and American scholastic publishers will become extremely active, the warned books will be revised, and new books will be written in competition for the enormous prize of the committee's final approval, an activity that a second review, after an interval of five or six years, will recognize and reward.

Such measures as these will be worth reams of essays in educational papers and Parents' Reviews, worth thousands of inspiring and suggestive lectures at pedagogic conferences. If, indeed, such essays and such lectures do any good at all. The more one looks into scholastic affairs the more one is struck not only by the futility but the positive mischievousness of much of what passes for educational liberalism. The school-master is criticised vehemently for teaching the one or two poor useless subjects he can in a sort of way teach, and practically nothing is done to help or equip him to teach anything else. By reason of this uproar, the world is full now of anxious muddled parents, their poor brains buzzing with echoes of Froebel, Tolstoy, Herbert Spencer, Ruskin, Herbart, Colonel Parker, Mr. Harris, Matthew Arnold, and the *Morning Post*, trying to find something better. They know nothing of what is right, they only know very, very clearly that the ordinary school is extremely wrong. They are quite clear they don't want "cram" (though they haven't the remotest idea what cram is), and they have a pretty general persuasion that failure at examination is a good test of a sound education. And in response to their bleating demand there grows a fine crop of Quack Schools; schools organized on lines of fantastic extravagance, in which bee-keeping takes the place of Latin, and gardening supersedes mathematics, in which boys play tennis naked to be cured of False Shame, and the numerical exercises called bookkeeping and commercial correspondence are taught to the sons of parents (who can pay a hundred guineas a year), as Commercial Science. The subjects of study in these schools come and go like the ravings of a disordered mind; "Greek History" (in an hour or so a week for a term) is followed by "Italian Literature," and this gives place to the production of a Shakesperian play that ultimately overpowers and disorganizes the whole curriculum. Ethical lessons and the school pulpit flourish, of course. A triennial walk to a chalk-pit is Field Geology, and vague half-holiday wanderings are Botany Rambles. "Art" of the copper punching variety replaces any decent attempt to draw, and an extreme expressiveness in music compensates for an almost deliberate slovenliness of technique. Even the ladies' seminaries of the Georgian days could scarcely have produced a parallel to the miscellaneous incapacity of the victim of these "modern" schools, and it becomes daily more necessary for those who have the interests of education at heart to disavow with the most unmistakable emphasis these catch-parent impostures.

With the other subjects under the headings of *A* and *B*, it is not necessary to deal at any length here. Drawing begins at home, and a child should have begun to sketch freely before the formal schooling commences. It is the business of the school to teach drawing and not to teach "art," which, indeed, is always an individual and spontaneous thing, and it need only concern itself directly with those aspects of drawing that require direction. Of course, an hour set aside from the school time in which boys or girls may do whatever they please with paper, ink, pens, pencils, compasses, and water-colour would be a most excellent and profitable thing, but that scarcely counts (except in the Quack Schools) as teaching. As a matter of fact, teaching absolutely spoils all that sort of thing. A course in model drawing and in perspective, however, is really a training in seeing things, it demands rigorous instruction and it must be the backbone of school drawing, and, in addition, studies may be made from flowers that would not be made without direction: topography (and much else) may be learnt by copying good explicit maps; chronology (to supplement the child's private reading of history) by the construction of time charts; and much history also by drawing and colouring historical maps. With geometrical drawing one passes insensibly into mathematics. And so much has been done not only to revolutionize the teaching of modern languages, but also to popularize the results, that I may content myself with a mere mention of the names of Rippmann, S. Alge, Hölzel, and Gouin as typical of the new ways.

There remains the question of *C*, the amount of Information that is to take a place in schooling. Now there is one "subject" that it would be convenient to include, were it only for the sake of the mass of exercise and illustration it supplies to the mathematical course, and that is the science of Physics. In addition, the science of physics, since it culminates in a clear understanding and use of the terminology of the aspects of energy and a clear sense of adequate causation, is fundamentally necessary to modern thought. Practical work is, no doubt, required for the proper understanding of physical science, and so far it must enter into schooling, but it may be pointed out here that in many cases the educational faddist is overdoing the manual side of science study to a ridiculous extent. Things have altered very much at the Royal College of Science, no doubt, since my student days, but fifteen years ago the courses in elementary physics and in elementary geology were quite childishly silly in this respect. Both these courses seemed to

H. G. Wells

have been inspired by that eminent educationist, Mr. Squeers, and the sequel to spelling "window" was always to "go and clean one." The science in each course in those days could have been acquired just as well in a fortnight as in half a year. One muddled away three or four days etching a millimetre scale with hydrofluoric acid on glass—to no earthly end that I could discover—and a week or so in making a needless barometer. In the course in geology, days and days were spent in drawing ideal crystalline forms and colouring them in water-colours, apparently in order to get a totally false idea of a crystal, and weeks in the patient copying of microscopic rock sections in water-colours. Effectual measures of police were taken to prevent the flight of the intelligent student from these tiresome duties. The mischief done in this way is very great. It deadens the average students and exasperates and maddens the eager ones. I am inclined to think that a very considerable proportion of what passes as "practical" science work, for which costly laboratories are built and expensive benches fitted, consists of very similar solemnities, and it cannot be too strongly urged that "practical" work that does not illuminate is mere waste of the student's time.

This physics course would cover an experimental quantitative treatment of the electric current, it would glance in an explanatory way at many of the phenomena of physical geography, and it would be correlated with a study of the general principles of chemistry. A detailed knowledge of chemical compounds is not a part of general education, it keeps better in reference books than in the non-specialized head, and it is only the broad conceptions of analysis and combination, and of the relation of energy to chemical changes, that have to be attained. Beyond this, and the application of map drawing to give accurate ideas and to awaken interest in geography and history, it is open to discussion whether any Fact subject need be taught as schooling at all. Ensure the full development of a man's mental capacity, and he will get his Fact as he needs it. And if his mind is undeveloped he can make no use of any fact he has. The subject called "Human Physiology" may be at once dismissed as absurdly unsuitable for school use. One is always meeting worthy people who "don't see why children should not know something about their own bodies," and who are not apparently aware that the medical profession after some generations of fairly systematic inquiry knows remarkably little. Save for some general anatomy, it is impossible to teach school-children anything true about the human body, because the explanation of almost any physiological process demands a knowledge of physical and chemical laws much sounder and subtler than the average child can possibly attain. And as for botany, geology, history, and geography (beyond the range already specified), these are far better relegated to the school library and the initiative of each child. Every child has its specific range of interest, and its specific way of regarding things. In geology, for example, one boy may be fascinated by the fossil hunting, another will find his interest in the effects of structure in scenery, and a third, with more imagination, will give his whole mind to the reconstruction of the past, and will pore over maps of Pleistocene Europe and pictures of Silurian landscape with the keenest appreciation. Each will be bored, or at least not greatly interested, by what attracts the others. Let the children have an easily accessible library—that is the crying need of nine hundred and ninety-nine out of a thousand schools to-day, a need every school-seeking parent may do something to remedy—and in that library let there be one or two good densely illustrated histories, illustrated travels, bound volumes of such a publication as Newnes' *Wide World Magazine* (I name these publications haphazard—there are probably others as good or better), Hutchinson and Co.'s *Living Animals of the World*, the Rev. H. N. Hutchinson's *Extinct Monsters*, the Badminton volumes on big game shooting, mountaineering, and yachting, Kerner's "Botany," collections of "The Hundred Best Pictures" sort, collections of views of towns and of scenery in different parts of the world, and the like. Then let the schoolmaster set aside five hours a week as the minimum for reading, and let the pupils read during that time just whatever they like, provided only that they keep silence and read. If the schoolmaster or school-mistress comes in at all here, it should be to stimulate systematic reading occasionally by setting a group of five or six pupils to "get up" some particular subject—a report on "animals that might still be domesticated," for example—and by showing them conversationally how to read with a slip of paper at hand, gathering facts. This sort of thing it is impossible to reduce to method and system, and, consequently, it is the proper field for the teacher's initiative. It is largely in order to leave time and energy for this that I am anxious to reduce the more rigorous elements in schooling to standard and text-book.

Now all this schooling need not take more than twenty hours a week for its backbone or hard-work portion, its English, mathematics, science, and exact drawing, and twelve hours a week for its easier, more individual employments of sketching, painting, and reading, and this leaves a large margin of time for military drill and for physical exercises. If we are to get the best result from the child's individuality, we must leave a large portion of that margin at the child's own disposal, it must be free to go for walks, to "muck about," as schoolboys say, to play games, and (within limits) to consort with companions of its own choosing—to follow its interests in short. It is in this direction that British middle-class education fails most signally at the present time. The English schoolboy and schoolgirl are positively hunted through their days. They do not play—using the word to indicate a spontaneous employment into which imagination enters—at all. They have games, but they are so regulated that the imagination is eliminated; they have exercises of various stereotyped sorts. They are taken to and fro to these things in the care of persons one would call ushers unhesitatingly were it not that they also pretended to teach. The rest of their waking time is preparation or supervised reading or walking under supervision. Their friendships are watched. They are never, never left alone. The avowed ideal of many boarding schoolmasters is to "send them to bed tired out." Largely this is due to a natural dread of accidents and scrapes, that will make trouble for the school, but there is also another cause. If I may speak frankly and entirely as an unauthoritative observer, I would say it is a regrettable thing that so large a proportion of British secondary schoolmasters and mistresses are unmarried. The normal condition of a healthy adult is marriage, and for all those who are not defective upon this side (and that means an incapacity to understand many things) celibacy is a state of unstable equilibrium and too often a quite unwholesome condition. Wherever there are celibate teachers I am inclined to suspect a fussiness, an unreasonable watchfulness, a disposition to pry, an exaggeration of what are called "Dangers," a painful idealization of "Purity." It is a part of the normal development of the human being to observe with some particularity certain phenomena, to entertain certain curiosities, to talk of them to trusted equals—*never*, be it noted, except by perversion to parents or teachers—and there is not the slightest harm in these quite natural things, unless they are forced back into an abashed solitude or associated by suggestion with conceptions of shame and disgust. That is what happens in too many of our girls' schools and preparatory schools to-day, and it is to that end mainly that youthful intimacies are discouraged, youthful freedom is restricted, and imagination and individuality warped and crippled. It is astonishing how much of their adolescence grown-up people will contrive to forget.

So much for schooling and what may be done to better it in this New Republican scheme of things. The upward continuation of it into a general College course is an integral part of a larger question that we shall discuss at a later stage, the larger question of the general progressive thought of the community as a whole.

VII

POLITICAL AND SOCIAL INFLUENCES

There can be few people alive who have not remarked on occasion that men are the creatures of circumstances. But it is one thing to state a belief of this sort in some incidental application, and quite another to realize it completely. Towards such a completer realization we have been working in these papers, in disentangling the share of inheritance and of deliberate schooling and training, in the production of the civilized man. The rest we have to ascribe to his world in general, of which his home is simply the first and most intimate aspect. In every developing citizen we have asserted there is a great mass of fluid and indeterminate possibility, and this sets and is shaped by the world about him as wax is shaped by a mould. It is rarely, of course, an absolutely exact and submissive cast that ensues; few men and women are without some capacity for question and criticism, but it is only very rare and obdurate material—only, as one says, a very original personality—that does not finally take its general form and direction in this way. And it is proposed in this paper to keep this statement persistently in focus, instead of dismissing it as a platitude and thinking no more about it at all after the usual fashion, while we examine certain broad social and political facts and conventions which constitute the general framework of the world in which the developing citizen is placed. I would submit that at the present time with regard to such things as church and kingdom, constitution and nationality, we are altogether too much enslaved by the idea of "policy," and altogether too blind to the remoter, deeper, and more lasting consequences of our public acts and institutions in moulding the next generation. It will not, I think, be amiss to pass beyond policy for a space, and to insist—even with heaviness—that however convenient an institution may be, however much it may, in the twaddle of the time, be a "natural growth," and however much the "product of a long evolution," yet, if it does not mould men into fine and vigorous forms, it has to be destroyed. We "save the state" for the sake of our children, that, at least, is the New Republican view of the matter, and if in our intentness to save the state we injure or sacrifice our children, we destroy our ultimate for our proximate aim.

Already it has been pointed out, with certain concrete instances, how the thing that is, asserts itself over the thing that is to be; already a general indication has been made of the trend of the argument we are now about to develop and define. That argument, briefly, is this, that to attain the ends of the New Republic, that is to say the best results from our birth possibilities, we must continually make political forms, social, political and religious formulæ, and all the rules and regulations of *life the clearest, simplest, and sincerest expression possible of what we believe about life and hope about life;* that whatever momentary advantage a generation may gain by accepting what is known to be a sham and a convention, by keeping in use the detected imposture and the flawed apparatus, is probably much more than made up for by the reaction of this acquiescence upon the future. As the typical instance of a convenient convention that I am inclined to think is now reacting very badly upon our future, the Crown of the British Empire, considered as the symbolical figurehead of a system of hereditary privilege and rule, serves extremely well. One may deal with this typical instance with no special application to the easy, kindly, amiable personality this crown adorns at the present time. It is a question that may be dealt with in general terms. What, we would ask, are the natural, inseparable concomitants of a system of hereditary rulers in a state, looking at the thing entirely with an eye to the making of a greater mankind in the world? How does it compare with the American conception of democratic equality, and how do both stand with regard to the essential truth and purpose in things?

To state these questions is like opening the door of a room that has long been locked and deserted. One has a lonely feeling. There are quite remarkably no other voices here, and the rusty hinges echo down empty passages that were quite threateningly full of men seventy or eighty years ago. But I am only one very insignificant member of a class of inquirers in England who started upon the question "why are we becoming inefficient?" a year or two ago, and from that starting point it is I came to this. . . . I do not believe therefore that upon this dusty threshold I shall stand long alone. We take most calmly the most miraculous of things, and it is only quite recently that I have come to see as amazing this fact, that while the greater mass of our English-speaking people is living under the profession of democratic Republicanism, there is no party, no sect, no periodical, no teacher either in Great Britain or America or the Colonies, to hint at a proposal to abolish the aristocratic and monarchical elements in the British system. There is no revolutionary spirit over here, and very little missionary spirit over there. The great mass of the present generation on both sides of the Atlantic takes hardly any interest in this issue at all. It is as if the question was an impossible one, outside the range of thinkable things. Or, as if the last word in this controversy was said before our grandfathers died.

But is that really so? It is permissible to suggest that for a time the last word had been said, and still to reopen the discussion now. All these papers, the very conception of New Republicanism, rests on the assumption—presumptuous and offensive though it must needs seem to many—that new matter for thought altogether, new apparatus and methods of inquiry, and new ends, have come into view since the early seventies, when the last Republican voices in England died away. We are enormously more aware of the Future. That, we have already defined as the essential difference of our new outlook. Our fathers thought of the Kingdom as it was to them, they contrasted with that the immediate alternative, and within these limits they were, no doubt, right in rejecting the latter. So, to them at any rate, the thing seemed judged. But nowadays when we have said the Kingdom is so and so, and when we have decided that we do not wish to convert it into a Republic upon the American or any other existing pattern before Christmas, 1904, we consider we have only begun to look at the thing. We have then to ask what is the future of the Kingdom; is it to be a permanent thing, or is it to develop into and give place to some other condition? We have to ask precisely the same question about the American democracy and the American constitution. Is that latter arrangement going to last for ever? We cannot help being contributory to these developments, and if we have any pretensions to wisdom at all, we must have some theory of what we intend with regard to these things; political action can surely be nothing but folly, unless it has a clear purpose in the future. If these things are not sempiternal, then are we merely to patch the fabric as it gives way, or are we going to set about rebuilding— piecemeal, of course, and without closing the premises or stopping the business, but, nevertheless, on some clear and comprehensive plan? If so, what is the plan to be? Does it permit us to retain in a more or less modified form, or does it urge us to get rid of, the British Crown? Does it permit us to retain or does it urge us to modify the American constitution? That is the form, it seems to me, in which the question of Republicanism as an alternative to existing institutions, must presently return into the field of public discussion in Great Britain; not as a question of political stability nor of individual rights this time, but as an aspect of our general scheme, our scheme to make the world more free and more stimulating and strengthening for our children and our children's children; for the children both of our bodies and of our thoughts.

It is interesting to recall the assumptions under which the last vestiges of militant Republicanism died out in Great Britain. As late as the middle years of the reign of Queen Victoria, there were many in England who were, and who openly

　　　　　H. G. Wells

professed themselves to be, Republicans, and there was a widely felt persuasion that the country was drifting slowly towards the constitution of a democratic republic. In those days it was that there came into being a theory, strengthened by the withdrawal of the Monarch from affairs, which one still hears repeated, that Great Britain was a "crowned republic," that the crown was no more than a symbol retained by the "innate good sense" of the British people, and that in some automatic way not clearly explained, such old-time vestiges of privilege as the House of Lords would presently disappear. One finds this confident belief in Progress towards political equality—Progress that required no human effort, but was inherent in the scheme of things—very strong in Dickens, for example, who spoke for the average Englishman as no later writer can be said to have done. This belief fell in very happily with that disposition to funk a crisis, that vulgar dread of vulgar action which one must regretfully admit was all too often a characteristic of the nineteenth century English. There was an idea among Englishmen that to do anything whatever of a positive sort to bring about a Republic was not only totally unnecessary but inevitably mischievous, since it evidently meant street fighting and provisional government by bold, bad, blood-stained, vulgar men, in shirt sleeves as the essential features of the process. And under the enervating influence of this great automatic theory—this theory that no one need bother because the thing was bound to come, was indeed already arriving for all who had eyes to see—Republicanism did not so much die as fall asleep. It was all right, Liberalism told us—the Crown was a legal fiction, the House of Lords was an interesting anachronism, and in that faith it was, no doubt, that the last of the Republicans, Mr. Bright and Mr. Joseph Chamberlain, "kissed hands." Then, presently, the frantic politics of Mr. Gladstone effected what probably no other human agency could have contrived, and restored the prestige of the House of Lords.

Practically the Crown has now gone unchallenged by press, pulpit, or platform speaker for thirty years, and as a natural consequence there is just now a smaller proportion of men under forty who call themselves Republicans even in private than there ever was since Plutarch entered the circle of English reading. To-day the Aristocratic Monarchy is an almost universally accepted fact in the British Empire, and it has so complete an air of unshakable permanence to contrast with its condition in the early nineteenth century that even the fact that it is the only really concrete obstacle to a political reunion of the English-speaking peoples at the present time, seems merely a fact to avoid.

There are certain consequences that must follow from the unchallenged acceptation of an aristocratic monarchy, consequences that do not seem to be sufficiently recognized in this connection, and it is to these that the reader's attention is now particularly drawn. There are a great number of British people who are more or less sincerely seeking the secret of national efficiency at present, and I cannot help thinking that sooner or later, in spite of their evident aversion, they will be forced to look into this dusty chamber of thought for the clue to the thing they need. The corner they will have to turn is the admission that no state and no people can be at its maximum efficiency until every public function is discharged by the man best able to perform it, and that no Commonweal can be near efficiency until it is endeavouring very earnestly to bring that ideal condition of affairs about. And when they have got round that corner they will have to face the fact that an Hereditary Monarchy is a state in which this principle is repudiated at a cardinal point, a state in which one position, which no amount of sophistication will prevent common men and women regarding as the most honourable, powerful, and responsible one of all, which is indeed by that very fact alone a great and responsible one, is filled on purely genealogical grounds. In a state that has also an aristocratic constitution this repudiation of special personal qualities is carried very much further. Reluctantly but certainly the seeker after national efficiency will come to the point that the aristocracy and their friends and connections *must* necessarily form a caste about the King, that their gradations *must* set the tone of the whole social body, and that their political position must enable them to demand

H. G. Wells

and obtain a predominating share in any administration that may be formed. So long, therefore, as your constitution remains aristocratic you must expect to see men of quite ordinary ability, quite ordinary energy, and no exceptional force of character, men frequently less clever and influential than their wives and lady friends, controlling the public services , a Duke of Norfolk managing so vital a business as the Post Office and succeeded by a Marquis of Londonderry, and a Marquis of Lansdowne organizing military affairs, and nothing short of a change in your political constitution can prevent this sort of thing. No one believes these excellent gentlemen hold these positions by merit or capacity, and no one believes that from them we are getting anything like the best imaginable services in these positions. These positions are held by the mere accident of birth, and it is by the mere accident of birth the great mass of Englishmen are shut out from the remotest hope of serving their country in such positions.

And this evil of reserved places is not restricted by any means to public control. You cannot both have a system and not have a system, and the British have a system of hereditary aristocracy that infects the whole atmosphere of English thought with the persuasion that what a man may attempt is determined by his caste. It is here, and nowhere else, that the clue to so much inefficiency as one finds it in contemporary British activity lies. The officers of the British Army instead of being sedulously picked from the whole population are drawn from a really quite small group of families, and, except for those who are called "gentleman rankers," to enlist is the very last way in the world to become a British officer. As a very natural corollary only broken men and unambitious men of the lowest class will consent to become ordinary private soldiers, except during periods of extreme patriotic excitement. The men who enter the Civil Service also, know perfectly well that though they may possess the most brilliant administrative powers and develop and use themselves with relentless energy, they will never win for themselves or their wives one tithe of the public honour that comes by right to the heir to a dukedom. A dockyard hand who uses his brains and makes a suggestion that may save the country thousands of pounds will get—a gratuity.

Throughout all English affairs the suggestion of this political system has spread. The employer is of a different caste from his workmen, the captain is of a different caste from his crew, even the Teachers' Register is specially classified to prevent "young gentlemen" being taught by the only men who, as a class, know how to teach in England, namely, the elementary teachers; everywhere the same thing is to be found. And while it is, it is absurd to expect a few platitudes about Freedom, and snobbishness, and a few pious hopes about efficiency, to counteract the system's universal, incessant teaching, its lesson of limited effort within defined possibilities. Only under one condition may such a system rise towards anything that may be called national vigour, and that is when there exists a vigorous Court which sets the fashion of hard work. A keen King, indifferent to feminine influence, may, for a time, make a keen nation, but that is an exceptional state of affairs, and the whole shape of the fabric gravitates towards relapse. Even under such an influence the social stratification will still, in the majority of cases, prevent powers and posts falling to the best possible man. In the majority of cases the best that can be hoped for, even then, will be to see the best man in the class privileged in relation to any particular service, discharging that service. The most efficient nation in the world to-day is believed to be Germany, which is—roughly speaking—an aristocratic monarchy, it is dominated by a man of most unkingly force of character, and by a noble tradition of educational thoroughness that arose out of the shames of utter defeat, and, as a consequence, a great number of people contrive to forget that the most dazzling display of national efficiency the world has ever seen followed the sloughing of hereditary institutions by France. One credits Napoleon too often with the vigour of his opportunity, with the force and strength it was his privilege to misdirect and destroy. And one forgets that this present German efficiency was paralleled in the eighteenth century by Prussia, whose aristocratic system first winded Republicans at

H. G. Wells

Valmy, and showed at Jena fourteen years after how much it had learnt from that encounter.

Now our main argument lies in this: that the great mass of a generation of children born into a country, all those children who have no more than average intelligence and average moral qualities, will accept the ostensible institutions of that country at their face value, and will be almost entirely shaped and determined by that acceptance. Only a sustained undertone of revolutionary protest can prevent that happening. They will believe that precedences represent real superiority, and they will honour what they see honoured, and ignore what they see treated as of no account. Pious sentiment about Equality and Freedom will enter into the reality of their minds as little as a drop of water into a greasy plate. They will act as little in general intercourse upon the proposition that "the man's the gowd for a' that," as they will upon the proposition that "man is a spirit" when it comes to the alternative of jumping over a cliff or going down by a ladder.

If, however, your children are not average children, if you are so happy as to have begotten children of exceptional intelligence, it does not follow that this fact will save them from conclusions quite parallel to those of the common child. Suppose they do penetrate the pretence that there is no intrinsic difference between the Royal Family and the members of the peerage on the one hand, and the average person in any other class on the other; suppose they discover that the whole scale of precedence and honour in their land is a stupendous sham;—what then? Suppose they see quite clearly that all these pretensions of an inviolate superiority of birth and breeding vanish at the touch of a Whitaker Wright, soften to a glowing cordiality before the sunny promises of a Hooley. Suppose they perceive that neither King nor lords really believe in their own lordliness, and that at any point in the system one may find men with hands for any man's tip, provided it is only sufficiently large! Even then!—How is that going to react upon our children's social conduct?

In ninety-nine cases out of a hundred they will accept the system still, they will accept it with mental reservations. They will see that to repudiate the system by more than a chance word or deed is to become isolated, to become a discontented alien, to lose even the qualified permission to do something in the world. In most cases they will take the oaths that come in their way and kiss the hands—just as the British elementary teachers bow unbelieving heads to receive the episcopal pat, and just as the British sceptic in orders will achieve triumphs of ambiguity to secure the episcopal see. And their reason for submission will not be absolutely despicable; they will know there is no employment worth speaking of without it. After all, one has only one life, and it is not pleasant to pass through it in a state of futile abstinence from the general scheme. Life, unfortunately, does not end with heroic moments of repudiation; there comes a morrow to the Everlasting Nay. One may begin with heroic renunciations and end in undignified envy and dyspeptic comments outside the door one has slammed on one's self. In such reflections your children of the exceptional sort, it may be after a youthful fling or two, a "ransom" speech or so, will find excellent reasons for making their peace with things as they are, just as if they were utterly commonplace. They know that if they can boast a knighthood or a baronetcy or a Privy Councillorship, they will taste day by day and every day that respect, that confidence from all about them that no one but a trained recluse despises. And life will abound in opportunities. "Oh, well!" they will say. Such things give them influence, consideration, power to do things.

The beginning of concessions is so entirely reasonable and easy! But the concessions go on. Each step upward in the British system finds that system more persistently about them. When one has started out under a King one may find amiable but whom one may not respect, admitted a system one does not believe in, when one has rubbed the first bloom off one's honour, it is infinitely easier to begin peeling the skin. Many a man whose youth was a dream of noble things, who was all for splendid achievements and the service of mankind, peers to-day, by virtue of such acquiescences, from between preposterous lawn sleeves or under a tilted coronet, sucked as dry of his essential honour as a spider sucks a fly.

But this is going too far, the reader will object! There must be concessions, there must be conformities, just as there must be some impurity in the water we drink and flaws in the beauty we give our hearts to, and that, no doubt, is true. It is no reason why we should drink sewage and kneel to grossness and base stupidity. To endure the worst because we cannot have the best is surely the last word of folly. Our business as New Republicans is not to waste our lives in the pursuit of an unattainable chemical purity, but to clear the air as much as possible. Practical ethics is, after all, a quantitative science. In the reality of life there are few absolute cases, and it is foolish to forego a great end for a small concession. But to suffer so much Royalty and Privilege as an Englishman has to do before he may make any effectual figure in public life is not a small concession. By the time you have purchased power you may find you have given up everything that made power worth having. It would be a small concession, I admit, a mere personal self-sacrifice, to pretend loyalty, kneel and kiss hands, assist at Coronation mummeries, and all the rest of it, in order, let us say, to accomplish some great improvement in the schools of the country, were it not for the fact that all these things must be done in the sight of the young, that you cannot kneel to the King without presenting a kneeling example to the people, without becoming as good a teacher of servility as though you were servile to the marrow. There lies the trouble. By virtue of this reaction it is that the shams and ceremonies we may fancy mere curious survivals, mere kinks and tortuosities, cloaks and accessories to-day, will, if we are silent and acquiescent, be halfway to reality again in the course of a generation. To our children they are not evidently shams; they are powerful working suggestions. Human institutions are things of life, and whatever weed of falsity lies still rooted in the ground has the promise and potency of growth. It will tend perpetually, according to its nature, to recover its old influence over the imagination, the thoughts, and acts of our children.

Even when the whole trend of economic and social development sets against the real survival of such a social and political system as the British, its pretensions, its shape and implications may survive, survive all the more disastrously because they are increasingly insincere. Indeed, in a sense, the British system, the pyramid of King, land-owning and land-ruling aristocracy, yeomen and trading middle-class and labourers, is dead—it died in the nineteenth century under the wheels of mechanism [Footnote: I have discussed this fully in *Anticipations*, Chapter III., Developing Social Elements.]—and the crude beginnings of a new system are clothed in its raiment, and greatly encumbered by that clothing. Our greatest peers are shareholders, are equipped by marriage with the wealth of Jews and Americans, are exploiters of colonial resources and urban building enterprises; their territorial titles are a mask and a lie. They hamper the development of the new order, but they cannot altogether prevent the emergence of new men. The new men come up to power one by one, from different enterprises, with various traditions, and one by one, before they can develop a sense of class distinction and collective responsibility, the old system with its organized "Society" captures them. If it finds the man obdurate, it takes his wife and daughters, and it waylays his sons. [Footnote: It is not only British subjects that are assimilated in this way, the infection of the British system, the annexation of certain social strata in the Republic by the British crown, is a question for every thoughtful American. America is less and less separate from Europe, and the social development of the United States cannot be a distinct process—it is inevitably bound up in the general social development of the English-speaking community. The taint has touched the American Navy, for example, and there are those who discourage promotion from the ranks—the essential virtue of the democratic state—because men so promoted would be at a disadvantage when they met the officers of foreign navies, who were by birth and training "gentlemen." When they met them socially no doubt was meant; in war the disadvantage might prove the other way about.] Because the hereditary kingdom and aristocracy of Great Britain is less and less representative of economic reality, more and more false to the real needs of the world, it does not follow that it will disappear, any more than malarial fever will disappear from a man's blood because it is irrelevant to the general purpose of his being. These things will only go when a sufficient number of sufficiently capable and powerful people are determined they shall go. Until that time they will remain with us, influencing things about them for evil, as it lies in their nature to do.

Before, however, any sufficiently great and capable body of men can be found to abolish these shams, these shams that must necessarily hamper and limit the development of our children, it is necessary that they should have some clear idea of the thing that is to follow, and the real security of these obsolete institutions lies very largely in the fact that at present the thing that is to follow does not define itself. It is too commonly assumed that the alternative to a more or less hereditary government is democratic republicanism of the American type, and the defence of the former consists usually in an indictment of the latter, complicated in very illogical cases by the assertion (drawn from the French instance) that Republics are unstable. But it does not follow that because one condemns the obvious shams of the British system that one must accept the shams of the United States. While in Great Britain we have a system that masks and hampers the best of our race under a series of artificial inequalities, the United States theory of the essential equality of all men is equally not in accordance with the reality of life. In America, just as in England, the intelligent child grows up to discover that the pretensions of public life are not justified, and quite equally to be flawed in thought and action by that discovery.

The American atmosphere has one great and indisputable superiority over the British: it insists upon the right of every citizen, it almost presents it as a duty, to do all that he possibly can do; it holds out to him even the highest position in the state as a possible reward for endeavour. Up to the point of its equality of opportunity surely no sane Englishman can do anything but envy the American state. In America "presumption" is not a sin. All the vigorous enterprise that differentiates the American from the Englishman in business flows quite naturally from that; all the patriotic force and loyalty of the common American, which glows beside the English equivalent as the sun beside the moon, glows even oppressively. But apart from these inestimable advantages I do not see that the American has much that an Englishman need envy. There are certainly points of inferiority in the American atmosphere, influences in development that are bad, not only in comparison with what is ideally possible, but even in comparison with English parallels.

For example, the theory that every man is as good as his neighbour, and possibly a little better, has no check for fools, and instead of the respectful silences of England there seems— to the ordinary English mind—an extraordinary quantity of crude and unsound judgments in America. One gets an impression that the sort of mind that is passively stupid in England is often actively silly in America, and, as a consequence, American newspapers, American discussions, American social affairs are pervaded by a din that in England we do not hear and do not want to hear. The real and steady development of American scientific men is masked to the European observer, and it must be greatly hampered by the copious silliness of the amateur discoverer, and the American crop of new religions and new enthusiasms is a horror and a warning to the common British intelligence. Many people whose judgments are not absolutely despicable hold a theory that unhampered personal freedom for a hundred years has made out of the British type, a type less deliberate and thorough in execution and more noisy and pushful in conduct, restless rather than indefatigable, and smart rather than wise. If ninety-nine people out of the hundred in our race are vulgar and unwise, it does seem to be a fact that while the English fool is generally a shy and negative fool anxious to hide the fact, the American fool is a loud and positive fool, who swamps much of the greatness of his country to many a casual observer from Europe altogether. American books, American papers, American manners and customs seem all for the ninety and nine.

Deeper and graver than the superficial defects of manner and execution and outlook to which these charges point, there are, one gathers, other things that are traceable to the same source. There is a report of profounder troubles in the American social body, of a disease of corruption that renders American legislatures feeble or powerless against the great business corporations, and of an extreme demoralization of the police force. The relation of the local political organization to the police is fatally direct, and that sense of ordered subordination to defined duties which distinguishes the best police forces of Europe fails. Men go into the police force, we are told, with the full intention of making it pay, of acquiring a saleable power.

There is probably enough soundness in these impressions, and enough truth in these reports and criticisms, to justify our saying that all is not ideally right with the American atmosphere, and that it is not to present American conditions we must turn in repudiating our British hereditary monarchy. We have to seek some better thing upon which British and American institutions may converge. The American personal and social character, just like the English personal and social character, displays very grave defects, defects that must now be reflected upon, and must be in course of acquisition by the children who are growing up in the American state. And since the American is still predominantly of British descent, and since he has not been separated long enough from the British to develop distinct inherited racial characteristics, and, moreover, since his salient characteristics are in sharp contrast with those of the British, it follows that the difference in his character and atmosphere must be due mainly to his different social and political circumstances. Just as the relative defects of the common British, their apathy, their unreasoning conservatism, and their sordid scorn of intellectual things is bound up with their politico-social scheme, so, I believe, the noisiness, the mean practicalness, and the dyspeptic-driving restlessness that are the shadows of American life, are bound up with the politico-social condition of America. The Englishman sticks in the mud, and the American, with a sort of violent meanness, cuts corners, and in both cases it is quite conceivable that the failure to follow the perfect way is really no symptom of a divergence of blood and race, but the natural and necessary outcome of the mass of suggestion about them that constitutes their respective worlds.

The young American grows up into a world pervaded by the theory of democracy, by the theory that all men must have an equal chance of happiness, possessions, and power, and in which that theory is expressed by a uniform equal suffrage. No man shall have any power or authority save by the free consent and delegation of his fellows—that is the idea—and to the originators of this theory it seemed as obvious as anything could be that these suffrages would only be given to those who did really serve the happiness and welfare of the greatest number. The idea was reflected in the world of business by a conception of free competition; no man should grow rich except by the free preference of a great following of customers. Such is still the American theory, and directly the intelligent young American grows up to hard facts he finds almost as much disillusionment as the intelligent young Englishman. He finds that in practice the free choice of a constituency reduces to two candidates, and no more, selected by party organizations, and the free choice of the customer to the goods proffered by a diminishing number of elaborately advertised businesses; he finds political instruments and business corporations interlocking altogether beyond his power of control, and that the two ways to opportunity, honour, and reward are either to appeal coarsely to the commonest thoughts and feelings of the vulgar as a political agitator or advertising trader, or else to make his peace with those who do. And so he, too, makes his concessions. They are different concessions from those of the young Englishman, but they have this common element of gravity, that he has to submit to conditions in which he does not believe, he has to trim his course to a conception of living that is perpetually bending him from the splendid and righteous way. The Englishman

H. G. Wells

grows up into a world of barriers and locked doors, the American into an unorganized, struggling crowd. There is an enormous premium in the American's world upon force and dexterity, and force in the case of common men too often degenerates into brutality, and dexterity into downright trickery and cheating. He has got to be forcible and dexterous within his self-respect if he can. There is an enormous discount on any work that does not make money or give a tangible result, and except in the case of those whose lot has fallen within certain prescribed circles, certain oases of organized culture and work, he must advertise himself even in science or literature or art as if he were a pill. There is no recognition for him at all in the world, except the recognition of—everybody. There will be neither comfort nor the barest respect for him, however fine his achievement, unless he makes his achievement known, unless he can make enough din about it, to pay. He has got to shout down ninety-nine shouting fellow-citizens. That is the cardinal fact in life for the great majority of Americans who respond to the stirrings of ambition. If in Britain capacity is discouraged because honours and power go by prescription, in America it is misdirected because honours do not exist and power goes by popular election and advertisement. In certain directions—not by any means in all—unobtrusive merit, soundness of quality that has neither gift nor disposition for "push," has a better chance in Great Britain than in America. A sort of duty to help and advance exceptional men is recognized at any rate, even if it is not always efficiently discharged, by the privileged class in England, while in America it is far more acutely felt, far more distinctly impressed upon the young that they must "hustle" or perish.

It will be argued that this enumeration of American and British defects is a mere expansion of that familiar proposition of the logic text-books, "all men are mortal." You have here, says the objector, one of two alternatives, either you must draw your administrators, your legislators, your sources of honour and reward from a limited, hereditary, and specially-trained class, who will hold power as a right, or you must rely upon the popular choice exercised in the shop and at the polling booth. What else can you have but inheritance or election, or some blend of the two, blending their faults? Each system has its disadvantages, and the disadvantages of each system may be minimized by education; in particular by keeping the culture and code of honour of your ruling class high in the former case and by keeping your common schools efficient in the latter. But the essential evils of each system are—essential evils, and one has to suffer them and struggle against them, as one has to struggle perpetually with the pathogenic bacteria that infest the world. The theory of monarchy is, no doubt, inferior to the democratic theory in stimulus, but the latter fails in qualitative effect, much more than the former. There, the objector submits, lies the quintessence of the matter. Both systems need watching, need criticism, the pruning knife and the stimulant, and neither is bad enough to justify a revolutionary change to the other. In some such conclusion as this most of the English people with whom one can discuss this question have come to rest, and it is to this way of looking at the matter that one must ascribe the apathetic acquiescence in the British hereditary system, upon which I have already remarked. There is a frank and excessive admission of every real and imaginary fault of the American system, and with the proposition that we are on the horns of a dilemma, the discussion is dismissed.

But are we indeed on the horns of a dilemma, and is there no alternative to hereditary government tempered by elections, or government by the ward politician and the polling booth? Cannot we have that sense and tradition of equal opportunity for all who are born into this world, that generous and complete acknowledgment of the principle of promotion from the ranks that is the precious birthright of the American, without the political gerrymandering, the practical falsification, that restricts that general freedom at last only to the energetic, and that subordinates quality to quantity in every affair of life? It is evident that for the New Republican to admit that the thing is indeed a dilemma, that there is nothing for it but to make the best of whichever bad thing we have at hand, that we cannot have all we desire but only a greater or a lesser moiety, is a most melancholy and hampering admission. And, certainly, no New Republican will agree without a certain mental struggle, without a thorough and earnest inquiry into the possibility of a third direction.

This matter has two aspects, it presents itself as two questions; the question first of all of administration, and the question of honour and privilege. What is it that the New Republican idea really requires in these two matters? In the matter of administration it requires that every child growing up in a state should feel that he is part owner of his state, completely free in his membership, and equal in opportunity to all other children—and it also wants to secure the management of affairs in the hands of the very best men, not the noisiest, not the richest or most skilfully advertised, but the best. Can these two things be reconciled? In the matter of honour and privilege, the New Republican idea requires a separation of honour from notoriety; it requires some visible and forcible expression of the essential conception that there are things more honourable than getting either votes or money; it requires a class and distinctions and privileges embodying that idea—and also it wants to ensure that through the whole range of life there shall not be one door locked against the effort of the citizen to accomplish the best that is in him. Can these two things be reconciled also?

I have the temerity to think that in both cases the conflicting requirements can be reconciled far more completely than is commonly supposed.

Let us take, first of all, the question of the reconciliation as it is presented in the administration of public affairs. The days have come when the most democratic-minded of men must begin to admit that the appointment of all rulers and officials by polling the manhood, or most of the manhood, of a country does not work—let us say perfectly—and at no level of educational efficiency does it ever seem likely to work in the way those who established it hoped. By thousands of the most varied experiments the nineteenth century has proved this up to the hilt. The fact that elections can only be worked as a choice between two selected candidates, or groups of candidates, is the unforeseen and unavoidable mechanical defect of all electoral methods with large electorates. Education has nothing to do with that. The elections for the English University members are manipulated just as much as the elections in the least literate of the Irish constituencies. [Footnote: There is a very suggestive book on this aspect of our general question, *The Crowd*, by M. Gustave le Bon, which should interest any one who finds this paper interesting. And the English reader who would like a fuller treatment of this question has now available also Ostrogorski's great work, *Democracy and the Organization of Political Parties*.] It is not a question of accidentals, but a question of the essential mechanism. Men have sought out and considered all sorts of devices for qualifying the present method by polling; Mills's plural voting for educated men will occur to the reader; Hare's system of vote collection, and the negative voting of Doctor Grece; and the defects of these inventions have been sufficiently obvious to prevent even a trial. The changes have been rung upon methods of counting; cumulative votes and the prohibition of plumping, and so on, have been tried without any essential modification of the results. There are various devices for introducing "stages" in the electoral process; the constituency elects electors, who elect the rulers and officers, for example, and there is also that futile attempt to bring in the non-political specialist, the method of electing governing bodies with power to "co-opt." Of course they "co-opt" their fellow politicians, rejected candidates, and so on. Among other expedients that people have discussed, are such as would make it necessary for a man to take some trouble and display some foresight to get registered as a voter or to pass an examination to that end, and such as would confront him with a voting paper so complex, that only a very intelligent and painstaking man would be able to fill it up without disqualification. It certainly seems a reasonable thing to require that the voter should be able at least to write out fully and spell correctly the name of the man of his choice. Except for the last, there is scarcely any of these things but its adoption would

H. G. Wells

strengthen the power of the political organizer, which they aim to defeat. Any complication increases the need and the power of organization. It is possible to believe—the writer believes—that with all this burthen of shortcomings, the democratic election system is still, on the whole, better than a system of hereditary privilege, but that is no reason for concealing how defective and disappointing its practical outcome has been, nor for resting contented with it in its present form. [Footnote: The statement of the case is not complete unless we mention that, to the method of rule by hereditary rulers and the appointment of officials by noble patrons on the one hand, and of rule by politicians exercising patronage on the other, there is added in the British system the Chinese method of selecting officials by competitive examination. Within its limits this has worked as a most admirable corrective to patronage; it is one of the chief factors in the cleanhandedness of British politicians, and it is continually importing fresh young men from outside to keep officialdom in touch with the general educated world. But it does not apply, and it does not seem applicable, to the broader issues of politics, to the appointment and endorsement of responsible rulers and legislators, where a score of qualities are of more importance than those an examination can gauge.]

Is polling really essential to the democratic idea? That is the question now very earnestly put to the reader. We are so terribly under the spell of established conditions, we are all so obsessed by the persuasion that the only conceivable way in which a man can be expressed politically is by himself voting in person, that we do all of us habitually overlook a possibility, a third choice, that lies ready to our hands. There is a way by means of which the indisputable evils of democratic government may be very greatly diminished, without destroying or even diminishing—indeed, rather enhancing—that invigorating sense of unhampered possibilities, that the democratic idea involves. There is a way of choosing your public servants of all sorts and effectually controlling public affairs on perfectly sound democratic principles, *without ever having such a thing as an election, as it is now understood, at all,* a way which will permit of a deliberate choice between numerous candidates—a thing utterly impossible under the current system—which will certainly raise the average quality of our legislators, and be infinitely saner, juster, and more deliberate than our present method. And, moreover, it is a way that is typically the invention of the English people, and which they use to-day in another precisely parallel application, an application which they have elaborately tested and developed through a period of at least seven or eight hundred years, and which I must confess myself amazed to think has not already been applied to our public needs. This way is the Jury system. The Jury system was devised to meet almost exactly the same problem that faces us to-day, the problem of how on the one hand to avoid putting a man's life or property into the hands of a Ruler, a privileged person, whose interest might be unsympathetic or hostile, while on the other protecting him from the tumultuous judgments of a crowd—to save the accused from the arbitrary will of King and Noble without flinging him to the mob. To-day it is exactly that problem over again that our peoples have to solve, except that instead of one individual affair we have now our general affairs to place under a parallel system. As the community that had originally been small enough and intimate enough to decide on the guilt or innocence of its members grew to difficult proportions, there developed this system of selecting by lot a number of its common citizens who were sworn, who were then specially instructed and prepared, and who, in an atmosphere of solemnity and responsibility in absolute contrast with the uproar of a public polling, considered the case and condemned or discharged the accused. Let me point out that this method is so universally recognized as superior to the common electoral method that any one who should propose to-day to take the fate of a man accused of murder out of the hands of a jury and place it in the hands of any British or American constituency whatever, even in the hands of such a highly intelligent constituency as one of the British universities, would be thought to be carrying crankiness beyond the border line of sanity.

Why then should we not apply the Jury system to the electoral riddle?

Suppose, for example, at the end of the Parliamentary term, instead of the present method of electing a member of Parliament, we were, with every precaution of publicity and with the most ingeniously impartial machine that could be invented, to select a Jury by lot, a Jury sufficiently numerous to be reasonably representative of the general feeling of the community and sufficiently small to be able to talk easily together and to do the business without debating society methods—between twenty and thirty, I think, might be a good working number—and suppose we were, after a ceremony of swearing them and perhaps after prayer or after a grave and dignified address to them upon the duty that lay before them, to place each of these juries in comfortable quarters for a few days and isolated from the world, to choose its legislator. They could hear, in public, under a time limit, the addresses of such candidates as had presented themselves, and they could receive, under a limit of length and with proper precautions for publicity, such documents as the candidates chose to submit. They could also, in public, put any questions they chose to the candidates to elucidate their intentions or their antecedents, and they might at any stage decide unanimously to hear no more of and to dismiss this or that candidate who encumbered their deliberations. (This latter would be an effectual way of suppressing the candidature of cranks, and of half-witted and merely symbolical persons.) The Jury between and after their interrogations and audiences would withdraw from the public room to deliberate in privacy. Their deliberations which, of course, would be frank and conversational to a degree impossible under any other conditions, and free from the dodges of the expert vote manipulator altogether, would, for example, in the case of several candidates of the same or similar political colours, do away with the absurdity of the split vote. The jurymen of the same political hue could settle that affair among themselves before contributing to a final decision.

This Jury might have certain powers of inquest. Provision might be made for pleas against particular candidates; private individuals or the advocates of vigilance societies might appear against any particular candidate and submit the facts about any doubtful affair, financial or otherwise, in which that candidate had been involved. Witnesses might be called and heard on any question of fact, and the implicated candidate would explain his conduct. And at any stage the Jury might stop proceedings and report its selection for the vacant post. Then, at the expiration of a reasonable period, a year perhaps, or three years or seven years, another Jury might be summoned to decide whether the sitting member should continue in office unchallenged or be subjected to a fresh contest.

This suggestion is advanced here in this concrete form merely to show the sort of thing that might be done; it is one sample suggestion, one of a great number of possible schemes of Election by Jury. But even in this state of crude suggestion, it is submitted that it does serve to show the practicability of a method of election more deliberate and thorough, more dignified, more calculated to impress the new generation with a sense of the gravity of the public choice, and infinitely more likely to give us good rulers than the present method, and that it would do so without sacrificing any essential good quality whatever inherent in the Democratic Idea. [Footnote: There are excellent possibilities, both in the United States and in this Empire, of trying over such a method as this, and of introducing it tentatively and piecemeal. In Great Britain already there are quite different methods of election for Parliament existing side by side. In the Hythe division of Kent, for example, I vote by ballot with elaborate secrecy; in the University of London I declare my vote in a room full of people. The British University constituencies, or one of them, might very readily be used as a practical test of this jury suggestion. There is nothing, I believe, in the Constitution of the United States to prevent any one State resorting to this characteristically Anglo-Saxon method of appointing its representatives in Congress. It is not only in political institutions that the method may be tried. Any societies or

H. G. Wells

institutions that have to send delegates to a conference or meeting might very easily bring this conception to a practical test. Even if it does not prove practicable as a substitute for election by polling, it might be found of some value for the appointment of members of the specialist type, for whom at present we generally resort to co-option. In many cases where the selection of specialists was desirable to complete public bodies, juries of educated men of the British Grand Jury type might be highly serviceable.] The case for the use of the Jury system becomes far stronger when we apply it to such problems as we now attempt to solve by co-opting experts upon various administrative bodies.

The necessity either of raising the quality of representative bodies or of replacing them not only in administration but in legislation by bureaucracies of officials appointed by elected or hereditary rulers, is one that presses on all thoughtful men, and is by no means an academic question needed to round off this New Republican theory. The necessity becomes more urgent every day, as scientific and economic developments raise first one affair and then another to the level of public or quasi-public functions. In the last century, locomotion, lighting, heating, education, forced themselves upon public control or public management, and now with the development of Trusts a whole host of businesses, that were once the affair of competing private concerns, claim the same attention. Government by hustings' bawling, newspaper clamour, and ward organization, is more perilous every day and more impotent, and unless we are prepared to see a government *de facto* of rich business organizers override the government *de jure*, or to relapse upon a practical oligarchy of officials, an oligarchy that will certainly decline in efficiency in a generation or so, we must set ourselves most earnestly to this problem of improving representative methods. It is in the direction of the substitution of the Jury method for a general poll that the only practicable line of improvement known to the present writer seems to lie, and until it has been tried it cannot be conceded that democratic government has been tried and exhaustively proved inadequate to the complex needs of the modern state.

So much for the question of administration. We come now to a second need in the modern state if it is to get the best result from the citizens born into it, and that is the need of honours and privileges to reward and enhance services and exceptional personal qualities and so to stir and ennoble that emulation which is, under proper direction, the most useful to the constructive statesman of all human motives. In the United States titles are prohibited by the constitution, in Great Britain they go by prescription. But it is possible to imagine titles and privileges that are not hereditary, and that would be real symbols of human worth entirely in accordance with the Republican Idea. It is one of the stock charges against Republicanism that success in America is either political or financial. In England, in addition, success is also social, and there is, one must admit, a sort of recognition accorded to intellectual achievement, which some American scientific men have found reason to envy. In America, of course, just as in Great Britain, there exists that very enviable distinction, the honorary degree of a university; but in America it is tainted by the freedom with which bogus universities can be organized, and by the unchallenged assumptions of quacks. In Great Britain the honorary degree of a university, in spite of the fact that it goes almost as a matter of course to every casual Prince, is a highly desirable recognition of public services. Beyond this there are certain British distinctions that might very advantageously be paralleled in America, the Fellowship of the Royal Society, for example, and that really very fine honour, as yet untainted by the class of men who tout for baronetcies and peerages, the Privy Council.

There are certain points in this question that are too often overlooked. In the first place, *honours and titles need not be hereditary*; in the second, *they need not be conferred by the political administration*; and, in the third, they are not only—as the French Legion of Honour shows—entirely compatible with, but *they are a necessary complement to the Republican Idea*.

H. G. Wells

The bad results of entrusting honours to the Government are equally obvious in France and Great Britain. They are predominantly given, quite naturally, for political services, because they are given by politicians too absorbed to be aware of men outside the political world. In Great Britain the process is modified rather than improved by what one knows as court influence. And in spite of the real and sustained efficiency of the Royal Society in distinguishing meritorious scientific workers, the French Academy, which has long been captured by aristocratic dilettanti, and the English Royal Academy of Arts, demonstrate the essential defects and dangers of a body which fills its own gaps. But there is no reason why a national system of honours and titles should not be worked upon a quite new basis, suggested by these various considerations. Let us, simply for tangibleness, put the thing as a concrete plan for the reader's consideration.

There might, for example, be a lowest stage which would include—as the English knighthood once included—almost every citizen capable of initiative, all the university graduates, all the men qualified to practice the responsible professions, all qualified teachers, all the men in the Army and Navy promoted to a certain rank, all seamen qualified to navigate a vessel, all the ministers recognized by properly organized religious bodies, all public officials exercising command; quasi-public organizations might nominate a certain proportion of their staffs, and organized trade-unions with any claim to skill, a certain proportion of their men, their "decent" men, and every artist or writer who could submit a passable diploma work; it would be, in fact, a mark set upon every man or woman who was qualified to do something or who had done something, as distinguished from the man who had done nothing in the world, the mere common unenterprising esurient man. It might carry many little privileges in public matters—for instance, it might qualify for certain electoral juries. And from this class the next rank might easily be drawn in a variety of ways. *In a modern democratic state there must be many fountains of honour.*

That is a necessity upon which one cannot insist too much. There must be no court, no gang, no traditional inalterable tribunal. Local legislative bodies, for example,—in America, state legislatures and in England, county councils,—might confer rank on a limited number of men or women yearly; juries drawn from certain special constituencies, from the roll of the medical profession, or from the Army, might assemble periodically to nominate their professional best, the Foreign or Colonial Office might confer recognition for political services, the university governing bodies might be entrusted with the power—just as in the middle ages many great men could confer knighthood. From among these distinguished gentlemen of the second grade still higher ranks might be drawn. Local juries might select a local chief dignitary as their "earl," let us say, from among the resident men of rank, and there is no reason why certain great constituencies, the medical calling, the engineers, should not specify one or two of their professional leaders, their "dukes." There are many occasions of local importance when an honourable figure-head is needed. The British fall back on the local hereditary peer or invite a prince, too often some poor creature great only by convention—and what the Americans do I do not know, unless they use a Boss. There are many occasions of something more than ceremonial importance when a responsible man publicly honoured and publicly known, and not a professional politician, is of the utmost convenience. And there are endless affairs, lists, gatherings, when the only alternative to rank is scramble. For myself I would not draw the line at such minor occasions for precedence. A Second Chamber is an essential part of the political scheme of all the English-speaking communities, and almost always it is intended to present stabler interests and a smaller and more selected constituency than the lower house. From such a life nobility as I have sketched a Second Chamber could be drawn much as the Irish representative peers in the House of Lords are drawn from the general peerage of Ireland. It would be far less party bound and far less mercenary than the American Senate, and far more intelligent and capable than the British House of Lords. And either of these bodies could be brought under a process of deliberate conversion in this direction with scarcely any revolutionary shock at all. [Footnote: In the case of the House of Lords, for example, the process of conversion might begin by extending the Scotch and Irish system to England, and substituting a lesser number of representative peers for the existing English peerage. Then it would merely revive a question that was already under discussion in middle Victorian times, to create non-hereditary peerages in the three kingdoms. The several Privy Councils might next be added to the three national constituencies by which and from which the representative peers were appointed, and then advisory boards might be called from the various Universities and organized professions, and from authoritative Colonial bodies to recommend men to be added to the voting peerage. Life peers already exist. The law is represented by life peers. The lords spiritual are representative life peers—they are the senior bishops, and they are appointed to represent a corporation— the Established Church. So a generally non-hereditary functional nobility might come into being without any violent break with the present condition of things. The conversion of the American Senate would be a more difficult matter, because the method of appointment of Senators is more stereotyped altogether, and, since 1800, unhappily quite bound up with the political party system. The Senate is not a body of varied and fluctuating origins into which new elements can be quietly inserted. An English writer cannot estimate how dear the sacred brace of Senators for each State may or may not be to the American heart. But the possibility of Congress delegating the power to appoint additional Senators to certain non-political bodies, or to juries of a specific constitution, is at least thinkable as the beginning of a movement that would come at last into parallelism with that in the British Empire.]

When these issues of public honour and efficient democratic administration have begun to move towards a definite solution, the community will be in a position to extend the operation of the new methods towards a profounder revolution, the control of private property. "We are all Socialists nowadays," and it is needless, therefore, to argue here at any length to establish the fact that beyond quite personal belongings all Property is the creation of society, and in reality no more than an administrative device. At present, in spite of some quite hideous and mischievous local aspects, the institution of Property, even in land and the shares of quasi-public businesses, probably gives as efficient a method of control, and even it may be a more efficient method of control than any that could be devised to replace it under existing conditions. We have no public bodies and no methods of check and control sufficiently trustworthy to justify extensive expropriations. Even the municipalization of industries needs to go slowly until municipal areas have been brought more into conformity with the conditions of efficient adminis-tration. Areas too cramped and areas that overlap spell waste and conflicting authorities, and premature municipalization in such areas will lead only to the final triumph of the private company. Political efficiency must precede Socialism. [Footnote: See Appendix I.] But there can be no doubt that the spectacle of irresponsible property is a terribly demoralizing force in the development of each generation. It is idle to deny that Property, both in Great Britain and America, works out into a practical repudiation of that equality, political democracy so eloquently asserts. There is a fatalistic submission to inferiority on the part of an overwhelming majority of those born poor, they hold themselves cheap in countless ways, and they accept as natural the use of wealth for wanton pleasure and purposes absolutely mischievous, they despair of effort in the public service, and find their only hope in gambling, sharp greedy trading, or in base acquiescences to the rich. The good New Republican can only regard our present system of Property as a terribly unsatisfactory expedient and seek with all his power to develop a better order to replace it.

There are certain lines of action in this matter that cannot but be beneficial, and it is upon these that the New Republican will, no doubt, go. One excellent thing, for example, would be to insist that beyond the limits of a reasonable amount of personal property, the community is justified in demanding a

H. G. Wells

much higher degree of efficiency in the property-holder than in the case of the common citizen, to require him or her to be not only sane but capable, equal mentally and bodily to a great charge. The heir to a great property should possess a satisfactory knowledge of social and economic science, and should have studied with a view to his great responsibilities. The age of twenty-one is scarcely high enough for the management of a great estate, and to raise the age of free administration for the owners of great properties, and to specify a superannuation age would be a wise and justifiable measure. [Footnote: Something of the sort is already secured in France by the power of the *Conseil de Famille* to expropriate a spendthrift.] There should also be a possibility of intervention in the case of maladministration, and a code of offences— habitual drunkenness, for example, assaults of various kinds— offences that established the fact of unfitness and resulted in deposition, might be drawn up. It might be found desirable in the case of certain crimes and misdemeanours, to add to existing penalties the transfer of all real or share properties to trustees. Vigorous confiscation is a particularly logical punishment for the proven corruption of public officers by any property owner or group of property owners. Rich men who bribe are a danger to any state. Beyond the limits of lunacy it might be possible to define a condition of malignancy or ruthlessness that would justify confiscation, attempts to form corners in the necessities of life, for example, could be taken as evidence of such a condition. All such measures as this would be far more beneficial than the immediate improvement they would effect in public management. They would infect the whole social body with the sense that property was saturated with responsibility and was in effect a trust, and that would be a good influence upon rich and poor alike.

Moreover, as public bodies became more efficient and more trustworthy, the principle already established in British social polity by Sir William Vernon Harcourt's Death Duties, the principle of whittling great properties at each transfer, might be very materially extended. Every transfer of property might establish a state mortgage for some fraction of the value of that property. The fraction might be small when the recipient was a public institution, considerable in the case of a son or daughter, and almost all for a distant relative or no kindred at all. By such devices the evil influence of property acquired by mere accidents would be reduced without any great discouragement of energetic, enterprising, and inventive men. And a man ambitious to found a family might still found one if he took care to marry wisely and train and educate his children to the level of the position he designed for them.

While the New Republican brings such expedients as this to bear upon property from above, there will also be the expedients of the Minimum Wage and the Minimum Standard of Life, already discussed in the third of these papers, controlling it from below. Limited in this way, property will resemble a river that once swamped a whole country-side, but has now been banked within its channel. Even when these expedients have been exhaustively worked out, they will fall far short of that "abolition of property" which is the crude expression of Socialism. There is a certain measure of property in a state which involves the maximum of individual freedom. Either above or below that Optimum one passes towards slavery. The New Republican is a New Republican, and he tests all things by their effect upon the evolution of man; he is a Socialist or an Individualist, a Free Trader or a Protectionist, a Republican or a Democrat just so far, and only so far, as these various principles of public policy subserve his greater end.

This crude sketch of a possible scheme of honour and privilege, and of an approximation towards the socialization of property will, at any rate, show that in this matter, as in the matter of political control, the alternative of the British system or the American system does not exhaust human possibilities. There is also the Twentieth Century System, which we New Republicans have to discover and discuss and bring to the test of experience. And for the sake of the education of our children, which is the cardinal business of our lives, we must refuse all convenient legal fictions and underhand ways, and see to it that the system is as true to the reality of life and to right and justice as we can, in our light and generation, make it. The child must learn not only from preacher and parent and book, but from the whole frame and order of life about it, that truth and sound living and service are the only trustworthy ways to either honour or power, and that, save for the unavoidable accidents of life, they are very certain ways. And then he will have a fair chance to grow up neither a smart and hustling cheat—for the American at his worst is no more and no less than that—nor a sluggish disingenuous snob—as the Briton too often becomes—but a proud, ambitious, clean-handed, and capable man.

VIII

THE CULTIVATION OF THE IMAGINATION

§ 1

In the closing years of the school period comes the dawn of the process of adolescence, and the simple egotism, the egotistical affections of the child begin to be troubled by new interests, new vague impulses, and presently by a flood of as yet formless emotions. The race, the species, is claiming the individual, endeavouring to secure the individual for its greater ends. In the space of a few years the almost sexless boy and girl have become consciously sexual, are troubled by the still mysterious possibilities of love, are stirred to discontent and adventure, are reaching out imaginatively or actively towards what is at last the recommencement of things, the essential fact in the perennial reshaping of the order of the world. This is indeed something of a second birth. At its beginning the child we have known begins to recede, the new individuality gathers itself together with a sort of shy jealousy, and withdraws from the confident intimacy of childhood into a secret seclusion; all parents know of that loss; at its end we have an adult, formed and determinate, for whom indeed the drama and conflict of life is still only beginning, but who is, nevertheless, in a very serious sense finished and made. The quaint, lovable, larval human being has passed then into the full imago, before whom there is no further change in kind save age and decay.

This development of the sexual being, of personal dreams, and

H. G. Wells

the adult imagination is already commencing in the early teens. It goes on through all the later phases of the educational process, and it ends, or, rather, it is transformed by insensible degrees into the personal realities of adult life.

Now this second birth within the body of the first differs in many fundamental aspects from that first. The first birth and the body abound in inevitable things; for example, features, gestures aptitudes, complexions, and colours, are inherited beyond any power of perversion; but the second birth is the unfolding not of shaped and settled things but of possibilities, of extraordinarily plastic mental faculties. No doubt there are in each developing individual dispositions towards this or that—tendencies, a bias in the texture this way or that—but the form of it all is extraordinarily a matter of suggestion and the influence of deliberate and accidental moulding forces. The universal Will to live is there, peeping out at first in little curiosities, inquiries, sudden disgusts, sudden fancies, the stumbling, slow realization that for this in a mysteriously predominant way we live, and growing stronger, growing presently, in the great multitude of cases, to passionate preferences and powerful desires. This flow of sex comes like a great river athwart the plain of our personal and egoistic schemes, a great river with its rapids, with its deep and silent places, a river of uncertain droughts, a river of overwhelming floods, a river no one who would escape drowning may afford to ignore. Moreover, it is the very axis and creator of our world valley, the source of all our power in life, and the irrigator of all things. In the microcosm of each individual, as in the microcosm of the race, this flood is a cardinal problem.

And from its very nature this is a discussion of especial difficulty, because it touches all of us—except for a few peculiar souls—so intimately and so disturbingly. I had purposed to call this paper "Sex and the Imagination," and then I had a sudden vision of the thing that happens. The vision presented a casual reader seated in a library, turning over books and magazines and casting much excellent wisdom aside, and then suddenly, as it were, waking up at that title, arrested, displaying a furtive alertness, reading, flushed and eager, nosing through the article. That in a vignette is the trouble in all this discussion. Were we angels—! But we are not angels; we are all involved. If we are young we are deep in it, whether we would have it so or not; if we are old, even if we are quite old, our memories still stretch out, living sensitive threads from our tender vanity to the great trouble. Detachment is impossible. The nearest we can get to detachment is to recognize that.

About this question the tragi-comic web of human absurdity thickens to its closest. When has there ever been a lucid view or ever will be of this great business? Here is the common madness of our species, here is all a tissue of fine unreasonableness—to which, no doubt, we are in the present paper infinitesimally adding. One has a vision of preposterous proceedings; great, fat, wheezing, strigilated Roman emperors, neat Parisian gentlemen of the latest cult, the good Saint Anthony rolling on his thorns, and the piously obscene Durtal undergoing his expiatory temptations, Mahomet and Brigham Young receiving supplementary revelations, grim men babbling secrets to schoolgirls, enamoured errand boys, amorous old women, debauchees dreaming themselves thoroughly sensible men and going about their queer proceedings with insane self-satisfaction, beautiful witless young persons dressed in the most amazing things, all down the vista of history—a Vision of Fair Women—looking their conscious queenliest, sentimentalists crawling over every aspect and leaving tracks like snails, flushed young blockheads telling the world "all about women," intrigue, folly—you have as much of it as one pen may condense in old Burton's Anatomy—and through it all a vast multitude of decent, respectable bodies pretending to have quite solved the problem—until one day, almost shockingly, you get their secret from a careless something glancing out of the eyes. Most preposterous of all for some reason is a figure—one is maliciously disposed to present it as feminine and a little unattractive, goloshed for preference, and saying in a voice of cultivated flatness, "Why cannot we be perfectly plain and sensible, and speak quite frankly about this matter?" The answer to which one conceives, would be near the last conclusions of Philosophy.

So much seethes about the plain discussion of the question of sexual institutions. One echoes the intelligent inquiry of that quite imaginary, libellously conceived lady in goloshes with a smile and a sigh. As well might she ask, "Why shouldn't I keep my sandwiches in the Ark of the Covenant? There's room!" "Of course there's room," one answers, "but—As things are, Madam, it is inadvisable to try. You see—for one thing— people are so peculiar. The quantity of loose stones in this neighbourhood."

The predominant feeling about the discussion of these things is, to speak frankly, Fear. We know, very many of us, that our present state has many evil aspects, seems unjust and wasteful of human happiness, is full of secret and horrible dangers, abounding in cruelties and painful things; that our system of sanctions and prohibitions is wickedly venial, pressing far more gravely on the poor than on the rich, and that it is enormously sapped by sentimentalities of various sorts and undermined and qualified by secret cults; it is a clogged and an ill-made and dishonest machine, but we have a dread, in part instinctive, in part, no doubt, the suggestion of our upbringing and atmosphere, of any rash alterations, of any really free examination of its constitution. We are not sure or satisfied where that process of examination may not take us; many more people can take machines to pieces than can put them together again. Mr. Grant Allen used to call our current prohibitions Taboos. Well, the fact is, in these matters there is something that is probably an instinct, a deeply felt necessity for Taboos. We know perhaps that our Taboos were not devised on absolutely reasonable grounds, but we are afraid of just how many may not collapse before a purely reasonable inquiry. We are afraid of thinking quite freely even in private. We doubt whether it is wise to begin, though only in the study and alone. "Why should we—? Why should we not—?" And the thought of a public discussion without limitations by a hasty myriad untrained to think, does, indeed, raise an image of consequences best conveyed perhaps by that fine indefinite phrase, "A Moral Chaos." These people who are for the free, frank, and open discussion assume so much; they either intend a sham with foregone conclusions, or they have not thought of all sorts of things inherent in the natural silliness of contemporary man.

On the whole I think a man or woman who is no longer a fabric of pure emotion may, if there is indeed the passion for truth and the clear sight of things to justify research, venture upon this sinister seeming wilderness of speculation, and I think, too, it is very probable the courageous persistent explorer will end at last not so very remote from the starting-point, but above it, as it were, on a crest that will give a wider view, reaching over many things that now confine the lower vision. But these are perilous paths, it must always be remembered. This is no public playground. One may distrust the conventional code, and one may leave it in thought, long before one is justified in leaving it either in expressed opinion or in act. We are social animals; we cannot live alone; manifestly from the nature of the question, here, at any rate, we must associate and group. For all who find the accepted righteousness not good enough or clear enough for them, there is the chance of an ironical destiny. We must look well to our company, as we come out of the city of the common practice and kick its dust from our superior soles. There is an abominable riff-raff gone into those thickets for purposes quite other than the discovery of the right thing to do, for quite other motives than our high intellectual desire. There are ugly rebels and born rascals, cheats by instinct, and liars to women, swinish unbelievers who would compromise us with their erratic pursuit of a miscellaneous collection of strange fancies and betray us callously at last. Because a man does not find the law pure justice, that is no reason why he should fake his gold to a thieves' kitchen; because he does not think the city a sanitary place, why he should pitch his tent on a dust-heap amidst pariah dogs. Because we criticize the old limitations that does not bind us to the creed of unfettered liberty. I very much doubt if, when at last the days for the sane complete discussion of our sexual problems come, it will give us anything at all in the way of "Liberty," as most people understand that word. In the place of the rusty old manacles, the chain and shot, the iron yoke, cruel, ill-fitting, violent implements from which it was yet possible to wriggle and escape to outlawry, it may be the world will discover only a completer restriction, will develop a scheme of neat gyves, light but efficient, beautifully adaptable to the wrists and ankles, never chafing, never oppressing, slipped on and worn until at last, like the mask of the Happy Hypocrite, they mould the wearer to their own identity. But for all that—gyves!

Let us glance for a moment or so now, in the most tentative fashion, at some of the data for this inquiry, and then revert from this excursion into general theory to our more immediate business, to the manner in which our civilized community at present effects the emotional initiation of youth.

The intellectual trouble in the matter, as it presents itself to me, comes in upon this, that the question does not lie in one plane. So many discussions ignore this fact, and deal with it on one plane only. For example, we may take the whole business on the plane of the medical man, ignoring all other considerations. On that plane it would probably be almost easy to reason out a working system. It never has been done by the medical profession, as a whole, which is fairly understandable, or by any group of medical men, which is the more surprising, but it would be an extremely interesting thing to have done and a material contribution to the sane discussion of this problem. It would not solve it but it would illuminate certain aspects. Let the mere physiological problem be taken. We want healthy children and the best we can get. Let the medical man devise his scheme primarily for that. Understand we are shutting our eyes to every other consideration but physical or quasi- physical ones. Imagine the thing done, for example, by a Mr. Francis Galton, who had an absolutely open mind upon all other questions. Some form of polygamy, marriage of the most transient description, with reproduction barred to specified types, would probably come from such a speculation.

But, in addition, a number of people who can have only a few children or none are, nevertheless, not adapted physiologically for celibacy. Conceive the medical man working that problem out upon purely materialistic lines and with an eye to all physiological and pathological peculiarities. The Tasmanians (now extinct) seem to have been somewhere near the probable result.

Then let us take one step up to a second stage of consideration, remaining still materialistic, and with the medical man still as our only guide. We want the children to grow up healthy; we want them to be taken care of. This means homes, homes of some sort. That may not abolish polygamy, but it will qualify it, it will certainly abolish any approach to promiscuity that was possible at the lowest stage, it will enhance the importance of motherhood and impose a number of limits upon the sexual freedoms of men and women. People who have become parents, at any rate, must be tied to the children and one another. We come at once to much more definite marriage, to an organized family of some sort, be it only Plato's state community or something after the Oneida pattern, but with at least a system of guarantees and responsibilities. Let us add that we want the children to go through a serious educational process, and we find at once still further limitations coming in. We discover the necessity of deferring experience, of pushing back adolescence, of avoiding precocious stimulation with its consequent arrest of growth. We are already face to face with an enlarged case for decency, for a system of suppressions and of complicated Taboos.

Directly we let our thoughts pass out of this physical plane and rise so high as to consider the concurrent emotions—and I suppose to a large number of people these are at least as important as the physical aspects—we come to pride, we come to preference and jealousy, and so soon as we bring these to bear upon our physical scheme, crumpling and fissures begin. The complications have multiplied enormously. More especially that little trouble of preferences. These emotions we may educate indeed, but not altogether. Neither pride nor preference nor jealousy are to be tampered with lightly. We are making men, we are not planning a society of regulated slaves; we want fine upstanding personalities, and we shall not get them if we break them down to obedience in this particular— for the cardinal expression of freedom in the human life is surely this choice of a mate. There is indeed no freedom without this freedom. Our men and women in the future must feel free and responsible. It seems almost instinctive, at least in the youth of the white races, to exercise this power of choice, not simply rebelling when opposition is offered to it, but *wanting to rebel*; it is a socially good thing, and a thing we are justified in protecting if the odds are against it, this passion for making the business one's very own private affair. Our citizens must not be caught and paired; it will never work like that. But in all social contrivances we must see to it that the freedoms we give are real freedoms. Our youths and maidens as they grow up out of the protection of our first taboos, grow into a world very largely in the hands of older people; strong men and experienced women are there before them, and we are justified in any effectual contrivance to save them from being "gobbled up"—against their real instincts. That works—the reflective man will discover—towards whittling the previous polygamy to still smaller proportions. Here, indeed, our present arrangements fail most lamentably; each year sees a hideous sacrifice of girls, mentally scarcely more than children—to our delicacy in discussion. We give freedom, and we do not give adequate knowledge, and we punish inexorably. There are a multitude of women, and not a few men, with lives hopelessly damaged by this blindfold freedom. So many poor girls, so many lads also, do not get a fair chance against the adult world. Things mend indeed in this respect; as one sign the percentage of illegitimate births in England has almost halved in fifty years, but it is clear we have much to revise before this leakage to perdition of unlucky creatures, for the most part girls no worse on the average, I honestly believe— until our penalties make them so—than other women, ceases. If our age of moral responsibility is high enough, then our age of complete knowledge is too high. But nevertheless, things are better than they were, and promise still to mend. All round we raise the age, the average age at marriage rises, just as, I believe, the average age at misconduct has risen. We may not be approaching a period of universal morality, but we do seem within sight of a time when people will know what they are doing.

That, however, is something of a digression. The intelligent inquirer who has squared his initially materialistic system of morals with the problems arising out of the necessity of sustaining pride and preference, is then invited to explore an adjacent thicket of this tortuous subject. It is, we hold, of supreme importance in our state to sustain in all our citizens, women as well as men, a sense of personal independence and responsibility. Particularly is this the case with mothers. An illiterate mother means a backward child, a downtrodden mother bears a dishonest man, an unwilling mother may even hate her children. Slaves and brutes are the sexes where women are slaves. The line of thought we are following out in these papers necessarily attaches distinctive importance to the woman as mother. Our system of morals, therefore, has to make it worth while and honourable to be a mother; it is particularly undesirable that it should be held to be right for a woman of exceptional charm or exceptional cleverness to evade motherhood, unless, perhaps, to become a teacher. A woman evading her high calling, must not be conceded the same claim upon men's toil and service as the mother-woman; more particularly Lady Greensleeves must not flaunt it over the housewife. And here also comes the question of the quality of jealousy, whether being wife of a man and mother of his children does not almost necessarily give a woman a feeling of exclusive possession in him, and whether, therefore, if we are earnest in our determination not to debase her, our last shred of polygamy does not vanish. From first to last, of course, it has been assumed that a prolific polygamy alone can be intended, for long before we have plumbed the bottom of the human heart we shall know enough to imagine what the ugly and pointless consequences of permitting sterile polygamy must be.

Then into all this tangle, whether as a light or an added confusion it is hard to say, comes the fact that while we are ever apt to talk of what "a woman" feels and what "a man" will do, and so contrive our code, there is, indeed, no such woman and no such man, but a vast variety of temperaments and dispositions, monadic, dyadic, and polymeric souls, and this sort of heart and brain and that. It is only the young fool and the brooding mattoid who believe in a special separate science of "women," there are all sorts of people, and some of each sort are women and some are men. With every stage in educational development people become more varied, or, at least, more conscious of their variety, more sensitively insistent upon the claim of their individualities over any general rules. Among the peasants of a countryside one may hope to order homogeneous lives, but not among the people of the coming state. It is well to sustain a home, it is noble to be a good mother, and splendid to bear children well and train them well, but we shall get no valid rules until we see clearly that life has other ways by which the future may be served. There are laws to be made and altered, there are roads and bridges to be built, figuratively and really; there is not only a succession of flesh and blood but of thought that is going on for ever. To write a fruitful book or improve a widely used machine is just as much paternity as begetting a son.

The last temporary raft of a logical moral code goes to pieces at this, and its separated spars float here and there. So I will confess they float at present in my mind. I have no System—I wish I had—and I never encountered a system or any universal doctrine of sexual conduct that did not seem to me to be reached by clinging tight to one or two of these dissevered spars and letting the rest drift disregarded, making a law for A, B, and C, and pretending that E and F are out of the question. That motherhood is a great and noble occupation for a good woman, and not to be lightly undertaken, is a manifest thing, and so also that to beget children and see them full grown in the world is the common triumph of life, as inconsequence is its common failure. That to live for pleasure is not only wickedness but folly, seems easy to admit, and equally foolish, as Saint Paul has intimated, must it be to waste a life of nervous energy in fighting down beyond a natural minimum our natural desires. That we must pitch our lives just as much as we can in the heroic key, and hem and control mere lasciviousness as it were a sort of leprosy of the soul, seems fairly certain. And all that love-making which involves lies, all sham heroics and shining snares, assuredly must go out of a higher order of social being, for here more than anywhere lying is the poison of life. But between these data there are great interrogative blanks no generalization will fill—cases, situations, temperaments. Each life, it seems to me, in that intelligent, conscious, social state to which the world is coming, must square itself to these things in its own way, and fill in the details of its individual moral code according to its needs. So it seems, at least, to one limited thinker.

To be frank, upon that common ground of decent behaviour, pride and self-respect, health and the heroic habit of thinking, we need for ourselves not so much rules as wisdom, and for others not, indeed, a foolish and indiscriminate toleration but at least patience, arrests of judgment, and the honest endeavour to understand. Now to help the imagination in these judgments, to enlarge and interpret experience, is most certainly one of the functions of literature. A good biography may give facts of infinite suggestion, and the great multitude of novels at present are, in fact, experiments in the science of this central field of human action, experiments in the "way of looking at" various cases and situations. They may be very misleading experiments, it is true, done with adulterated substances, dangerous chemicals, dirty flasks and unsound balances; but that is a question of their quality and not of their nature, they are experiments for all that. A good novel may become a very potent and convincing experiment indeed. Books in these matters are often so much quieter and cooler as counsellors than friends. And there, in truth, is my whole mind in this matter.

Meanwhile, as we work each one to solve his own problems, the young people are growing up about us.

§ 2

How do the young people arrive at knowledge and at their interpretation of these things? Let us for a few moments at least, put pretence and claptrap aside, and recall our own youth. Let us recognize that this complex initiation is always a very shy and secret process, beyond the range of parent and guardian. The prying type of schoolmaster or schoolmistress only drives the thing deeper, and, at the worst, blunders with a hideous suggestiveness. It is almost an instinct, a part of the natural modesty of the growing young, to hide all that is fermenting in the mind from authoritative older people. It would not be difficult to find a biological reason for that. The growing mind advances slowly, intermittently, with long pauses and sudden panics, that is the law of its progress; it feels its way through three main agencies, firstly, observation, secondly, tentative, confidential talk with unauthoritative and trusted friends, and thirdly, books. In the present epoch observation declines relatively to books; books and pictures, these dumb impersonal initiators, play a larger and a larger part in this great awakening. Perhaps for all but the children of the urban poor, the furtive talk also declines and is delayed; a most desirable thing in a civilizing process that finds great advantage in putting off adolescence and prolonging the average life.

Now the furtive talk is largely beyond our control, only by improving the general texture of our communal life can we effectually improve the quality of that. But we may bear in mind that factor of observation, and give it a casting vote in any decision upon public decency. That is all too often forgotten. Before Broadbeam, the popular humorist, for example, flashes his glittering rapier upon the County Council for suppressing some vulgar obscenity in the music-halls, or tickles the ribs of a Vigilance Association for its care of our hoardings, he should do his best to imagine the mental process of some nice boy or girl he knows, "taking it in." To come outright to the essential matter of this paper, we are all too careless of the quality of the stuff that reaches the eyes and ears of our children. It is not that the stuff is knowledge, but that it is knowledge in the basest and vulgarest colourings, knowledge without the antiseptic quality of heroic interpretation, debased, suggestive, diseased and contagious knowledge.

How the sexual consciousness of a great proportion of our young people is being awakened, the curious reader may see for himself if he will expend a few pennies weekly for a month or so upon the halfpenny or penny "comic" papers which are bought so eagerly by boys. They begin upon the facts of sex as affairs of nodding and winking, of artful innuendo and scuffles in the dark. The earnest efforts of Broadbeam's minor kindred to knock the nonsense out of even younger people may be heard at almost any pantomime. The Lord Chamberlain's attempts to stem the tide amaze the English Judges. No scheme for making the best of human lives can ignore this system of influences.

What could be done in a sanely ordered state to suppress this sort of thing?

There immediately arises the question whether we are to limit art and literature to the sphere permissible to the growing youth and "young person." So far as shop windows, bookstalls, and hoardings go, so far as all general publicity goes, I would submit the answer is Yes. I am on the side of the Puritans here, unhesitatingly. But our adults must not walk in mental leading strings, and were this world an adult world I doubt if there is anything I would not regard as fit to print and publish. But cannot we contrive that our adult literature shall be as free as air while the literature and art of the young is sanely expurgated?

There is in this matter a conceivable way, and as it is the principal business of these papers to point out and discuss such ways, it may be given here. It will be put, as for the sake of compact suggestion so much of these papers is put, in the form of a concrete suggestion, a sample suggestion as it were. This way, then, is to make a definition of what is undesirable matter for the minds of young people, and to make that cover as much suggestive indecency and coarseness as possible, to cover everything, indeed, that is not *virginibus puerisque*, and to call this matter by some reasonably inoffensive adjective, "adult," for example. One might speak of "adult" art, "adult" literature, and "adult" science, and the report of all proceedings under certain specified laws could be declared "adult" matter. In the old times there was an excellent system of putting "adult" matter into Latin, and for many reasons one regrets that Latin. But there is a rough practical equivalent to putting "adult" matter into Latin even now. It depends upon the fact that very few young people of the age we wish to protect, unless they are the children of the imbecile rich, have the spending of large sums of money. Consequently, it is only necessary to state a high minimum price for periodicals and books containing "adult" matter or "adult" illustrations, and to prosecute everything below that limit, in order to shut the flood-gates upon any torrent of over-stimulating and debasing suggestions there may be flowing now. It should be more clearly recognized in our prosecutions for obscenity, for example, that the gravity of the offence is entirely dependent upon the accessibility of the offensive matter to the young. The application of the same method to the music-hall, the lecture-theatre, and the shelves of the public library, and to several other sources of suggestion would not be impossible. If the manager of a theatre saw fit to produce "adult" matter without excluding people under the age of eighteen, let us say, he would have to take his chance, and it would be a good one, of a prosecution. This latter expedient is less novel than the former, and it finds a sort of precedent in the legislative restriction of the sale of drink to children and the protection of children's morals under specific unfavourable circumstances.

There is already a pretty lively sense in our English-speaking communities of the particular respect due to the young, and it is probable that those who publish these suggestive and stimulating prints do not fully realize the new fact in our social body, that the whole mass of the young now not only read but buy reading matter. The last thirty or forty years have established absolutely new relations for our children in this direction. Legislation against free art and free writing is, and one hopes always will be, intensely repugnant to our peoples. But legislation which laid stress not on the indecorum but on the accessibility to the young, which hammered with every clause upon that note, is an altogether different matter. We want to make the pantomime writer, the proprietor of the penny "comic," the billsticker, and the music-hall artist extremely careful, punctiliously clean, but we do not want, for example, to pester Mr. Thomas Hardy.

Yet there is danger in all this. The suppression of premature and base suggestions must not overleap itself and suppress either mature thought (which has been given its hemlock not once but many times on this particular pretext) or the destruction of necessary common knowledge. If we begin to hunt for suggestion and indecency it may be urged we shall end by driving all these things underground. Youth comes to adult life now between two dangers, vice, which has always threatened it, and morbid virtue, which would turn the very heart of life to ugliness and shame. How are we, or to come closer to the point, how is the average juryman going to distinguish between these three things; between advisable knowledge and corruptingly presented knowledge, and unnecessary and undesirable knowledge? In practice, under the laws I have sketched, it is quite probable the evil would flourish extremely, and necessary information would be ruthlessly suppressed. Many of our present laws and provisions for public decency do work in that manner. The errand-boy may not look at the Venus de Medici, but he can cram his mind with the lore of how "nobs" run after ballet girls, and why Lady X locked the door. One can only plead here, as everywhere, no law, no succinct statement can save us without wisdom, a growing general wisdom and conscience, coming into the detailed administration of whatever law the general purpose has made.

Beside our project for law and the state, it is evident there is scope for the individual. Certain people are in a position of exceptional responsibility. The Newsagents, for example, constitute a fairly strong trade organization, and it would be easy for them to think of the boy with a penny just a little more than they do. Unfortunately such instances as we have had of voluntary censorship will qualify the reader's assent to this proposition. Another objection may be urged to this distinction between "adult" and general matter, and that is the possibility that what is marked off and forbidden becomes mysterious and attractive. One has to reckon with that. Everywhere in this field one must go wisely or fail. But what is here proposed is not so much the suppression of information as of a certain manner of presenting information, and our intention is at the most delay, and to give the wholesome aspect first.

Let us leave nothing doubtful upon one point; the suppression of stimulus must not mean the suppression of knowledge. There are things that young people should know, and know fully before they are involved in the central drama of life, in the serious business of love. There should be no horrifying surprises. Sane, clear, matter-of-fact books setting forth the broad facts of health and life, the existence of certain dangers, should come their way. In this matter books, I would insist, have a supreme value. The printed word may be such a quiet counsellor. It is so impersonal. It can have no conceivable personal reaction with the reader. It does not watch its reader's face, it is itself unobtrusively unabashed and safer than any priest. The power of the book, the possible function of the book in the modern state is still but imperfectly understood. It need not be, it ought not, I think, to be, a book specifically on what one calls delicate questions, that would be throwing them up in just the way one does not want them thrown up; it should be a sort of rationalized and not too technical handbook of physiological instruction in the College Library— or at home. Naturally, it would begin with muscular physiology, with digestion, and so on. Other matters would come in their due place and proportion. From first to last it would have all that need be known. There is a natural and right curiosity on these matters, until we chase it underground.

Restriction alone is not half this business. It is inherent in the purpose of things that these young people should awaken sexually, and in some manner and somewhere that awakening must come. To ensure they do not awaken too soon or in a fetid atmosphere among ugly surroundings is not enough. They cannot awaken in a void. An ignorance kept beyond nature may corrupt into ugly secrecies, into morose and sinister seclusions, worse than the evils we have suppressed. Let them awaken as their day comes, in a sweet, large room. The true antiseptic of the soul is not ignorance, but a touch of the heroic in the heart and in the imagination. Pride has saved more men than piety, and even misconduct loses something of its evil if it is conceived upon generous lines. There lurks a capacity for heroic response in all youth, even in contaminated youth. Before five-and-twenty, at any rate, we were all sentimentalists at heart.

And the way to bring out these responses?

Assuredly it is not by sermons on Purity to Men Only and by nasty little pamphlets of pseudo-medical and highly alarming information stuffed into clean young hands [Footnote: See Clouston's *Mental Diseases*, fifth edition, p. 535, for insanity caused by these pamphlets; see also p. 591 *et seq.* for "adolescent" literature.]—ultra "adult" that stuff should be—but in the drum and trumpet style the thing should be done. There is a mass of fine literature to-day wherein love shines clean and noble. There is art telling fine stories. There is a possibility in the Theatre. Probably the average of the theatre-goer is under rather than over twenty-two. Literature, the drama, art; that is the sort of food upon which the young imagination grows stout and tall. There is the literature and art of youth that may or may not be part of the greater literature of life, and upon this mainly we must depend when our children pass from us into these privacies, these dreams and inquiries that will make them men and women. See the right stuff is near them and the wrong stuff as far as possible away, chase cad and quack together, and for the rest, in this matter—*leave them alone.*

IX

THE ORGANIZATION OF THE
HIGHER EDUCATION

When we digressed to the general question of the political, social, and moral atmosphere in which the English-speaking citizen develops, we left the formal education of the average child, whose development threads through these papers and holds them together, at about the age of fifteen and at the end of the process of Schooling. We have now to carry on that development to adult citizenship. It is integral in the New Republican idea that the process of Schooling, which is the common atrium to all public service, should be fairly uniform throughout the social body, that although the average upper-class child may have all the advantages his conceivably better mental inheritance, his better home conditions, and his better paid and less overworked teachers may give him, there shall be no disadvantages imposed upon the child of any class, there shall be no burking of the intellectual education for any purpose whatever. To keep poor wretches in serfdom on the land by depriving them of all but the most rudimentary literary education, as a very considerable element in the new Nature Study Movement certainly intends, is altogether antagonistic to New Republican ideas, and there must be no weeding out of capable and high-minded teachers by filtering them through grotesque and dishonouring religious tests—dishonouring because compulsory, whatever the real faith of the teacher may be. And at the end of the Schooling period there must begin a process of sorting in the mass of the national youth—as far as possible, regardless of their social origins—that will go on throughout life. For the competition of public service must constitute the Battle for Existence in the civilized state. All-round inferiority in school life—failure not simply at this or that or at the total result (which, indeed, may be due very often to the lopsidedness of exceptional gifts) but failure all along the line—is a mark of essential inferiority. A certain proportion of boys and girls will have shown this inferiority, will have done little with any of their chances in or out of school during their school life, and these—when they are poorer-class children—will very naturally drop out of the educational process at this stage and pass into employment suited to their capacity, employment which should not carry with it any considerable possibility of prolific marriage. A really well-contrived leaving-school examination—and it must be remembered that the theory and science of examinations scarcely exists as yet—an examination which would take account of athletic development and moral influence (let us say provisionally by the vote of fellow-pupils) and which would be so contrived as to make specially high quality in one department as good as all-round worth—could effect this first classification. It would throw out the worst of the duffers and fools and louts all along the social scale. What is to become of the rejected of the upper and wealthy class is, I admit, a difficult problem as things are to-day. At present they carry a loutish ingredient to the public schools, to the Army, to Oxford and Cambridge, and it is open to question whether it would not be well to set aside one public school, one especially costly university, and one gentlemen's regiment of an attractively smart type, into which this mass of expensive slackness might be drained along a channel of specially high fees, low standards, and agreeable social conditions. That, however, is a quite subsidiary question in this discussion. A day may come, as I have already suggested, when it will be considered as reasonable to insist upon a minimum mental qualification for the administration of property as for any other form of power in the state. Pride and their many advantages— of which one is quite conceivably an average essential superiority—will probably ensure a satisfactory result from the

H. G. Wells

Schooling process in the case of a much greater proportion of better-class than of lower-class boys and girls. [Footnote: In most big public schools, I am told, there is a system of superannuation about sixteen, but I know nothing of the provision for those who are weeded out.]

From the mass who show a satisfactory result at the end of the Schooling process, the functional manhood and womanhood of our peoples have to be developed, and we have now to discuss the nature of the second phase of education, the phase that should be the mental parallel and accompaniment of physical adolescence in all the citizens who are to count for strength in the state. There is a break in the whole development of the human being at this age, and it may very well be paralleled by a break in methods and subjects of instruction. In Great Britain, in the case of the wealthier classes, schooling and puerile discipline is prolonged altogether too far, largely through the gross incapacity of our secondary teachers. These men are unable, boring away day after day, week after week, year after year, with vain repetitions, imbecile breaks and new beginnings, through all the vast period from eleven or twelve until twenty, to achieve that mastery of Latin and Greek which was once the necessary preliminary to education, and which has become at last, through the secular decline in scholastic energy and capacity due to the withdrawal of interest in these studies, the unattainable educational ideal. These classical pedagogues, however, carry the thing up to three or four and twenty in the Universities—though it is inconceivable that any language spoken since the antediluvian age of leisure, can need more than ten years to learn—and if they could keep the men until forty or fifty they would still be fumbling away at the keys to the room that was ransacked long ago. But with educated men as teachers and practical handbooks to help, and practical examiners to guide them, there is no reason whatever why the great mass of the linguistic training of the citizen, in the use of his own and any other necessary language, should not be done for good and all by fourteen, why he should not have a fairly complete mastery of form and quantity through mathematical training and drawing, and why the way should not be clear and immediate for the development of that adult mental edifice of which this is the foundation.

By fourteen the power of abstract reasoning and of an analytical treatment of things is in existence, the learner is now less to be moulded and more to be guided than he was. We want now to give this mind we have established, the most stimulating and invigorating training we can, we want to give it a sane coherent view of our knowledge of the universe in relation to itself, and we want to equip it for its own special work in the world. How, on the basis of the Schooling we have predicated, are these ends to be attained?

Now let us first have it perfectly clear that this second stage in development lies no more completely within the idea of College than the former lay completely within the idea of School. In the general discussion of these things we are constantly faced by the parallel error to that we have tried to dissipate in regard to schools, the error that the Professor and his Lecture and (in the case of experimental sciences) his Laboratory make, or can make, the man, just precisely in the same way that the Schoolmaster or Schoolmistress is supposed to be omnipotent in the education of the boy or girl. And, unhappily, the Professor, unless he is a man of quite exceptional mental power for a Professor, shares this groundless opinion. The Schoolmaster is under-educated in regard to his work, and incapable of doing it neatly; the Professor is too often over-specialized and incapable of forming an intelligent, modest idea of his place in education; and the same consequence flows from the defect of either, an attempt to use an improperly large portion of the learner's time and energy. Over-direction, and what one may call intellectual sectarianism, are faults from which few College courses are free to- day. The Professor stands between his students and books, he says in lectures in his own way what had far better be left for other men's books to tell, he teaches his beliefs without a court of appeal. Students are kept writing up their notes of his not very brilliant impromptus, and familiarizing themselves with his mental constitution instead of the subject of study. They get no training in the use of books as sources of knowledge and ideas, albeit such a training is one of the most necessary of all acquisitions for an efficient citizen, and whatever discussion the modern student indulges in is all too often treated rather as presumption to be discouraged than as the most necessary and hopeful of mental processes. Our Universities and Colleges are still but imperfectly aware of the recent invention of the Printed Book; and its intelligent use in this stage of education has made little or no headway against their venerable traditions. That things are only understood by being turned over in the mind and looked at from various points of view is, of course, altogether too modern a conception for our educationists. At the London Royal College of Science, for example, which is an exceptionally new and efficient College, there is no properly organized escape from the orthodoxy of the lecture-theatre, no circulating library whatever available to the students, no library, that is, which will ensure a copious supply and exchange of the best books on each subject, and, consequently, even to look up an original paper that has been quoted or discussed, involves an expenditure of time that is practically prohibitive of the thing as a general practice. [Footnote: There are three very fine libraries in the adjacent South Kensington Museum, especially available to students, but, like almost all existing libraries, they are managed in most respects on lines conceived when a copy of a book was an almost unique thing made specially by the copyist's hand. However much a book is in demand, however cheap its price of publication may be, no library in England, unless it is a modern subscription library, ever gets duplicate copies. This is the cause of the dearness of serious books; they are bought as rarities, and have to be sold in the same spirit. But when libraries learn to buy by the dozen and the hundred, there is no reason why the sort of book now published at 10s. 6d. should not be sold at a shilling from the beginning.] The Professors, being busy and important men, lecture from their particular standpoints, and having lectured, bolt; there is no provision whatever for the intelligent discussion of knotty points, and the only way to get it is to buttonhole a demonstrator and induce him to neglect his task of supervising prescribed "practical" work in favour of educational talk. Let us, therefore, in view of this state of affairs, deal with the general question how a branch of thought and knowledge may be most beneficially studied under modern conditions, before discussing the more particular question what subjects should or should not be undertaken.

Now the full statement not only of what is known of a subject, but of its difficulties, dark places, and conflicting aspects should be luminously set forth in the College text-books, large, well-written, well-illustrated books by one or several hands, continually revised and kept abreast of the advance of knowledge by capable and critical-minded young men. Such books are essential and cardinal in proper modern teaching. The country may be speckled with universities until they are as thick as public-houses, and each may be provided with its score or so of little lecturers, and if it does not possess one or more good general text-books in each principal subject then all this simply means that a great number of inadequate, infertile little text-books are being dictated, one by each of these lecturers. Not the course of lectures, but the sound, full text-book should be the basis of College instruction, and this should be supplemented by a greater or lesser number of more or less controversial pamphlets or books, criticising, expanding or correcting its matter or putting things in a different and profitable way. This text-book should be paralleled in the case of experimental science by a hand-book of illustrative and explanatory laboratory work. Portions of the book could be set for preparation at each stage in the course with appropriate experiments, students could submit difficulties in writing to be dealt with by the Professor in conversational lectures, and the reading of the students could be checked by periodic examinations upon cardinal parts, and supplemented, if these examinations showed it to be necessary, by dissertations upon special issues of difficulty. Upon the matters that were distinctively his "subject," or upon his points of disagreement with the general issues of the book, the Professor might lecture in the accepted way. This is surely the proper method of work

H. G. Wells

for adolescent students in any subject, in philology just as much as in comparative anatomy, and in history just as much as in economics. The cheapening of printing, paper, and, above all, of illustration has done away with the last excuse for the vocal course of instruction and the lecturer's diagrams. But it has not done away with them.

It is one of the most curious of human phenomena, this persistence of tradition against what one might have imagined the most destructive facts, and in no connection is this aspect more remarkable than in all that concerns the higher stages of education. One might think that somewhere in the seventeenth century it would have been recognized at the Seats of Learning that thought and knowledge were progressive things, and that a periodic revision of courses and syllabuses, a periodic recasting of work and scope, a re-arrangement of chairs and of the appliances of the faculties, was as necessary to the continued healthy existence of a University as periodic meals and sleep and exercise are necessary to a man. But even today we are founding Universities without any provision for this necessary change, and the chances are that in a century or so they will present just as much backwardness and illiteracy as do the ordinary graduation organizations of Oxford and Cambridge today, that a hundred years from now the past graduates of ripe old Birmingham, full of spite against newfangled things "no fellow can understand," will be crowding up to vote against the substitution of some more modern subject for "Huxley"—"Huxley" they will call the subject, and not Comparative Anatomy, on the model of "Euclid"—or for the retention of compulsory "Commercial Geography of the Nineteenth Century," or "Longhand Bookkeeping" in the Little Go. (And should any germinating noble founder read these pages I would implore him with all the earnestness that is possible in printed matter, to provide that every fifty years, let us say, the whole of his prospective foundation shall go into solution, shall re-apportion its funds and reorganize the entire mechanism of its work.)

The idea that a text-book should be regularly reset and

reprinted is still quite foreign to the Professorial mind, as, indeed, is the idea that the care of text-books and publications is a University function at all. No one is startled by a proposal to apply £800 or £1000 a year to a new chair in any subject, but to apply that sum yearly as a standing charge to the revision and perfection of a specific text-book would seem, even today, quite fantastically extravagant to most University men. Yet what could be more obviously helpful to sound and thorough teaching than for a University, or a group of Universities, to sustain a Professor in each of the chief subjects of instruction, whose business would be neither teaching as it is now understood, nor research, but the critical and exhaustive editing of the College text-book of his subject, a text-book which would stand in type at the University Press, which would be revised annually and reprinted annually, primarily for the use of the matriculated students of the University and incidentally for publication. His business would be not only to bring the work up to date and parallel with all the newest published research and to invite and consider proposals of contributions and footnotes from men with new views and new matter, but also to substitute for obscure passages fuller and more lucid expositions, to cut down or relegate to smaller type passages of diminishing importance and to introduce fresh and more efficient illustrations, and his work would be carried on in consultation with the General Editor of the University Press who would also be a specialist in modern printing and book-making, and who would be constantly taking up, trying, and adopting fresh devices of arrangement, and newer, better, and cheaper methods of printing and illustration. It would not merely raise the general efficiency of the College work of adolescents very greatly to have this series of textbooks living and growing in each subject at one or (better) at several Universities or grouped Universities, but in each subject the periodic change in these books would afford a most valuable corrective to the influence of specialized work by keeping the specialist worker easily in touch with the current presentation of his science as a whole.

The text-book, however good, and the lecturer, however able, are only one of two necessary factors in College work, the reciprocal element is the students' activity. Unless the students are actively engaged not simply in taking in what they are told, but in rearranging it, turning it over, trying and testing it, they are doing little good. We recognize this quite abundantly in the laboratory nowadays, but we neglect it enormously in the more theoretical study of a subject. The facts of a subject if it is a science may be got at in the most thorough way by handling in the laboratory, but the ideas of a subject must be handled in discussion, reproduction and dispute. Examinations, examinations by teachers who understand this very fine art, in which the student is obliged to restate, apply, and use the principles of his subject, are of the utmost value in keeping the mind active and not simply receptive. They are just as good and as vitally necessary as examination papers which merely demand definitions and lists and bald facts are bad. And then there might be discussions—if the Professor were clever enough to conduct them. If the students of a class could be induced to submit propositions for discussion, from which a topic could be selected, and could then be made to prepare for a disputation to which all would have to contribute, with the Professor as a controlling influence in the chair to check facts and logic and to conclude, it would have the value of a dozen lectures. But Professors who are under the burthen of perhaps ninety or a hundred lectures a year cannot be expected to do anything of this sort. Directed reading, conferences on knotty points, special lectures followed by the questioning of the lecturer, discussions upon matters of opinion, laboratory work when needful, fairly frequent test examinations, and a final examination for places, are the proper ingredients of a good modern College course, and in the necessity of leaving the Professor's energies free for the direction of all this really educational work, lies another reason for that complete, explicit, well-arranged text-book upon which I am insisting.

Coming back now from these general propositions about books and teaching to our mass of young people about fifteen years old, our adolescent nation, who have accomplished their Schooling and are ready for the College phase, we have to consider what subjects they are to be taught, and how far they are to go with these subjects. Whether they are to give all or part of their time to these College studies, whether they are going to pursue them in evening classes or before breakfast in the morning or during the livelong day is a question of secondary conveniences that may very well be disregarded here. We are concerned with the general architecture now, and not with the tactical necessities of the clerk of the works. [Footnote: But I may perhaps point out here how integral to a sane man-making scheme is the raising of the minimum age at which children may work. A day will come, I hope, when even the partial employment of children under fifteen will be prohibited, and when, as Mr. Sidney Webb suggested some time ago, employment up to the age of twenty-one will be limited to so few hours a week—his suggestion was thirty—as to leave a broad margin for the more or less compulsory college work and physical training that are becoming essential to the modern citizen.]

We need waste little time nowadays, I submit, in disposing of Encyclopaedic conceptions of College Education, conceptions that played a part in almost all educational schemes— Bentham's stupendous Chrestomathia is the fearful example— before the middle nineteenth century. We are all agreed in theory, at any rate, that to know one subject or group of subjects exhaustively is far better than a universal smattering, that the ideal of education is more particularly "all about something" with "something about everything" in a very subordinate place. The fact remains that the normal curriculum of our higher schools and colleges is a pointless non-educational miscellany, and the average graduate in Arts knows something, but not enough, of science, mathematics, Latin, Greek, literature, and history; he has paid tribute to several conflicting schemes of education, and is a credit to none. We have to get rid of this state of affairs, and we have to provide (i) a substantial mental training which shall lead at last to a broad and comprehensive view of things, and which shall be a training in generalization, abstraction, and the examination of evidence, stimulating and disciplining the imagination and developing the habit of patient, sustained, enterprising and thorough work, and (ii) we have to add a general culture, a circle of ideas about moral, aesthetic, and social matters that shall form a common basis for the social and intellectual life of the community. The former of these two elements must at some stage develop—after two or five or seven or some such period of years, which may be different in different cases—into the special training for the definite function of the individual in the social body, whether as engineer, business manager, doctor, priest, journalist, public administrator, professional soldier, or what not. And before we ask what must constitute (i) it may be well to define the relation between the first and the second section of the College stage of education.

It is (i) that will constitute the essential *work* of the College, which will be the especial concern of the Professorial staff, which will "count" in examinations, and I conceive it as occupying typically four full working days in the week, four good, hard-driving days, and no more, of the students' time. The remaining three, so far as they are not engaged by physical exercise, military training, and mere amusement, must be given to (ii), which I imagine an altogether more general, discursive, various, and spontaneous series of activities. To put the thing briefly, with the use of a convenient slang word (i), is "grind," and (ii) is general culture, elements that are altogether too greatly confused in adolescent education. A large number of people will consider it right and proper that (ii) on the seventh day of the week should become devotional exercise or religious thought and discussion. I would submit that under (ii) there should be formally recognized certain extremely valuable educational influences that are at present too often regarded as irregular or improper invasions of school and college work, the collegiate debating society, for example, private reading, experimental science outside the curriculum, and essays in various arts. It should be possible to provide a certain definite number of hours weekly in which the student should be required merely to show that he was doing something of a developmental kind, he would have his choice between the Library—every College ought to have a good and not too priggishly conceived Library, in which he might either read or write—or the music master, the debating society, the museum, the art studio, the dramatic society, or any concern of the sort that the College authorities had satisfactory reason for supposing to be alive and efficient. In addition (ii) should include certain minor but necessary studies not included in (i), but pursued for all that with a certain insistence, taught or directed, and controlled perhaps by examinations. If, for example, the acquisition of a foreign language was a part of the preliminary schooling, it could be kept alive by a more fastidious study in the higher grade. For the making of the good, all-round, average citizen (i) will be the essential educational factor, but for the boy or girl with a dash of genius (ii) will rise from the level of culture to that of a great opportunity.

What subject or group of subjects is to constitute (i)? There are at least three, and quite probably beyond the very limited range of my knowledge there are other, arrangements of studies that can be contrived to supply this essential substantial part of the College course. Each suffices completely, and I would hesitate to express any preference for one or the other. Each has its special direction towards certain sorts of adult function, and for that reason it may be suggested that the secondary education of an English-speaking country might very well afford all three (or more) types of secondary course. The small schools might specialize upon the type locally most desirable, the larger might group its triplicate (or quadruplicate) system of sustained and serious courses about a common Library and the common arrangements for Section ii. of the College scheme.

The first of these possible College courses, and the one most likely to be useful and fruitful for the mass of the male population in a modern community, is an expansion of the Physics of the Schooling stage. It may be very conveniently spoken of as the Natural Philosophy, course. Its backbone will be an interlocking arrangement of Mathematics, Physics, and

H. G. Wells

the principles of Chemistry, and it will take up as illustrative and mind-expanding exercises, Astronomy, Geography, and Geology conceived as a general history of the Earth. Holding the whole together will be the theory of the Conservation of Energy in its countless aspects and a speculative discussion of the constitution of matter. A certain minimum of Historical and Political reading and of general "Library" would be insisted upon in Section ii. This could be made a quite noble and spacious course of instruction extending over from three to five years, from fourteen or fifteen up to eighteen or twenty-one (or even longer in the case of those partially employed); its less successful products would drop out—it might be before completion—to take up the work of more or less skilled artisans and technical workers, and its more successful ones would pass some of them into the technical colleges for special industries with a view to business direction, into special study for the engineering trades, for the profession of soldiering, [Footnote: I may perhaps explain that my conception of military organization is a universal service of citizens —non-professional soldiers—who will be trained—possibly in boyhood and youth, to shoot very well indeed, to ride either horses or bicycles, and to take up positions and move quickly and easily in organized bodies, and, in addition, a special graduated profession of soldiers who will be in their various ranks engineers, gunners, special-force men of various sorts, and, in the higher ranks, masters of all the organization and methods necessary for the rapid and effective utilization of the non-professional manhood of the country, of volunteers, militia, or short-service enlistment levies, drawn from this general supply, and of all the machinery of communication, provisioning, and so forth. They will not be necessarily the "social superiors" of their commands, but they will naturally exercise the same authoritative command in warfare that a doctor does in a sick-room.] or for the naval and mercantile services, or into research and the literature of science. Some also would pass on to study for the profession of medicine through more special work in Chemistry and Physiology, and some with a proclivity for drawing and design would become architects, designers of appliances, and the like. The idea of the ordinary development of this course is not so very remote from what already exists in Great Britain as the Organized Science School, but, as with all these courses, it would be done in varying degrees of thoroughness and extension under varying conditions. This is the first of my three alternative College courses.

The second course will probably seem less acceptable to many readers, but all who are qualified to speak will testify to its enormous educational value. It is what one may speak of as the Biological Course. Just as the conception of Energy will be the central idea of the Natural Philosophy course, so the conception of Organic Evolution will be the central idea of the Biological Course. A general review of the whole field of Biology—not only of the Natural History of the present but of the geological record—in relation to the known laws and the various main theories of the evolutionary process will be taken, and in addition some special department, either the Comparative Anatomy of the Vertebrata chiefly, or of the plants chiefly, or of several Invertebrated groups chiefly, will be exhaustively worked out in relation to these speculations. The first of these alternatives is not only probably the most invigorating mental exercise of the three but bears also more directly upon the practical concerns of life. Physiology will be taken up in relation to this special exhaustive study, and the "Elementary Physics of the Schooling" stage will be prolonged up into a treatment of Chemistry with especial reference to biological problems. Through such a course as this students might pass to the study of medicine just as well as through Natural Philosophy, and the medical profession would profit by the clash of the two types of student. The biological course, with its insistence upon heredity and physiological facts, would also give the very best and gravest preparation in the world for the practical concerns of motherhood. From it students would pass on illuminated to the study of psychology, philosophical science, and educational method. The training in the discussion of broad generalization, and much of the fact involved, would be a most excellent preliminary to special theological study and also to the advanced study of economics and political science. From this course also artists of various sorts would escape through the avenue of Section ii. which, by the by, would have to involve Historical Reading. So much for my second suggested College course.

The third of these three alternative courses is the History course, done extensively in relation to general geography, economic theory, and the general evolution of the world, and intensively in relation to British or American history, and perhaps to some particular period. Out of it would spring a thorough study of the development of English literature and also of the legal systems of the English-speaking peoples. This course also would be a way of approach to philosophical science, to theology, to the thorough study of economic and political science, and possibly it would contribute a larger proportion of its students to imaginative literature than either of the two preceding courses. It would also be the natural preliminary course to the special study of law and so a source of politicians. In the Section ii. of this course a light but lucid treatment of the great generalizations of physical and biological science would be desirable. And from this course also the artist would break away.

Conceivably there are other courses. The course in Mathematics as one sees it given to the Cambridge Tripos men, and what is called the Classical course, will occur to the reader. Few people, however, are to be found who will defend the exclusively mathematical "grind" as a sound intellectual training, and so it need not be discussed here. The case, however, is different with the classical course. It is alleged by those who have had the experience that to learn Latin and Greek more or less thoroughly and then to stumble through one or two Latin and Greek authors "in the original" has an educational value surpassing any conceivable alternative. There is a mysterious benefit from one's private translation however bad that no other translation however good can impart. Plato, for example, who has certainly in the very best translations, quite perceptibly no greater mind than Lord Bacon, Newton, Darwin, or Adam Smith, becomes god-like to all who pass beyond the Little-Go. The controversy is as old as the Battle of the Books, a quite interminable wrangle, which I will not even attempt to summarize here. For my own part I believe all this defence of the classics on the part of men with classical education is but one more example of that human weakness that splashes Oxford metaphysical writings with needless tags and shreds of Greek and set Demetrius the silversmith bawling in the streets. If the reader is of another opinion there is no need to convert him in this present argument, provided only that he will admit the uselessness of his high mystery for the training of the larger mass of modern men. By his standards they are beneath it. A convention upon this issue between the two parties therefore is attainable. Let us admit the classical course for the parents who like and can afford this sort of thing for their sons and daughters. Let us withdraw all objections to its endowment, unless it is quite excessive endowment. Let the classical be the senior service, and the classical professor, to use his own queer way of putting things, *primus inter pares*. That will make four courses altogether, the Classical, the Historical, the Biological, and the Physical, for one or more of which all the secondary schools and colleges in that great English-speaking community at which the New Republic aims should be organized. [Footnote: One may, however, suggest one other course as possible under special conditions. There is one sort of art that requires not only a very rigorous and exhaustive training, but also an early commencement, and that is music, at once the most isolated and the most universal of arts. Exceptional gifts in the direction of music will have appeared in the schooling stage, and it is quite conceivable that the college phase for those who are destined for a musical career should have as its backbone a "grind" in the theory and practice of music, with languages and general culture relegated to a Section ii.]

It may be objected that this is an idealized proposal, and that existing conditions, which are, of course, the material out of which new conditions are to be made do not present anything like this form. As a matter of fact, if only the reader will allow for a certain difference in terminology, they do. What I have here called Schooling is, so far as the age of the pupils go, typically presented in Great Britain by what is called the elementary school, and in America by the public school, and certain schools that unanalytical people in England, mistaking a social for an educational difference, seem disposed to class with secondary schools, the inferior Grammar Schools, the cheaper private schools, and what are called Preparatory Schools, [Footnote: As things are, there is no doubt a considerable advantage in the child from a good home going on to a good preparatory school instead of entering a public elementary school, and the passage above must not be misread as a sweeping condemnation of such establishments.] are really also elementary schools. The latter have more social pretension and sometimes far less efficiency than a Government Elementary School, but that is all the difference. All these schools admit of a gradual approximation to the ideal of schooling already set forth in the sixth of these papers. Some are already within a measureable distance of that ideal. And above these elementary schools, above the School grade proper, and answering to what is here called College, there is a great variety of day and evening schools of the most varied description which agree all of them in the presentation of a second phase in the educational process beginning about the age of thirteen to sixteen and going on to nineteen and twenty. In Great Britain such institutions are sometimes called secondary schools and sometimes colleges, and they have no distinct boundary line to separate them from the University proper, on the one hand, or the organized Science Schools and the Higher Grade Board Schools and evening classes of the poorer sort. The Universities and medical schools are, indeed, hampered with work quite similar to that of secondary schools and which the secondary schools have failed to do, the Cambridge undergraduate before his Little-Go, the London University medical student before his Preliminary Scientific Examination, are simply doing the belated work of this second stage. And there is, I doubt not, a similar vague complexity in America. But through the fog something very like the boundary line here placed about fourteen is again and again made out; not only the general requirements for efficient education, but the trend of present tendency seems to be towards a scheme of three stages in which a first stage of nine or ten years of increasingly serious Schooling (Primary Education), from a very light beginning about five up to about fourteen, is to be followed by a second stage of College education (Secondary Education), from fourteen or sixteen to an upward boundary determined by class and various facilities, and this is to be succeeded by a third stage, which we will now proceed to consider in detail.

Let us make it clear at once that this third stage is a much ampler thing than the graduation or post graduation work of a university. It may or it may not include that as an ingredient. But the intention is to express all those agencies (other than political, social, and economic forces, and the suggestions that arise from them), that go to increase and build up the mental structure of the man or woman. This includes the pulpit, so far as it is still a vehicle for the importation of ideas and emotions, the stage, books that do anything more than pass the time, newspapers, the Grove and the Agora. These all, in greater or lesser degrees, work powerfully together to make the citizen. They work most powerfully, of course, in those plastic unsettled years that last from adolescence to the middle twenties, but often in very slowly diminishing intensity right into the closing decades of middle age. However things may have been in the quieter past when newspapers did not exist, when creeds were rigid, plays mere spectacles to be seen only "in Town," and books rare, the fact remains that to-day everybody goes much further and learns far more than any of the professedly educational agencies can be held accountable for. There was a time, perhaps, when a man really did "settle down" intellectually, at the end of his days of learning, when the only way—outside the libraries and households of a few princely personages—to go on thinking and to participate in the secular development of ideas, was to go to a University and hear and dispute. But those days have gone for a hundred years at least. They have gone by, and the strange thing is that a very large proportion of those who write and talk about education have not discovered they have gone by, and still think and talk of Universities as though they were the only sources and repositories of wisdom. They conjure up a vision in my mind of an absent-minded water-seller, bearing his precious jars and crying his wares knee-deep, and going deeper into a rising stream. Or if that does not seem just to the University in the past, an image of a gardener, who long ago developed a novel variety of some great flower which has now scattered its wind-borne seed everywhere, but who still proffers you for sale in a confidential, condescending manner a very little, very dear packet of that universal commodity. Until the advent of Mr. Ewart (with his Public Libraries' Act), Mr. Passmore Edwards, and Mr. Andrew Carnegie, the stream of endowment for research and teaching flowed just as exclusively to the Universities as it did in Tudor times.

Let us deal, then, first with the finally less important and more formal portion of the third stage in the educational process; that is to say, with the University Course. One may conceive that so far as positive teaching and learning go, a considerable proportion of the population will never pass beyond the second stage at all. They will fail to keep up in the course of that stage, or they will branch off into the special development of some special aptitude. The failures will gravitate into positions a little better perhaps, but analogous to those taken up by the failures of the Schooling phase. The common clerks and common shop-hands, for example, would come out here. The others, who fall out without completing their College course, but who may not be College failures at all, will be all sorts of artists and specializing persons of that type. A great many girls, for economic and other reasons, will probably never get beyond the College stage. They will pass from the Biological and Historical courses into employment, or marry, or enter domestic life. But what may finally become a much larger proportion of New Republican citizens will either from the beginning, taking the College course in the evening, or after a year or so of full attendance at the College course, start also upon the third-grade work, the preparation for the upper ranks of some technical and commercial employment, for the systematic and liberal instruction that will replace the old rule-of-thumb apprenticeship. One can imagine a great variety of methods of combining the apprenticeship phase of serious occupation with the College course. Many waking up to the demands of life may do better for themselves with a desperately clutched College course of evening classes than others who will have progressed comfortably in day Colleges. There should be opportunity by means of scholarship openings for such cases of a late awakening to struggle back into the higher education. There may be every gradation from such students to those who will go completely and exhaustively through the College and who will then go on at one and twenty or two and twenty to equally complete and exhaustive work in the third grade. One imagines the third grade in its completeness as a most varied choice of thorough studies carried on for three or four years after eighteen or twenty-one, special schools of medicine, law, engineering, psychology, and educational science, economics and political science, economics and commercial science, philosophy and theology, and physical science. Quite apart from the obvious personal limitation, the discussion of the method of dealing specifically with each of these subjects would be too diversified and special a theme to occupy me now. The larger fact to which attention has to be given is this: that all these studies and all the technical study and such like preparation at lower levels of the third stage must be as it were floating in a common body of Thought, which is the unifying principle, the common initiative, the real common life of the truly civilized state, and that this body of Thought is no longer to be contained within the form of a University. It is the larger of the two things. And the last question, therefore, in these speculations is the general organization of that body of Thought, that is to say of contemporary literature, using the word in its widest sense to cover all that is good in journalism, all untechnical speculative, philosophical writing, all that is true and new in the drama, in poetry, fiction or any other distinctly literary form, and all scientific publication that is not purely a matter of recording or technical working out, all scientific publication that is, that deals with general ideas.

There was a time when the higher education was conceived of

H. G. Wells

as entirely a matter of learning. To endow chairs and teachers, and to enable promising scholars to come and hear the latter was the complete organization of the higher education. It is within quite recent years that the conception of endowing research for its own sake, leaving the Research Professor free altogether from direct teaching or with only a few good pupils whose work consisted chiefly in assimilating his ideas and helping with his researches, has become at all widely acceptable. Indirectly, of course, the Research Professor is just as much a teacher as the Teaching Professor, because his results become accessible as he writes them. Our work now is to broaden both the conception of research and of teaching, to recognize that whatever imports fresh and valid ideas, fresh and valid aspects—not simply of chemical and physical matters, but of aesthetic, social, and political matters, partakes of the honour and claims of research—and that whatever conveys ideas and aspects vividly and clearly and invigoratingly, not simply by word of mouth but by book or picture or article, is teaching. The publication of books, the whole business of bringing the contemporary book most efficiently home to the general reader, the business of contemporary criticism, the encouragement and support of contemporary writers, *is just as vitally important in the modern state as the organisation of Colleges and Schools*, and just as little to be left to the enterprise of isolated individuals working primarily upon commercial lines for gain.

There are two aspects of this question. There is the simpler one of getting an abundance of good books, classical and contemporary, and of good publications distributed everywhere through the English-speaking world, and there is the more subtle and complex problem of getting, stimulating, and sustaining the original writers and the original critics and investigators upon whom the general development of contemporary thought, upon whom indeed the progress of the world finally depends. The latter problem may be reserved for the next paper, and here we will deal simply with the question of access and distribution.

For the present we must assume the quality of the books; all that sort of question must be deferred for our final discussion. We will simply speak of good books, serious books, on the one hand, and of light and merely amusing books on the other, in an intentionally vague way. The former sort of books is our present concern; pleasure as an end, pleasure except as necessary recuperation, is no affair for the state.

Books are either bought or borrowed for reading, and we have to consider what can be done to secure the utmost efficiency in the announcement, lending and selling of books. We have also to consider the best possible means of distributing periodicals. We have particularly to consider how books specifically "good," or "thorough," or "serious," and periodicals that are "sound" and "stimulating" are to be made as widely and invitingly accessible as possible. The machinery we have in hand are the booksellers and the newsvendors, the circulating libraries, the post-office, and the free public libraries that are now being energetically spread throughout the land [by men who, in this aspect, answer very closely to the conception of New Republicans as it is here unfolded], and to bring and keep all this machinery to the very highest level of efficiency is integral to the New Republican scheme of activity.

It may be objected that the organization of bookselling and publishing is the discussion of trivial details in the intellectual life of a people, but indeed that is not so. It is a constant trouble, a perpetual drain upon the time and energy of every man who participates in that life, to get the books that are necessary to the development of his thoughts. The high price of books, burthensome as it is, is the lesser evil, the great trouble is the trouble of access. There are a great number of people now who read nothing at all, or only promiscuous fiction, who would certainly become real readers were books of any other sort attractively available. These things are not trivial. The question of book distribution is as vitally important to the intellectual health of a modern people as are open windows in cases of phthisis. No nation can live under modern conditions unless its whole population is mentally

H. G. Wells

aerated with books.

That allusion to the predominance of fiction brings one round to the question of the Public Library. One is constantly reading attacks on these new and most promising institutions, and always these attacks base themselves on the fact that the number of novels taken out was so many times, so many hundred times greater than the number of "serious books." Follows nonsense about "scrappy" reading, shallowness of the public mind, and so forth. In Great Britain public pomposities take up the strain and deliver large vague, foolish discourses on our intellectual decline. It occurs to none of these people—nothing, indeed, ever does seem to occur to this sort of people—to inquire if a man or woman *can* get serious reading from a public library. An inspection of a Public Library Catalogue reveals, no doubt, a certain proportion of "serious" books available, but, as a rule, that "serious side" is a quite higgledy-piggledy heap of fragments. Suppose, for example, an intelligent mechanic has a proclivity for economic questions, he will find no book whatever to guide him to what literature there may be upon those questions. He will plunge into the catalogue, and discover perhaps a few publications of the Cobden Club, Henry George's *Progress and Poverty*, J. S. Mill's *Autobiography*, Ruskin's *Unto This Last, The Statesman's Year Book for 1895*, and a text-book specially adapted to such and such an examination by the tutors of some Correspondence College. What can you expect from such a supply but a pitiful mental hash? What is the most intelligent of mechanics likely to secure for himself from this bran pie? Serious subjects are not to be read in this wild disorderly way. But fiction can be. A novel is fairly complete in itself, and in sticking to novels, the Public Library readers show, I submit, a better literary sense and a finer intellectual feeling than the muddle-headed, review-inspired, pretentious people who blame them.

But manifestly the Public Libraries ought to be equipped for serious reading. Too many of them are covers without meat, or, at least, with nothing to satisfy a respectable mind hunger. And the obvious direct method to equip them is to organize an

Association, to work, if possible, with the Librarians, and get this "serious" side of the Libraries, this vitally important side, into better order. A few men with a little money to spend could do what is wanted for the whole English-speaking world. The first business of such an Association would be to get "Guides" to various fields of human interest written, guides that should be clear, explicit Bibliographies, putting all the various writers into their relationships one to another, advising what books should be first taken by the beginner in the field, indicating their trend, pointing out the less technical ones and those written obscurely. Differential type might stamp the more or less important works. These Guides ought to go to every Public Library, and I think also that all sorts of people would be eager to buy them if they were known to be comprehensive, intelligent, and inclusive. They might even "pay." Then I would suggest this Association should make up lists of books to present an outline course or a full course corresponding to each Guide. Where books were already published in a cheap edition, the Association would merely negotiate with the publisher for the special supply of a few thousand copies of each. Where books were modern and dear the Association would negotiate with publisher and author, for the printing of a special Public Library Edition. They would then distribute these sets of books either freely or at special rates, three or four sets or more to each Library. In many cases the Association would probably find it preferable to print its editions afresh, with specially written introductions, defining the relationship of each book to the general literature of the subject. [Footnote: In America Mr. George Iles is already organizing the general appraisement of books for the public library reader in a most promising manner. *The Bibliography of the Literature of American History*, with an appraisal of each book, which has appeared under his direction, is edited by Mr. Larned, and is a most efficient performance; it is to be kept up to date by Mr. P. P. Wells, librarian of the Yale Law School. It includes an appendix by Professor Channing, of Harvard, which is on the lines of the "Guides" I suggest, though scarcely so full as I should like them. This appendix is reprinted separately for five cents, and it is almost all English public

H. G. Wells

librarians and libraries need so far as American history goes. The English Fabian Society, I may note, publishes a sixpenny bibliography of social and economic science, but it is a mere list for local librarians, and of little use to the uninitiated reader.]

Such an Association in the present state of publishing would become—in Great Britain, at any rate—quite inevitably a Publishing Association. A succession of vigorous, well-endowed Voluntary Publishing Associations is a quite vital necessity in the modern state. A succession is needed because each age has its unexpected new needs and new methods, and it would not be a bad idea to endow such associations with a winding-up clause that would plump them, stock, unspent capital, and everything except perhaps a pension fund for the older employés, into the funds of some great Public Library at the end of thirty or forty years. Several such Associations have played, or are still playing a useful part in British affairs, but most of them have lost the elasticity of youth. Lord Brougham's Society for the Diffusion of Useful Knowledge was one of the earliest, and we have today, for example, the Society for the Promotion of Christian Knowledge, the Catholic Truth Society, the Rationalist Press Association, and the Fabian Society. There is a real need to-day for one—indeed there is room for several—Publishing Associations that would set themselves to put bright modern lights into these too often empty lanterns, the Public Libraries. So lit, Great Britain and America would have in them an instrument of public education unparalleled in the world, infinitely better adapted to the individualistic idiosyncrasy of our peoples than any imitation of German colleges can possibly be. Propaganda of all sorts could be diverted to this purpose. Persons of imperialistic tendencies might well consider the advisability of Guides to good geographical and historical reading and sets of travel books, and of geographical and historical works. Americanisers might consider the possibility of sets that would help the common British to a clearer idea of America, and Americans to a realization that the British Islands are something more than three obscure patches of land entirely covered by a haughty peerage and a slightly absurd but historically interesting Crown. . . . Indeed, whatever you want thought or believed, I would say, *give books!*

But the good New Republican would have a wider scope for his Publishing Association than to subdue it to this specific doctrine or that. It is not the opinion makes the man; it is not the conclusion makes the book. We live not in the truth, but in the promise of the truth. Sound thinking, clearly and honestly set forth, that is the sole and simple food of human greatness, the real substance and the real wealth of nations; the key that will at last unlock the door to all we can dream of or desire.

H. G. Wells

X

THOUGHT IN THE MODERN STATE

These speculations upon the possibilities and means of raising the average human result have brought us at last to the problem of increasing the amount of original intellectual activity in the state, as a culminating necessity. That average child who threads our speculations has been bred and fed, we now suppose, educated in school and college, put under stimulating political and social conditions and brought within reach and under the influence of the available literature of the time, and he is now emerging into adult responsibility. His individual thought and purpose has to swim in and become part of the general thought and purpose of the community. If that general flow of thought is meagre, his individual life will partake of its limitations. As the general thought rises out of its pools and narrow channels towards a wide flood, so each individual becomes more capable of free movements and spacious co-operations towards the general end. We have bred our citizen and trained him only to waste all his energy at last; he is no better than the water in an isolated dry-season pool in the bed of a tropical river, unless he can mingle in the end with the general sea of thought and action.

Thought is the life, the spontaneous flexibility of a community. A community that thinks freely and fully throughout its population is capable of a thousand things that are impossible in an unthinking mass of people. The latter, collectively considered, is a large rigid thing, a lifeless thing, that will break rather than bend, that will die rather than develop. Its inevitable end is dust and extinction. Look at the thing from the baser level of political conceptions, and still that floating tide of thought is a necessity. With thought and gathered knowledge things that mean tumult, bloodshed, undying hatreds, schisms and final disaster to uncivilized races, are accomplished in peace; constitutional changes, economic reorganizations, boundary modifications and a hundred grave matters. Thought is the solvent that will make a road for men through Alpine difficulties that seem now unconquerable, that will dissolve those gigantic rocks of custom and tradition that loom so forbiddingly athwart all our further plans. For three thousand years and more the Book has been becoming more and more the evident salvation of man. If our present civilization collapse, it will collapse as all previous civilizations have collapsed, not from want of will but from the want of organization for its will, for the want of that knowledge, that conviction, and that general understanding that would have kept pace with the continually more complicated problems that arose about it. [Footnote: Dr. Beattie Crozier, in his most interesting and suggestive *History of Intellectual Development*, terms the literary apparatus that holds a people together to a common purpose, the "Bible" of that people, and suggests that the "Bible" of a modern people should be the History of Civilization. His work expresses by very different phrases and methods a line of thought closely akin to the thesis of this paper.]

One writes "our present civilization" and of previous civilizations, but indeed no civilizations have yet really come into existence. Tribes have aggregated into nations, nations have aggregated into empires, and then, after a struggle, has come a great confusion of thought, a failure to clarify a common purpose, and disintegration. Each successive birth has developed a more abundant body of thought, a more copious literature than the last, each has profited by the legacy of the previous failure, but none have yet developed enough. Mankind has been struggling to win this step of a permanent civilized state, and has never yet attained any sort of permanency—unless perhaps in China. And that sole imperfect permanency was based primarily upon a literature. A literature is the triumphant instrument of the invincible culture of the Jews. Through the whole volume of history the thoughtful reader cannot but exclaim, again and again, "But if they had only understood one another, all this bloodshed, all this crash, disaster, and waste of generations could have been avoided!" Our time has come, and we of the European races are making our struggle in our turn. Slavery still fights a guerilla war in factory and farm, cruelty and violence peep from every slum, barbaric habits, rude barbaric ways of thinking, grossness and stupidity are still all about us. And yet in many ways we seem to have got nearer to the hope of permanent beginnings than any of those previous essays in civilization. Collectively we know a great deal more, and more of us are in touch with the general body of knowledge than was ever the case at any earlier stage. Assuredly we know enough to hope that we have passed the last of the Dark Ages. But though we hope, we deal with no certainties, and it is upon the broadening and increase of the flow of ideas that our hope depends.

At present this stream of thought and common understanding is not nearly so wide and deep as it might conceivably become, as it must become if indeed this present civilization is to be more than another false start. Our society [Footnote: *Anticipations*, Chapter III. Developing Social Elements.] has ceased to be homogeneous, and it has become a heterogeneous confusion without any secure common grounds of action, under the stress of its own material achievements. For the lack of a sufficient literature we specialize into inco-ordinated classes. A number of new social types are developing, ignorant of each other, ignorant almost of themselves, full of mutual suspicions and mutual misunderstandings, narrow, limited, and dangerously incapable of intelligent collective action in the face of crises. The medical man sees nothing beyond his profession; he misunderstands the artist, the divine, and the engineer. The engineer hates and despises the politician, the lawyer misses the aims of the medical man, the artist lives angrily in a stuffy little corner of pure technique; none of them read any general literature at all except perhaps a newspaper. Each thinks parochially in his own limits, and, except for his specialty, is an illiterate man. It is absolutely necessary to the progress of our civilization that these isolations should be overcome, that the community should become aware of itself collectively and should think as a whole. And the only thing that can overcome these isolations and put the mass of intelligent men upon a common basis of understanding, is an abundant and almost universally influential contemporary literature.

We have already discussed the possibility of developing the innervation of the state, the distribution of books, the stimulation and direction of reading, and all the peripheral aspects of literature, and we come now to the difficult and intricate problem of whether we can do anything, and what it is we may do, to stimulate the central thought. Can we hope to improve the conditions of literary production, to make our literature more varied, quintessential and abundant, to enforce it with honour and help, to attract to its service every man and woman with gifts of value, and to make the most of these gifts?

Quite a number of people will assert that those things that constitute literature come and go beyond the control and will of man, they will speak of Shakespeare as being a sort of mystical consequence, of Roger Bacon or Newton as men independent of circumstances, inevitably great. And if they are by way of being comic writers—the word "humorist," as Schopenhauer long since pointed out, is a stolen lion's skin for these gentry—they will become extremely facetious about the proposed school for Bacons and Shakespeares. But a little reflection will convince the reader that none of the great figures of the past appeared without certain conditions being added to their inherent powers. In the first place, they had to be reasonably sure of a sympathetic and intelligent atmosphere, however limited in extent—there was no Plato in the heroic age, and no Newton during the Heptarchy—and in the second, the medium, language or what not, had to be ready for their use. In the third place they needed personally a certain minimum of training and preparation, and in the fourth they had to feel that for some reason—not necessarily a worldly one—the thing was "worth while." Given a "developer" of these ingredients, and they appeared. But without this developer they would not have appeared, and it is therefore reasonable to suppose, first, that a great number of men of a quality as rare as were those who constitute the unparalleled roll of English intellectual greatness, lived and died undeveloped before ever the developer was compounded at all, and that even in the last few hundred years the necessary combination has fallen upon so small an area of our racial life as to have missed far more than it has hit. The second of these papers is, indeed, an attempt to present quite convincingly what the comic man will probably regard as his effectual objection, that inherent tendency cannot be produced at will. But that the developer may conceivably be made in much greater quantities and spread much wider than it is at present is an altogether different thing. There are, one submits, enormous reserves of intellectual force unworked and scarcely touched, even to-day.

We have already discussed the means and possibilities of a net of education that should sweep through the whole social body, and of the creation of an atmosphere more alert and active than our present one. We have now to consider how the greatest proportion of those born with exceptional literary powers may be picked out and induced to exercise those powers to the utmost. Let us admit at once that this is a research of extraordinary subtlety and complexity, that there are ten thousand ways of going wrong, and perhaps mischievously wrong. That one may submit, is not a sufficient reason for abandonment and despair. To take an analogous case, it may be a complex and laborious thing to escape out of a bear-pit into which one has fallen, but few people will consider that a reason for inaction. Even if they had small hope of doing anything effectual they might find speculation and experiments in escape, a congenial way of passing the time. It is the sort of project one should only abandon at the final and conclusive proof of its impossibility. Exactly the same principle applies to human destinies and the saving of other lives than our own. As a matter of fact, the enterprise is not at all a hopeless one if it is undertaken honestly, warily, and boldly.

Let us consider the lines upon which men must go to ensure the greatest possible growth of original thought in the state, original thought of which what scientific men call Research is only one phase.

Before we can consider how we may endow him and equip him and help him, we have to consider how we may find the original thinker, and we have, if we can, to define him and to discover whatever we can of his methods and habits, his natural history as it were. We are attempting generalization about a class of remarkably peculiar and difficult persons. They are persons either of great intellectual power or simply of great imaginative power, whose bias and quality it is to apply these exceptional powers not directly and simply to their personal advancement and enrichment, but primarily through philosophical, scientific, or artistic channels, to the increase of knowledge or of wisdom or of both. And here is the peculiar point in this problem, they are men who put, or who wish to put the best of themselves and most of themselves into occupations and interests that do not lead to practical results, that often for the individual in open competition and the market fail more or less completely to "pay." Their activities, of course, pay tremendously at last for the race, but that is not their personal point of application. They take their lives and their splendid powers, they waste themselves in remote and inaccessible regions and bring back precious things that immediately any sharp commercial-minded man will turn into current coin for himself and the use of the world.

There are certain things follow naturally from this remote concentration, and we must persistently keep them in mind. These men of exceptional mental quality, if they are really to do what they are specially fitted to do, with all their power, will be unable to give their personal affairs, their personal advancement, sustained attention. In a democratic community whose principle is "hustle," in a leisurely monarchy where only opulence, a powerful top-note, and conspicuous social gifts succeed, they will have either to neglect or taint their special talent in order to survive. It does not follow that because a man's special qualities and inclinations are towards, let us say, illuminating inquiries into the constitution of matter, or profound and beautiful or simply beautiful renderings of his individual vision of life, that he is indifferent to or independent of honour, of all the freedoms to do and to rest from doing that come with wealth, or of the many lures and pleasures of life. Posthumous Fame is losing its attractiveness in an age which has discovered excellent reasons for doubting whether after all *ære perennius* was not rather too strong a figure. However powerful the impulse to think, to state and create, there comes a point—often a point a long way from starvation—at which a genius will stop working. Your man of scientific, literary, or artistic genius will not work below his conception of the endurable minimum, the minimum of hope and honour and attention as well as of material things, any more than a coal-heaver will—and we live in a period when the Standard of Life tends to rise. To secure these things which most men make the entire objective of their lives is, or should be, an irrelevancy to the man of exceptional gifts. This means an enormous handicap for him. Unless, therefore, we endow him and make life easy for him so long as he does his proper work, he will have either to pervert his powers more or less completely to these irrelevant ends, or if his powers do not admit of such perversion, he will have no use for them whatever. He will take some subordinate place in the world as a rather less than average man and, it may be, find the leisure to give just an amateurish ineffectual expression of the thing he might have been.

Now this is the case with a great deal of scientific and artistic work, and with nearly all literature at the present time, throughout the English-speaking community. There are a few sciences slightly endowed, there are a few arts patronized with some intelligence and generosity, and for the rest there is nothing for it, for the man who wants to do these most necessary and vital things, but to hammer some at least of his precious gold into the semblance of a brass trumpet and to devote a certain proportion of his time and energy to blowing that trumpet and with that air of conscious modesty the public is pleased to consider genuine, proclaiming the value of his wares. Some men seem able to do this sort of thing without any deterioration in quality and some with only a partial deterioration, but the way of self-advertisement is on a slippery slope, and it has brought many a man of indisputable gifts to absolute vulgarity and ineffectiveness of thought and work. At the best it is a shameful business, this noise and display, for all that Scott and Dickens were past masters in the art. And some men cannot do it at all. Moreover, what the good man may do with an effort, the energetic quack, whose only gift is simulation, can do infinitely better. It is only in the unprofitable branches of intellectual work that the best now holds the best positions unchallenged. In the really popular branches of artistic work every honourable success draws a parasitic swarm of imitators like fish round bread in a pool. In the world of thought, far more than in the world of politics, the polling method, the democratic method has broken down, the method that will only permit an author to write—unless his subject is one that allows him to hold a Professorial Chair—on condition that he can get a publisher to induce the public to buy a certain minimum number of copies of each of his works, a method that will give him no rest, once he is in the full swing of "production," until the end, no freedom to change his style or matter, lest he should lose that paying following by the transition or the pause.

Now before we can discuss how else we can deal with those who constitute the current thought of the community, we must consider how we are to distinguish what is worth sustaining from what is not.

This is the public aspect of Criticism. It is the mineralogy of literature and art. At present Criticism, as a public function, is discharged by private persons, usually anonymous and frequently mysterious, and it is discharged with an astonishing ineffectiveness. Nowhere in the whole English-speaking world is there anything one can compare to a voice and a judgment—much less any discussion between reputable voices. There are periodicals professing criticism, but most of them have the effect of an omnibus in which disconnected heterogeneous people are continually coming and going, while the conductor asks first one of his fluctuating load and then another haphazard for an opinion on this or that. The branch of literature that has first to be put on a sound footing is critical literature. The organization into efficiency of the criticism of contemporary work one is forced to believe an almost necessary preliminary to the hopeful treatment of the rest of the current of thought.

There is, of course, also the suggestion that an English Academy of Letters might be of great service in discounting vulgar "successes" and directing respect and attention to literary achievements. One may doubt whether such an Academy as a Royal Charter would give the world would be of any service at all in this connection. But Mr. Herbert Trench has suggested recently that it might be possible to organize a large Guild of literary men and women, which would include all capable writers, and from which a sort of Academy could be elected, either by a general poll or, I would suggest, by a Jury of Election or successive Juries confirming one another. The New Republican would like to see such a Guild not purely English, but Anglo-American, or in duplicate for the two countries. With a very carefully chosen nucleus and some little elaboration in the admission of new members—whose works might be submitted to the report of a critical jury—such a Guild might be made fairly representative of literary capacity. Election, one may suggest, should be involuntary. There would be a number of literary men, one fears—great men some of them—who would absolutely refuse to work with any such body, and from the first the Guild would have to determine to make such men unwilling members, members to whom all the honours and privileges of the Guild would be open whenever they chose to abandon their attitude of scorn or distrust. Such a Guild would furnish a useful constituency, a useful jury-list. It could be used to recommend writers for honours, to check the distribution of public pensions for literary services, perhaps even to send a member or so to the Upper Chamber. It is, at any rate, an experiment worth trying.

But such a Guild at best is only one of many possible expedients in this matter. Another is for a few people of means to subsidize a magazine for the exhaustive criticism of contemporary work for a few years. Quite a small number of people, serious in this matter, a couple of thousand or so, could float such a magazine by the simple expedient of guaranteeing subscriptions. [Footnote: It may be suggested that among other methods of putting the criticism of contemporary literature upon a better footing is one that might conceivably be made to pay its own expenses. There is so much room for endowments nowadays that where one can get at the purse of the general public one should certainly prefer it to that of the generous but overtaxed donor. The project would require a strong endowment, but that endowment might be of the nature of a guarantee fund, and might in the end return unimpaired to the lender. The suggestion is the establishment of a well-planned and reasonably cheap monthly or weekly critical magazine, written on a level at present unattainable—chiefly because of the low rate of payment for all literary criticism. There can be no doubt among those who read much among literary and quasi-literary periodicals in English that there is a very considerable amount of high critical ability available. Buried and obscured to an ineffectual degree among much that is formal, foolish, and venial, there is to be found to-day a really quite remarkable number of isolated reviews, criticisms and articles in which style is apparent, in which discrimination shines fitfully, in which there is the unmistakable note of honest enthusiasm for good work. For the most part, such criticism bears also the marks of haste—as, indeed, it must do when a review as long as the column of a daily paper, a day's work, that is, of steady writing, earns scarcely a pound. But the stuff is there. Scarcely a number of the *Academy*, or the *Spectator*, scarcely a week of the *Morning Post*, the *Daily News*, or the *Daily Chronicle*, but there is a review, or a piece of a review, that has the stigmata of literature. And this suggestion is that some of these writers shall be got together, shall be paid at least as well as popular short-story writers are paid, shall each have a definite department marked out under a trustworthy editor, and be pledged to limit their work to the pages of this new critical magazine. Their work would be signed, and there they would be, conspicuously urged to do the best that was in them, *apropos* of more or less contemporary books and writers. They would have leisure for deliberate judgments, for the development of that consistency of thought which the condition of journalism renders so impossible. This review would mean for them status, reputation, and opportunity. They would deal with contemporary fiction, with contemporary speculative literature, and with the style, logic, methods and vocabulary of scientific and philosophical writers. Their work would form the mass of the magazine, but there would also be (highly paid) occasional writers, towards whose opinions the regular staff would very carefully define their attitude. The project, of course, in foolish hands, might be very foolishly misinterpreted. It might be quite easy to drive a team of egregious asses in this way over contemporary work, leaving nothing but hoof-marks and injuries, but we are assuming the thing to be efficiently done. It is submitted that such a magazine, patiently and generously sustained for a few years, would at last probably come to pay its way. Unless the original selection of the staff was badly done, it would by sheer persistent high quality win its way to authority with the reading public, and so fill its covers with a swelling mass of advertisement pages. And once it paid, then forthwith a dozen rivals would be in the field, all of them, of course, also paying highly for critical matter and competing for critics of standing. Such an enterprise would be a lever for criticism through the whole of our literary world.]

Then it should also be possible to endow university lectureships and readerships in contemporary criticism, lectureships and readerships in which questions of style and method could be illustrated by quotation (not necessarily of a flattering sort) from contemporary work. Why should there not be an endowment which would enable a man of indisputable critical capacity to talk through an illuminating course, to sit before a little pile of marked books and reading sometimes here and sometimes there and talking between, to distinguish the evil from the good? What a wholesome thing to have Mr. Henley, for example, at that in the place of some of the several specialists who will lecture you so admirably on the Troubadours! How good to hear Mr. Frederic Harrison (with some one to follow) adjusting all our living efforts to the scale of the divine Comte, and Mr. Walkley and Mr. Herbert Paul making it perfectly clear that a dead dog is better than a living lion, by demonstrations on the lion. Criticism to-day is all too much in the case of that doctor whose practice was deadly, indeed, but his post-mortems admirable! No doubt such lectures would consist at times of highly contentious matter, but what of that? There could be several chairs. It would not be an impossible thing to set a few Extension Lecturers afloat upon the same channel. We have now numerous courses of lectures on the Elizabethan Dramatists and the evolution of the Miracle Play, and the people who listen to this sort of thing will depart straight away to recreate their souls in the latest triumph of vehement bookselling. Why not base the literary education of people upon the literature they read instead of upon literature that they are scarcely more in touch with than with Chinese metaphysics? A few carefully chosen pages of contemporary rubbish, read with a running comment, a few carefully chosen pages of what is, comparatively, not rubbish, a little lucid discussion of effects and probabilities, would do more to quicken the literary sense of the average person than all the sham enthusiasm about Marlowe and Spenser that was ever concocted. There are not a few authors who would be greatly the better and might even be subsequently grateful for a lecture upon themselves in this style. Let no one say from this that the classics of our tongue are depreciated here. But the point is, that for people who know little of history, little of our language, whose only habitual reading is the newspaper, the popular novel, and the

H. G. Wells

sixpenny magazine, to plunge into the study of works written in the language of a different period, crowded with obsolete allusions, and saturated with obsolete ideas and extinct ways of thinking, is pretentious and unprofitable, and that most of such Extension Lecturing is fruitless and absurd. And I appeal to these two facts in confirmation, to the thousands of people who every year listen to such lectures and to the hundreds of thousands of copies of our national classics sold by the booksellers, on the one hand, and on the other to the absolute incapacity of our public to judge any new literary thing or to protect itself in any way from violently and vulgarly boomed rubbish of the tawdriest description. Without a real and popular criticism of contemporary work as a preliminary and basis, the criticism and circulation of the classics is quite manifestly vain.

By such expedients very much might be done for the literary atmosphere. By endowing a critical review or so, by endowing a few chairs and readerships in contemporary criticism, by organizing a Guild of Literature and a system of exemplary honours for literature, by stimulating the general discussion of contemporary work through lectures and articles, criticism could, I believe, be made "worth while" to an extent that is now scarcely imaginable, and there might be created an atmosphere of attention, appreciation, and judgment that would be in itself extraordinarily stimulating to all forms of literary effort. Of course all this sort of thing may be done cheaply, stupidly, dishonestly, and vulgarly, and one imagines the shy and exquisite type of mind recoiling from the rude sanity of these suggestions. But, indeed, they need not be done any other way than finely and well. People whose conception of what is good in art and literature is inseparable from rarity ought, I submit, to collect stamps. At an earlier phase in this series of discussions there was broached a project for an English Language Society, which would set itself to do or get done a number of services necessary to the teaching and extension of the language of our universal peoples. With such a Society those who undertook this project for the habilitation of criticism would necessarily co-operate and interlock.

It is upon this basis of an organized criticism and of a well-taught and cherished language that the English literature of the Twentieth Century, the literature of analysis and research, and the literature of creative imagination, has to stand. Upon such a basis it becomes possible to consider the practicability of the endowment of general literature. For to that at last we come. I submit that it is only by the payment of authors, and if necessary their endowment in a spacious manner, and in particular by the entire separation of the rewards of writing from the accidents of the book market, that the function of literature can be adequately discharged in the modern state. The laws of supply and demand break down altogether in this case. We have to devise some means of sustaining those who discharge this necessary public function in the progressive state.

There are several general propositions in this matter that it may be worth while to state at this point. The first is that both scientific generalization and literature proper have been and are and must continue to be the product of a quite exceptionally heterogeneous aggregation of persons. They are persons of the most various temperaments, of the most varied lop-sidedness, of the most various special gifts, and the most various social origins, having only this in common, the ability to add to the current of the world's thought. They are not to be dealt with as though they were a class of persons all of exceptional general intelligence, of exceptional strength of character, or of exceptional sanity. To do that, would be to hand over literature from the man of genius to the man of talent. A single method of selection, help, honour, and payment, measurement by one general standard cannot, therefore, be accepted as a solution. There must not be any one single central body, any authoritative single control, for such a body or authority would inevitably develop a "character" in its activity and greet with especial favour (or with especial disfavour) certain types. In this case, at any rate, organization is not centralization, and it is also not uniformity. The proposition may indeed be thrown out that the principle of Many Channels (a principle involving the repudiation both of the monarchical and the democratic idea) is an essential one to go upon in all questions of honour and promotion in the modern state. And not only Many Channels, but Many Methods. Whatever the value of that as a universally valuable proposition, it certainly applies here.

And next we may suggest that we must take great care that we pay for the thing we need and not for some subsidiary qualification of less value. The reward must be directly related to the work, and independent of all secondary considerations. It must have no taint of charity. The recipient must not have to show that he is in want. Because a writer or investigator is a sober, careful body and quite solvent in a modest way, that is no reason why we should not pay him stimulatingly for his valuable contributions to the general mind, or because he is a shiftless seeker of misfortunes, why we should pay him in excess. But pay him anyhow. Almost scandalous private immorality, I submit, should not bar the literary worker from his pay any more than it justifies our stealing his boots. We must deal with immorality as immorality, and with work as work. Above all, at the present time, we must keep clearly in view that popularity has no relation to literary, philosophic or scientific value, it neither justifies nor condemns. At present, except in the case of certain forms of research and in relation to the altogether too charitable-looking British Civil List, we make popularity the sole standard by which a writer may be paid. The novelist, for example, gets an income extraordinarily made up of sums of from sixpence to two shillings per person sufficiently interested to buy his or her books. The result is entirely independent of real literary merit. The sixpences and shillings are, of course, greatly coveted, and success in getting them on anything like a magnificent scale makes a writer, good or bad, vehemently hated and abused, but the hatred and abuse—unaccompanied as they are by any proposals for amelioration—are hardly less silly than the system. And for our present purpose it really does not matter if the fortunate persons who interest the great public are or are not overpaid. Our concern is with the underpaid, and with all this affair of mammoth editions and booming only as it affects that aspect. We are concerned with the exceptional man's necessities and not with his luxuries. The fly of envy in the True Artist's ointment may, I think, very well stop there until magnanimity becomes something more of a cult in the literary and artistic worlds than it is at the present time.

This, perhaps, is something of a digression from our second general proposition, that we must pay directly for the work itself. But it leads to a third proposition. The whole history of literature and science abundantly shows that no critical judgment is more than an approximation to the truth. Criticism should be equal to the exposure of the imitator and the pure sham, of course, it should be able to analyze and expose these types, but above that level is the disputed case. At the present time in England only a very few writers or investigators hold high positions by anything approaching the unanimous verdict of the intelligent public—of that section of the public that counts. In the department of fiction, for example, there is a very audible little minority against Mr. Kipling, and about Mr. George Moore or Mr. Zangwill or Mr. Barrie one may hear the most diverse opinions. By the test of blackballing, only the unknown would survive. The valuation is as erratic in many branches of science. The development of criticism will diminish, but it certainly will not end, this sort of thing, and since our concern is to stimulate rather than punish, we must do just exactly what we should not do if we were electing men for a club, we must include rather than exclude. I am told that Americans remark in relation to University endowments, "we speculate in research," and that will serve for only a slight exaggeration of this third proposition. So long as we get most of the men of exceptional mental gifts in the community under the best conditions for their work, it scarcely matters if, for each one of them, we get four or five shams or mere respectabilities upon our hands. Respectabilities and shams have a fatal facility for living on the community anyhow, and there is no more reason in not doing these things on their account than there would be in burning a house down to get rid of cockroaches and rats. The rat poison of sound criticism—to follow that analogy—is the remedy here. And if the respectability lives, his work at any rate dies.

H. G. Wells

But if the reward must be directly for the work, it must not have any quantitative relation to the output of work. It is quality we want, not quantity; we want absolutely to invert the abominable conditions of the present time by which every exercise of restraint costs an author a fine. It is my personal conviction that almost every well-known living writer is or has been writing too much. "No book, no income" is practically what the world says to an author, and the needy authors make a pace the independent follow; there is no respect for fine silences, if you cease you are forgotten. The literature of the past hundred years is unparalleled in the world's history in this feature that the greater portion of it is or has been written under pressure. It was the case with Scott, the case with Dickens, Tennyson, even with Browning, and a host of other great contributors to the edifice. No one who loves Dickens and knows anything of the art he practised but deplores that evil incessant demand that never permitted him to revise his plans, to alter, rearrange and concentrate, that never released him from the obligation to touch dull hearts and penetrate thick skins with obtrusive pathos and violent caricature.

Once embarked upon his course, he never had a moment for reconstruction. He had no time to read, no time to think. A writer nowadays has to think in books and articles; to read a book he must criticize or edit it; if he dare attempt an experiment, a new departure, comes his agent in a panic. Every departure from the lines of his previous success involves chaffering, unless he chance to be a man of independent means. When one reflects on these things it is only amazing that the average book is not more copious and crude and hasty than it is, and how much in the way of comprehensive and unifying work is even now in progress. There are all too many books to read. It would be better for the public, better for our literature, altogether better, if this obligation to write perpetually were lifted. Few writers but must have felt at times the desire to stop and think, to work out some neglected corner of their minds, to admit a year's work as futile and thrust it behind the fire, or simply to lie fallow, to camp and rest the horses. Let us, therefore, pay our authors as much not to write as though they wrote; instead of that twenty or thirty volumes, which is, I suppose, the average product, let us require a book or so, worth having. Which means, in fact, that we must find some way of giving an author, once he has proved his quality, a fixed income quite irrespective of what he does. We might, perhaps, require evidence that he was doing some work now and then, we might prohibit alien occupations, but for my own part I do not think even that is necessary. Most authors so sustained will write, and all will have written. We are presupposing, be it remembered, the stimulus of honours and criticism and of further honours and further emoluments.

Finally, in making schemes for the endowment of original mental activity, we must not ignore the possibility of a perversion that has already played its part in the histories of painting and music, and that is the speculative financing of promising candidates for these endowments. If we are going to make research, criticism, and creation "worth while" we must see to it that in reality we are not simply making it worth while for Solomons and Moses to "spot" the early promise, to stimulate its modesty, to help it to its position, and to draw the major profits of the enterprise. The struggling young man of exceptional gifts who is using his brains not to make his position but to do his destined work, is by that at a great disadvantage in dealing with the business man, and it is to the interest of the community that he should be protected from his own inexperience and his own self-distrust. The average Whitechapel Jew could cheat a Shakespeare into the workhouse in no time, and our idea is rather to make the world easy for Shakespeares than to hand it over to the rat activities of the "smart" business man.

Freedom of Contract is an idea no one outside a debating society dreams of realizing in the state. We protect tenants from landlords in all sorts of ways, our law overrides all sorts of bargains, and in the important case of marriage we put almost all the conditions outside bargaining and speculative methods altogether by insisting upon one universal contract or none.

We protect women who are physically and economically weak in this manner, not so much for their own good as the good of the race. The state already puts literary property into a class apart by limiting its duration. At a certain point, which varies in different circumstances, copyright expires. It is possible for an author, whose fame comes late, to be present as a row of dainty volumes in half the comfortable homes in the world, while his grandchildren beg their bread. The author's blood is sacrificed to the need the whole world has of cheap access to his work. And since we do him this injury for the sake of our intellectual life, it is surely not unreasonable to interfere for his benefit also if that subserves the greater end.

Now there are two ways at least in which the author may be and should be protected from the pressure of immediate necessities. The first of these is to render his copyright in his work inalienably his, to forbid him to make any bargain by which the right to revise, abbreviate, or alter what he has written passes out of his hands, and to make every such bargain invalid. He would be free himself to alter or to endorse alterations, but to yield no *carte blanche* to others. He would be free also to make whatever bargain he chose for the rights of publication. But, and this is the second proposal, no bargain he made should be valid for a longer period than seven years from the date of its making. Every seven years his book would come back into his control, to suppress, revise, resell, or do whatever he liked to do with it. Only in one way could he escape this property, and that would be by declaring it void and making his copyright an immediate present to the world. And upon this proposal it is possible to base one form—and a very excellent form—of paying for the public service of good writing and so honouring men of letters and thought, and that is by buying and, more or less, completely extinguishing their copyrights, and so converting them into contemporary classics.

Throughout these papers a disposition to become concrete has played unchecked. Always definite proposals have been preferred to vague generalizations, and here again it will be convenient to throw out an almost detailed scheme—simply as an illustration of the possibilities of the case. I am going to suggest to the reader that to endow a thousand or so authors, as authors, would be a most wise and admirable proceeding for a modern statesman, and I would ask him before he dismisses this suggestion as absurd and impossible, to rest contented with no vague rejection but to put to himself clearly why the thing should under present conditions be absurd and impossible. Always in the past the need of some organ for the establishment and preservation of a common tone and substance of thought in the state has been recognized; commonly this organ has taken the form of a Church, a group of Churches (as in America) or an educational system (as in China). But all previous schemes of social and political organization have been static, have aimed at a permanent state. Our modern state we know can only live by adaptation, and we have to provide not a permanent but a developing social, moral and political culture. Our new scheme must include not only priests and teachers but prophets and seekers. Literature is a vitally necessary function of the modern state.

Let us waive for the moment the subtle difficulty that arises when we ask who are the writers of literature, the guides and makers of opinion, the men and women of wisdom, insight, and creation, as distinguished from those who merely resonate to the note of the popular mind; let us assume that this is determined, and let us make a scheme in the air to support these people under such conditions as will give us their best. Suppose the thing done boldly, and that for every hundred thousand people in our population we subsidize an author—if we can find as many. Suppose we give him some sort of honour or title and the alternative of going on writing under copyright conditions—which many popular favourites would certainly prefer—or of giving up his copyrights to the public and receiving a fixed income, a respectable mediocre income, £800 or £1000 for example.

That means four hundred or more subsidized authors for Great Britain, which would work out, perhaps, as eighteen or twenty every year, and a proportionate number for America

H. G. Wells

and the Colonial States of the British Empire. Suppose, further, that from this general body of authors we draw every year four or five of the seniors to form a sort of Academy, a higher stage of honour and income; this would probably give something under a hundred on this higher stage. Taking the income of the two stages as £1000 and £2000 respectively, this would work out at about £500,000 a year for Great Britain—a quite trivial addition to what is already spent on educational work. A scheme that would provide for widows and children whose education was unfinished, and for the official printing and sale of correct texts of the books written, would still fall within the dimensions of a million pounds. I am assuming this will be done quite in addition to the natural growth of Universities and Colleges, to the evolution of great text-books and criticism, and to the organization and publication of special research in science and letters. This is to be an endowment specifically for unspecialized literature, for untechnical philosophy that is, and the creative imagination.

It must not be imagined that such an endowment would be a new payment, by the community. In all probability we are already paying as much, or more, to authors, in the form of royalties, of serial fees, and the like. We are paying now with an unjust unevenness—we starve the new and deep and overpay the trite and obvious. Moreover, the community would have something in exchange for its money; it would have the copyright of the works written. It may be suggested that by a very simple device a large proportion of these payments could be recovered. Suppose that all books, whether copyright or not, and all periodicals sold above a certain price—sixpence, let us say—had to bear a defaced stamp of— for example—a halfpenny for each shilling of price. This would probably yield a revenue almost sufficient to cover these literary pensions. In addition the books of the pensioned authors might bear an additional stamp as the equivalent of the present royalty.

The annual selection of eighteen or twenty authors might very well be a dispersed duty. One or two each might be appointed in some way by grouped Universities, or by three or four of the Universities taken in rotation, by such a Guild of Authors as we have already considered, by the British Academy of History and Philosophy, by the Royal Society, by the British Privy Council. The Jury system would probably be of very great value in making these appointments.

That is a rough sketch of a possible scheme—presented in the most open-minded way. It would not meet all conceivable cases, so it would need to be supplemented in many directions; moreover, it is presented with hideous crudity, but for all that, would not something of the sort work well? How would it work? There would certainly be a great diminution in the output of written matter from the thousand or more recognized writers this would give us, and almost as certainly a great rise in effort and deliberation, in distinction, quality, and value in their work. This would also appear in the work of their ambitious juniors. Would it extinguish anything? I do not see that it would. Those who write trivially for the pleasure of the public would be just as well off as they are now, and there would be no more difficulty than there is at present for those who begin writing. Less, indeed; for the thousand subsidized writers, at least, would not be clamorously competing to fill up magazines and libraries; they might set a higher and more difficult standard, but they would leave more space about them. The thing would scarcely affect the development of publishing and book distribution, nor injure nor stimulate—except by raising the standard and ideals of writing—newspapers, magazines, and their contributors in any way.

I do not believe for one moment the thing would stop at such a subsidized body of authors, such a little aristocracy of thought, as this project presents. But it would be an efficient starting-point. There are those who demand a thinking department for Army and Navy; and that idea admits of extension in this direction, this organized general literature of mine would be the thinking organization of the race. Once this deliberate organization of a central ganglion of interpretation and presentation began, the development of the brain and nervous system in the social body would proceed apace. Each step made would enable the next step to be wider and bolder. The general innervation of society with books and book distributing agencies would be followed by the linking up of the now almost isolated mental worlds of science, art, and political and social activity in a system of intercommunication and sympathy.

We have now already in the history of the world one successful experiment in the correlation of human endeavour. Compare all that was accomplished in material science by the isolated work of the great men before Lord Verulam, and what has been done since the system of isolated inquiry gave place to a free exchange of ideas and collective discussion. And this is only one field of mental activity and one aspect of social needs. The rest of the intellectual world is still unorganized. The rest of the moral and intellectual being of man is dwarfed and cowed by the enormous disproportionate development of material science and its economic and social consequences. What if we extend that same spirit of organization and free reaction to the whole world of human thought and emotion? That is the greater question at which this project of literary endowment aims.

It may seem to the reader that all this insistence upon the supreme necessity for an organized literature springs merely from the obsession of a writer by his own calling, but, indeed, that is not so. We who write are not all so blinded by conceit of ourselves that we do not know something of our absolute personal value. We are lizards in an empty palace, frogs crawling over a throne. But it is a palace, it is a throne, and, it may be, the reverberation of our ugly voices will presently awaken the world to put something better in our place. Because we write abominably under pressure and for unhonoured bread, none the less we are making the future. We are making it atrociously no doubt; we are not ignorant of that possibility, but some of us, at least, would like to do it better. We know only too well how that we are out of touch with scholarship and contemplation. We must drive our pens to live and push and bawl to be heard. We must blunder against men an ampler training on either side would have made our allies, we must smart and lose our tempers and do the foolish things that are done in the heat of the day. For all that, according to our lights, we who write are trying to save our world in a lack of better saviours, to change this mental tumult into an order of understanding and intention in which great things may grow. The thought of a community is the life of that community, and if the collective thought of a community is disconnected and fragmentary, then the community is collectively vain and weak. That does not constitute an incidental defect, but essential failure. Though that community have cities such as the world has never seen before, fleets and hosts and glories, though it count its soldiers by the army corps and its children by the million, yet if it hold not to the reality of thought and formulated will beneath these outward things, it will pass, and all its glories will pass, like smoke before the wind, like mist beneath the sun; it will become at last only one more vague and fading dream upon the scroll of time, a heap of mounds and pointless history, even as are Babylon and Nineveh.

XI

THE MAN'S OWN SHARE

In this manner it is that the initial proposition of New Republicanism works itself out. It shapes into the rough outline of an ideal new state, a New Republic, a great confederation of English-speaking republican communities, each with its non-hereditary aristocracy, scattered about the world, speaking a common language, possessing a common literature and a common scientific and, in its higher stages at least, a common educational organization, and it indicates in crude, broad suggestions the way towards that state from the present condition of things. It insists as a cardinal necessity, not indeed as an end but as an indispensable instrument by which this world state must be made and sustained, upon a great, a contemporary, and a universally accessible literature, a literature not simply of thought and science but of power, which shall embody and make real and living the sustaining dreams of the coming time, and which shall draw together and bring into intelligent correlation all those men and women who are working now discontentedly and wastefully towards a better order of life. For, indeed, a great number of men and women are already working for this New Republic, working with the most varied powers and temperaments and formulæ, to raise the standard of housing and the standard of living, to enlarge our knowledge of the means by which better births may be attained, to know more, to educate better, to train better, to write good books for teachers, to organize our schools, to make our laws simpler and more honest, to clarify our political life, to test and reorganize all our social rules and conventions, to adjust property to new conditions, to improve our language, to increase intercourse of all sorts, to give our ideals the justice of a noble presentation; at a thousand points the New Republic already starts into being. And while we scattered pioneers and experimenters piece together our scattered efforts into a coherent scheme, while we become more and more clearly conscious of our common purpose, year by year the old order and those who have anchylosed to the old order, die and pass away, and the unhampered children of the new time grow up about us.

In a few years this that I call New Republicanism here, under I know not what final name, will have become a great world movement conscious of itself and consistent within itself, and we who are making now the crude discovery of its possibility will be working towards its realization in our thousand different ways and positions. And coming to our help, to reinforce us, to supersede us, to take the growing task out of our hands will come youth, will come our sons and daughters and those for whom we have written our books, for whom we have taught in our schools, for whom we have founded and ordered libraries, toiled in laboratories, and in waste places and strange lands; for whom we have made saner and cleaner homes and saner and cleaner social and political arrangements, foregoing a hundred comfortable acquiescences that these things might be done. Youth will come to take over the work from us and go on with it in a bolder and ampler manner than we in these limited days dare to attempt.

Assuredly youth will come to us, if this is indeed to be the dawn of a new time. Without the high resolve of youth, without the constant accession of youth, without recuperative power, no sustained forward movement is possible in the world. It is to youth, therefore, that this book is finally addressed, to the adolescents, to the students, to those who are yet in the schools and who will presently come to read it, to those who being still plastic can understand the infinite plasticity of the world. It is those who are yet unmade who must become the makers. After thirty there are few conversions and fewer fine beginnings; men and women go on in the path they have marked out for themselves. Their imaginations have become firm and rigid even if they have not withered, and there is no turning them from the conviction of their brief experience that almost all that is, is inexorably so. Accomplished things obsess us more and more. What man or woman over thirty in Great Britain dares to hope for a republic before it is time to die? Yet the thing might be. Or for the reunion of the English-speaking peoples? Or for the deliverance of all of our blood and speech from those fouler things than chattel slavery, child and adolescent labour? Or for an infantile death-rate under ninety in the thousand and all that would mean in the common life? These and a hundred such things are coming now, but only the young know how near they may be brought to us. As for us others, we plant a tree never believing we shall eat the fruit, we build a house never hoping to live therein. The desert, we believe in our hearts, is our home and our destined grave, and whatever we see of the Promised Land we must see through the eyes of the young.

With each year of their lives they come more distinctly into conscious participation with our efforts. Those soft little creatures that we have figured grotesquely as dropping from an inexorable spout into our world, those weak and wailing lumps of pink flesh more helpless than any animal, for whom we have planned better care, a better chance of life, better conditions of all sorts, those laval souls who are at first helpless clay in our hands, presently insensibly have become helpers beside us in the struggle. In a little while they are beautiful children, they are boys and girls and youths and maidens, full of the zest of new life, full of an abundant, joyful receptivity. In a little while they are walking with us, seeking to know whither we go, and whither we lead them, and why. Our account of the men-makers is not complete until we add to birth and school and world, the increasing element of deliberate co-operation in the man or woman we are seeking to make. In a little while they are young men and women, and then men and women, save for a fresher vigour, like ourselves. For us it comes at last to fellowship and resignation. For them it comes at last to responsibility, to freedom, and to introspection and the searching of hearts. We must if we would be men-makers, as the first and immediate part of the business, correct and finish ourselves. The good New Republican must needs ask and ask repeatedly: What have I done and what am I doing with myself while I tamper with the lives of others? His self-examination will be no monstrous egotism of perfectibility, indeed, no virtuosity of virtue, no exquisite retreat and slinking "out of the race, where that immortal garland is to be run for, not without dust and heat." But he will seek perpetually to gauge his quality, he will watch to see himself the master of his habits and of his powers; he will take his brain, blood, body, and lineage as a trust to be administered for the world. To know all one can of one's self in relation to the world about one, to think out all one can, to take nothing for granted except by reason of one's unavoidable limitations, to be swift, indeed, but not hasty, to be strong but not violent, to be as watchful of one's self as it is given one to be, is the manifest duty of all who would subserve the New Republic. For the New Republican, as for his forerunner the Puritan, conscience and discipline must saturate life. He must be ruled by duties and a certain ritual in life. Every day and every week he must set aside time to read and to think, to commune with others and himself, he must be as jealous of his health and strength as the Levites of old. Can we in this generation make but a few thousands of such men and women, men and women who are not afraid to live, men and women with a common faith and a common understanding, then, indeed, our work will be done. They will in their own time take this world as a sculptor takes his marble and shape it better than all our dreams.

APPENDIX

A PAPER ON ADMINISTRATIVE AREAS READ BEFORE THE FABIAN SOCIETY

[Footnote: I am indebted to Mr. E. R. Pease for some valuable corrections.—H. G. W.]

Let me begin this paper upon the question of Scientific Administrative areas in relation to municipal undertakings by defining the sort of Socialism I profess. Because, you know, it is quite impossible to conceal that there are very many different sorts of socialism, and your society is, and has long been, a remarkably representative collection of the various types. We have this much in common, however, that we insist upon and hammer home and never lose sight of the fact that Property is a purely provisional and law-made thing, and that the law and the community which has given may also, at its necessity, take away. The work which the Socialist movement has done is to secure the general repudiation of any idea of sacredness about property. But upon the extent to which it is convenient to sanction a certain amount of property, and the ways in which existing excesses of property are to be reduced, Socialists differ enormously. There are certain extreme expressions of Socialism that you will connect with the names of Owen and Fourier, and with Noyes's "History of American Socialism," in which the abolition of monopoly is carried out with logical completeness to the abolition of marriage, and in which the idea seems to be to extend the limits of the Family and of intimate intercourse to include all humanity. With these Socialisms I have nothing in common. There are a large number of such questions concerning the constitution of the family upon which I retain an open and inquiring mind, and to which I find the answers of the established order, if not always absolutely incorrect, at any rate glaringly incomplete and totally inadequate; but I do not find the answers of these Socialistic Communities in any degree more satisfactory.

There are, however, more limited Socialisms, systems which deal mainly with economic organizations, which recognize the rights of individuals to possessions of a personal sort, and which assume without detailed discussion the formation of family groups within the general community. There are limited socialisms whose repudiation of property affects only the common interests of the community, the land it occupies, the services in which all are interested, the necessary minimum of education, and the sanitary and economic interaction of one person or family group upon another; socialisms which, in fact, come into touch with an intelligent individualism, and which are based on the attempt to ensure equality of opportunity and freedom for complete individual development to every citizen. Such socialists look not so much to the abolition of property as to the abolition of inheritance, and to the intelligent taxation of property for the services of the community. It is among such moderate socialists that I would number myself. I would make no hard and fast rule with regard to any portion of the material and apparatus used in the service of a community. With regard to any particular service or concern, I would ask, Is it more convenient, more likely to lead to economy and efficiency, to let this service rest in the hands of some single person or group of persons who may offer to do the service or administer the concern, and whom we will call the owners, or to place it in the hands of some single person or group of persons, elected or chosen by lot, whom we will call the official or group of officials? And if you were to suggest some method of election that would produce officials that, on the whole, were likely to manage worse than private owners, and to waste more than the private owner's probable profits, I should say then by all means leave the service or concern in private hands.

You see upon this principle the whole question of the administration of any affair turns upon the question, Which will give the maximum efficiency? It is very easy to say, and it stirs the heart and produces cheering in crowded meetings to say, "Let everything be owned by all and controlled by all for the good of all," and for the general purposes of a meeting it is quite possible to say that and nothing more. But if you sit down quietly by yourself afterwards and try and imagine things being "owned by all and controlled by all for the good of all," you will presently arrive at the valuable discovery in social and political science that the phrase means nothing whatever. It is also very striking, on such rhetorical occasions, to oppose the private owner to the community or the state or the municipality, and to suppose all the vices of humanity concentrated in private ownership, and all the virtues of humanity concentrated in the community, but indeed that clear and striking contrast will not stand the rough-and-tumble of the workaday world. A little examination of the matter will make it clear that the contrast lies between private owners and public officials—you must have officials, because you can't settle a railway time-table or make a bridge by public acclamation—and even there you will find it is not a simple question of the white against black order. Even in our state to-day there are few private owners who have absolute freedom to do what they like with their possessions, and there are few public officials who have not a certain freedom and a certain sense of proprietorship in their departments, and in fact, as distinguished from rhetoric, there is every possible gradation between the one thing and the other. We have to clear our minds of misleading terms in this affair. A clipped and regulated private ownership—a private company, for example, with completely published accounts, taxed dividends, with a public representative upon its board of directors and parliamentary powers—may be an infinitely more honest, efficient, and controllable public service than a badly elected or badly appointed board of governors of officials. We may—and I for one do—think that a number of public services, an increasing number of public services, can be best administered as public concerns. Most of us here to-night are, I believe, pretty advanced municipalizers. But it does not follow that we believe that any sort of representative or official body pitched into any sort of area is necessarily better than any sort of private control. The more we are disposed to municipalize, the more incumbent it is upon us to search out, study, and invent, and to work to develop the most efficient public bodies possible. And my case to-night is, that the existing local government bodies, your town councils, borough councils, urban district boards, and so forth, are, for the purposes of municipalization, far from being the best possible bodies, and that even your county councils fall short, that by their very nature all these bodies must fall far short of the highest possible efficiency, and that as time goes on they must fail even more than they do now to discharge the duties we Fabians would like to thrust upon them. And the general reason upon which I would have you condemn these bodies and seek for some newer and ampler ones before you press the municipalization of public concerns to its final trial, is this—that their areas of activity are impossibly small.

The areas within which we shape our public activities at present, derive, I hold, from the needs and conditions of a past order of things. They have been patched and repaired enormously, but they still preserve the essential conceptions of a vanished organization. They have been patched and repaired first to meet this urgent specific necessity and then that, and never with any comprehensive anticipation of coming needs, and at last they have become absolutely impossible. They are like fifteenth-century houses which have been continuously occupied by a succession of enterprising but short-sighted and close-fisted owners, and which have now been, with the very slightest use of lath-and-plaster partitions and geyser hot-water apparatus, converted into modern residential flats. These local government areas of to-day represent for the most part what were once distinct, distinctly organized, and individualized communities, complete minor economic systems, and they preserve a tradition of what was once administrative convenience and economy. To-day, I submit, they do not represent communities at all, and they become more wasteful and more inconvenient with every fresh change in economic necessity.

This is a double change. Let me first of all say a word in justification for my first assertion that existing areas do not represent communities, and then pass to a necessary consequence or so of this fact. I submit that before the railways, that is to say in the days in which the current conception of local government areas arose, the villages, and still more the boroughs, and even the counties, were practically complete minor economic systems. The wealth of the locality was, roughly speaking, local; rich people resided in contact with their property, other people lived in contact with their work, and it was a legitimate assumption that a radius of a mile or so, or of a few miles, circumscribed most of the practical interests of all the inhabitants of a locality. You got rich and poor in visible relationships; you got landlord and tenant, you got master and workman all together. But now, through a revolution in the methods of locomotion, and chiefly through the making of railways, this is no longer true. You can still see the villages and towns separated by spaces of fields and physically distinct, but it is no longer the case that all who dwell in these old limits are essentially local inhabitants and mutually interdependent as once they would have been. A large proportion of our population to-day, a large and an increasing proportion, has no localized interests at all as an eighteenth-century person would have understood locality.

Take for example Guildford, or Folkestone, and you will find that possibly even more than half the wealth in the place is non-local wealth—wealth, that is, having no relation to the local production of wealth—and that a large majority of the more educated, intelligent and active inhabitants derive their income, spend their energies, and find their absorbing interests outside the locality. They may rent or own houses, but they have no reality of participation and little illusion of participation in any local life. You will find in both towns a considerable number of hotels, inns, and refreshment places which, although they are regulated by local magistrates upon a basis of one license to so many inhabitants, derive only a small fraction of their profits from the custom of the inhabitants. You find too in Folkestone, as in most seaside places, a great number of secondary schools, drawing scarcely a pupil from the neighbourhood. And on the other hand you will find labour in both towns, coming in by a morning train and going out at night. And neither of these instances is an extreme type. As you come in towards London you will find the proportion of what I would call non-local inhabitants increasing until in Brixton, Hoxton, or West Ham you will find the really localized people a mere thread in the mass of the population. Probably you find the thinnest sham of a community in the London boroughs, where a clerk or a working man will shift his sticks from one borough to another and move on to a third without ever discovering what he has done. It is not that all these people do not belong to a community, but that they belong to a larger community of a new type which your administrators have failed to discover, and which your working theory of local government ignores. This is a question I have already written about with some completeness in a book published a year or so ago, and called "Anticipations," and in that book you will find a more lengthy exposition than I can give here and now of the nature of this expansion. But the gist of the argument is that the distribution of population, the method of aggregation in a community, is determined almost entirely by the available means of locomotion. The maximum size of any community of regular daily intercourse is determined by the length of something that I may best suggest to your mind by the phrase—the average possible suburban journey in an hour. A town, for example, in which the only method of progression is on foot along crowded ways, will be denser in population and smaller in area than one with wide streets and a wheeled traffic, and that again will be denser and compacter than one with numerous tubes, trams, and light railways. Every improvement in locomotion forces the suburban ring of houses outward, and relieves the pressure of the centre. Now, this principle of expanding communities

H. G. Wells

holds not only in regard to towns, but also on the agricultural country side. There, also, facilities for the more rapid collection of produce mean finally the expansion and coalescence of what were previously economic unities.

Now if, while this expansion of the real communities goes on, you keep to the old boundary lines, you will find an increasing proportion of your population straddling those lines. You will find that many people who once slept and worked and reared their children and worshipped and bought all in one area, are now, as it were, delocalized; they have overflowed their containing locality, and they live in one area, they work in another, and they go to shop in a third. And the only way in which you can localize them again is to expand your areas to their new scale.

This is a change in human conditions that has been a very distinctive event in the history of the past century, and it is still in progress. But I think there is excellent reason for supposing that for practical purposes this change, made by the railway and the motor, this development of local locomotion, will reach a definite limit in the next hundred years. We are witnessing the completion of a great development that has altered the average possible suburban journey in an hour from one of four or five miles to one of thirty miles, and I doubt very much whether, when every tendency of expansion has been reckoned with, this average hour journey will ever get much beyond sixty or seventy miles an hour. A radius of four or five miles marked the maximum size of the old community. A radius of a hundred miles will certainly mark the maximum of the new community. And so it is no effectual answer to my general argument to say that a revision of administrative areas always has been and always will be a public necessity. To a certain extent that always has been and always will be true, but on a scale in no way comparable to the scale on which it is true to-day, because of these particular inventions. This need in its greatness is a peculiar feature of the present time, and a peculiar problem of the present time. The municipal areas that were convenient in the Babylonian, ancient Egyptian, or

Roman empires were no larger and no smaller than those that served the purpose of seventeenth-century Europe, and I believe it is highly probable—I think the odds are in favour of the belief—that the most convenient administrative areas of the year 2000 will be no larger and no smaller than those for many subsequent centuries. We are, in this respect, in the full flow of a great and permanent transition. And the social and political aspect of the change, is this steadily increasing proportion of people—more especially in our suburban areas—who are, so far as our old divisions go, delocalized. They represent, in fact, a community of a new sort, the new great modern community, which is seeking to establish itself in the room of the dwindling, little, highly localized communities of the past.

Now what are the practical consequences of this large and increasing non-local element in your old local government areas? First, there is this. The non-local people do not follow, have neither the time, nor the freedom, nor the stimulus of sufficient interests to follow, local politics. They are a sort of Outlanders. Local politics remain therefore more and more in the hands of the dwindling section of people whose interests really are circumscribed by the locality. These are usually the small local tradesmen, the local building trade, sometimes a doctor and always a solicitor; and the most energetic and active and capable of these, and the one with the keenest eye to business, is usually the solicitor. Whatever you put into the hands of a local authority—education, lighting, communications—you necessarily put into the hands of a group of this sort. Here and there, of course, there may be variations; an organized labour vote may send in a representative, or some gentleman of leisure and philanthropic tastes, like Mr. Bernard Shaw, may confer distinction upon local deliberations, but that will not alter the general state of affairs. The state of affairs you must expect as the general rule, is local control by petty local interests, a state of affairs that will certainly intensify in the years to come, unless some revision of areas can be contrived that will overtake the amplifying interests of the delocalized section of the population.

Let me point out what is probably the result of a dim recognition of this fact by the non-local population, and that is the extreme jealousy of rates and municipal trading by the less localized paying classes in the community. That is a question we Socialists, believing as we do all of us at least in the abstract theory of municipalization, must particularly consider. The easy exasperation of the £1000-a-year man at the rates and his extreme patience under Imperial taxation is incomprehensible, unless you recognize this fact of his delocalization. Then at once it becomes clear. He penetrates the pretences of the system to a certain extent; and he is infuriated by the fact of taxation without representation, tempered by a mysteriously ineffective voting paper left at his door. I myself, as one of the delocalized class, will confess he has my sympathy. And those who believe in the idea of the ultimate municipalization of most large industries, will continue to find in this non-localized class, working especially through the medium of Parliament, a persistent and effective obstruction to all such projects, unless such a rectification of areas can be contrived as will overtake the delocalization and the diffusion of interests that has been and is still going on. I will confess that it seems to me that this opposition between the localized and the non-localized classes in the future, or to be more correct, the opposition between the man whose ideas and life lie in a small area, and the man whose ideas and life lie in a great area, is likely to give us that dividing line in politics for which so many people are looking to-day. For this question of areas has its Imperial as well as its local side. You have already seen the Liberal party split upon the Transvaal question; you yourselves have—I am told—experienced some slight parallel tendency to fission, and it is interesting to note that this was, after all, only another aspect of this great question of areas, which I would now discuss in relation to municipal trading. The small communities are fighting for existence and their dear little ways, the synthetic great communities are fighting to come into existence, and to absorb the small communities. And curiously enough at our last meeting you heard Mr. Belloc, with delightful wit and subtlety, expounding the very antithesis of the conceptions I am presenting to-night. Mr.

Belloc—who has evidently never read his Malthus—dreams of a beautiful little village community of peasant proprietors, each sticking like a barnacle to his own little bit of property, beautifully healthy and simple and illiterate and Roman Catholic and *local*, local over the ears. I am afraid the stars in their courses fight against such pink and golden dreams. Every tramway, every new twopenny tube, every light railway, every improvement in your omnibus services, in your telephonic services, in your organization of credit, increases the proportion of your delocalized class, and sucks the ebbing life from your old communities into the veins of the new.

Well, you may say, no doubt this is right so far as it goes; existing local government areas do not represent real countries, but still these local government devices are of service for cutting up and distributing administrative work. But that is exactly what they are not. They are worse when you consider them in regard to function, than when you consider them in regard to representation. Since our conceptions of what constitutes a local administrative area were developed there has arisen the problems of water supply and of organized sewage, of railways, tramways, and communications generally, and of lighting and telephonic intercourse; there hangs over us, though the average local authority has no eyes to see it, the necessity of adapting our roads to accommodate an increasing new traffic of soft-tyred vehicles, and it is not improbable that heating by wholesale, either by gas or electricity, will presently be also possible and desirable. For all these things we need wide views, wide minds and wide areas, and still more do we want wide views for the business of education that is now also coming into the sphere of local administration.

It happens that I have had an object-lesson in this matter of local government; and indeed it is my object-lesson that has led to this paper to-night. I live upon the boundary line of the Sandgate Urban District Board, a minute authority with a boundary line that appears to have been determined originally about 1850 by mapping out the wanderings of an intoxicated excursionist, and which—the only word is interdigitates—with

H. G. Wells

the borough of Folkestone, the Urban District of Cheriton, and the borough of Hythe. Each of these bodies is by way of being a tramway authority, each is at liberty to secure powers to set up generating stations and supply electricity, each is a water authority, and each does its own little drainage, and the possibilities of friction and litigation are endless. The four places constitute an urban area greatly in need of organized intercommunication, but the four authorities have never been able to agree upon a scheme; and now Folkestone is concerning itself with the project of a little internal tramway system all of its very own. Sandgate has succumbed to the spell of the South Eastern Railway Company, and has come into line with a project that will necessitate a change of cars at the Folkestone boundary. Folkestone has conceded its electrical supply to a company, but Sandgate, on this issue, stands out gallantly for municipal trading, and proposes to lay down a plant and set up a generating station all by itself to supply a population of sixteen hundred people, mostly indigent. In the meanwhile, Sandgate refuses its inhabitants the elementary convenience of the electric light, and when, quite inadvertently, I connected across the convolutions of the boundary with the Folkestone supply, my life was darkened by the threat of impossible litigation. But if Folkestone repudiates municipal enterprise in the matter of lighting, I gather it does not do so in the matter of telephones; and there has been talk of a neat little Folkestone telephonic system competing against the National Telephone Company, a compact little conversazione of perhaps a hundred people, rate sustained. And how is the non-local inhabitant to come into these things? The intelligent non-local inhabitant can only save his two or three pounds of contribution to this folly or that by putting in twenty or thirty pounds' worth of work in local politics. He has no local connections, no local influence, he hasn't a chance against the plumber. When the house I occupy was built, it was a mere interposition of Providence that the drain did not go southward into a Folkestone sewer instead of northward into Sandgate. Heaven knows what would have happened if it had! I and my neighbours are by a special concession permitted to have water from the Folkestone source. By incessant vigilance we do, I believe, usually succeed in deducting the Folkestone water rate from the Sandgate general rate which covers water, but the wear and tear is enormous. However, these are details, dear to my heart, but the merest marginal comments to my argument. The essential fact is the impracticable silliness of these little divisions, the waste of men, the waste of nervous energy, the waste of administrative energy they involve. I am convinced that in the case of almost any public service in the Folkestone district with our present boundaries, the administrative waste will more than equal the profit of a private company with parliamentary powers overriding our local authorities; that if it is simply a choice between these little bodies and a company (of the common type even), then in lighting, locomotion, and indeed in almost any general public service, I would say, "give me the company." With companies one may hope to deal later; they will not stand in the way of developing saner areas, but an obstinate little authority clutching everything in its hands, and led by a clerk naturally interested in litigation, and who is also something of an expert in political organization, will be an altogether harder thing to supersede.

This difficulty in greater or lesser degree is everywhere. In the case of poor law administration in particular, and also in the case of elementary education, the whole country displays what is another aspect of this same general phenomenon of delocalization; the withdrawal of all the wealthier people from the areas that are specializing as industrial centres, and which have a rising population of poor workers, to areas that are specializing as residential, and which have, if anything, a falling proportion of poor labourers. In a place like West Ham or Tottenham you find starved schools and an abundant delocalized industrial population, and, by way of contrast, at Guildford or Farnham for example, you will find enormously rich delocalized people, belonging to the same great community as these workers, who pay only the most trivial poor rate and school rate for the benefit of their few immediate neighbours, and escape altogether from the burthens of West Ham. By treating these places as separate communities you

H. G. Wells

commit a cruel injustice on the poor. So far as these things go, to claim convenience for the existing areas is absurd. And it is becoming more and more evident that with tramways, with lighting, with electric heating and force supply, and with the supply of water to great populations, there is an enormous advantage in large generating stations and large areas; that these things must be handled in areas of hundreds of square miles to be efficiently done.

In the case of secondary and higher education one discovers an equal stress and incompatibility. At present, I must point out, even the boundaries of the projected educational authority for London are absurdly narrow. For example, in Folkestone, as in every town upon the south coast, there are dozens of secondary schools that are purely London schools, and filled with London boys and girls, and there are endless great schools like Tonbridge and Charterhouse outside the London area that are also London schools. If you get, for example, a vigorous and efficient educational authority for London, and you raise a fine educational system in the London area, you will find it incomplete in an almost vital particular. You will give the prosperous middle class and the upper class of London the alternative of good teaching and bad air, or of what very probably, under tolerant local authorities, will be relatively bad teaching and open air and exercise out of London. You will have to tax this influential class of people for the magnificent schools they in many cases will be unable to use. As a consequence, you will find again all the difficulties of their opposition, practically the same difficulties that arise so naturally in the way of municipal trading. I would suggest that it would be not only logical but politic, for the London Educational Authority, and not the local authority, to control every secondary school wherever it happened to be, which in an average of years drew more than half its attendance from the London area. That, however, by the way. The point more material to my argument here is that the educational organization of the London area, the Thames valley, and the southern counties are inseparable; that the question of local locomotion is rapidly becoming impossible upon any smaller basis than such an area; that roads, light railways, drainage, water, are all clamouring now to be dealt with on the big scale; and that the more you cut this great area up, the more you leave it in the hands of the localized men, the more you sin against efficiency and the light.

I hope that you will consider this first part of my case proved. And now I pass on to the more debatable question—the nature of the new divisions that are to replace the old. I would suggest that this is a matter only to be answered in detail by an exhaustive analysis of the distribution of population in relation to economic standing, but I may perhaps just indicate roughly what at a first glance I imagine would be one suitable local government area. Let me remind you that some years ago the Conservative party, in an outbreak of intelligence, did in a sort of transitory way see something of what I have been trying to express to-night, and created the London County Council— only to quarrel with it and hate it and fear it ever since. Well, my proposal would be to make a much greater area even than the London County, and try to include in it the whole system of what I might call the London-centred population. I believe If you were to take the whole valley of the Thames and its tributaries and draw a line along its boundary watershed, and then include with that Sussex and Surrey, and the east coast counties up to the Wash, you would overtake and anticipate the delocalizing process almost completely. You would have what has become, or is becoming very rapidly, a new urban region, a complete community of the new type, rich and poor and all sorts and aspects of economic life together. I would suggest that watersheds make excellent boundaries. Let me remind you that railways, tramways, drain-pipes, water-pipes, and high-roads have this in common—they will not climb over a watershed if they can possibly avoid doing so, and that population and schools and poor tend always to distribute themselves in accordance with these other things. You get the minimum of possible overlap—such overlap as the spreading out of the great midland city to meet London must some day cause—in this way. I would suggest that for the regulation of sanitation, education, communications, industrial control, and poor relief, and for the taxation for these purposes, this area should be one, governed by one body, elected by local constituencies that would make its activities independent of imperial politics. I propose that this body should replace your county councils, boards of guardians, urban and rural district councils, and all the rest of them altogether; that you should elect it, perhaps triennially, once for all. For any purpose of a more local sort, local water-supply systems, local tramway systems—the tramways between Brighton and Shoreham, for example—this body might delegate its powers to subordinate committees, consisting, it has been suggested to me by Mrs. Sidney Webb, of the members for the local constituencies concerned, together with another member or so to safeguard the general interests, or perhaps with an appointed expert or so in addition. These committees would submit their detailed schemes for the approval of committees appointed by the general body, and they would be controllable by that body. However, there is no need for detailed scheming here and now. Let us keep to the main idea.

I submit that such a mammoth municipality as this will be, on the one hand, an enormously more efficient substitute for your present little local government bodies, and on the other hand, will be able to take over a considerable proportion of the detailed work and a considerable proportion of the detailed machinery, of your overworked and too extensive central machinery, your local government board, education department, and board of trade. It will be great enough and fine enough to revive the dying sentiment of local patriotism, and it will be a body that will appeal to the ambition of the most energetic and capable men in the community. They will be picked men, to a much greater extent than are your guardians, your urban district councillors and town councillors and so on, at present, because there will be perhaps a hundred or a couple of hundred of them in the place of many thousands. And I venture to think that in such a body you may confidently hope to find a collective intelligence that may be pitted against any trust or board of directors the world is likely to produce.

I suggest this body as a sort of concrete sample of the thing I have in mind. I am quite open to hear and accept the most far-reaching modification of this scheme; it is *the idea of the scale* that I wish particularly to enforce. Municipalize on this scale, I would say, and I am with you altogether. Here is something distinctly and clearly subserving that making of mankind upon which all sane social and political proposals must ultimately base themselves. But to put more power, and still more power in the hands of these petty little administrative bodies that we have to-day, is, I submit, folly and darkness. If the existing areas are to remain the same, then, on the whole, my vote is against municipal trading, and on the whole, with regard to light, to tramways and communications, to telephones, and indeed to nearly all such public services, I would prefer to see these things in the hands of companies, and I would stipulate only for the maximum publicity for their accounts and the fullest provision for detailed regulation through the Board of Trade.

H. G. Wells

ABOUT THE AUTHOR

 **H. G. Wells** (September 21, 1866 – August 13, 1946), born Herbert George Wells, was an English writer best known for such science fiction novels as The Time Machine, The War of the Worlds, The Invisible Man, and The Island of Doctor Moreau. He was a prolific writer of both fiction and non-fiction, and produced works in many different genres, including contemporary novels, history, and social commentary. He was also an outspoken socialist. His later works become increasingly political and didactic, and only his early science fiction novels are widely read today. Wells, along with Hugo Gernsback and Jules Verne, is sometimes referred to as "The Father of Science Fiction".

Herbert George Wells, the fifth and last child of Joseph Wells (a former domestic gardener and at the time shopkeeper and cricketer) and his wife Sarah Neal (a former domestic servant), was born at Atlas House, 47 High Street, Bromley, Kent. The family was of the impoverished lower-middle-class.

A defining incident of young Wells's life is said to be an accident he had in 1874, when he was seven years old, which left him bedridden with a broken leg. To pass the time he started reading, and soon became devoted to the other worlds and lives to which books gave him access; they also stimulated his desire to write.

Choose from Thousands of 1stWorldLibrary Classics By

A. M. Barnard	Booth Tarkington	Edward Everett Hale
Ada Leverson	Boyd Cable	Edward J. O'Biren
Adolphus William Ward	Bram Stoker	Edward S. Ellis
Aesop	C. Collodi	Edwin L. Arnold
Agatha Christie	C. E. Orr	Eleanor Atkins
Alexander Aaronsohn	C. M. Ingleby	Eleanor Hallowell Abbott
Alexander Kielland	Carolyn Wells	Eliot Gregory
Alexandre Dumas	Catherine Parr Traill	Elizabeth Gaskell
Alfred Gatty	Charles A. Eastman	Elizabeth McCracken
Alfred Ollivant	Charles Amory Beach	Elizabeth Von Arnim
Alice Duer Miller	Charles Dickens	Ellem Key
Alice Turner Curtis	Charles Dudley Warner	Emerson Hough
Alice Dunbar	Charles Farrar Browne	Emilie F. Carlen
Allen Chapman	Charles Ives	Emily Bronte
Alleyne Ireland	Charles Kingsley	Emily Dickinson
Ambrose Bierce	Charles Klein	Enid Bagnold
Amelia E. Barr	Charles Hanson Towne	Enilor Macartney Lane
Amory H. Bradford	Charles Lathrop Pack	Erasmus W. Jones
Andrew Lang	Charles Romyn Dake	Ernie Howard Pie
Andrew McFarland Davis	Charles Whibley	Ethel May Dell
Andy Adams	Charles Willing Beale	Ethel Turner
Angela Brazil	Charlotte M. Braeme	Ethel Watts Mumford
Anna Alice Chapin	Charlotte M. Yonge	Eugene Sue
Anna Sewell	Charlotte Perkins Stetson	Eugenie Foa
Annie Besant	Clair W. Hayes	Eugene Wood
Annie Hamilton Donnell	Clarence Day Jr.	Eustace Hale Ball
Annie Payson Call	Clarence E. Mulford	Evelyn Everett-green
Annie Roe Carr	Clemence Housman	Everard Cotes
Annonaymous	Confucius	F. H. Cheley
Anton Chekhov	Coningsby Dawson	F. J. Cross
Archibald Lee Fletcher	Cornelis DeWitt Wilcox	F. Marion Crawford
Arnold Bennett	Cyril Burleigh	Fannie E. Newberry
Arthur C. Benson	D. H. Lawrence	Federick Austin Ogg
Arthur Conan Doyle	Daniel Defoe	Ferdinand Ossendowski
Arthur M. Winfield	David Garnett	Fergus Hume
Arthur Ransome	Dinah Craik	Florence A. Kilpatrick
Arthur Schnitzler	Don Carlos Janes	Fremont B. Deering
Arthur Train	Donald Keyhoe	Francis Bacon
Atticus	Dorothy Kilner	Francis Darwin
B.H. Baden-Powell	Dougan Clark	Frances Hodgson Burnett
B. M. Bower	Douglas Fairbanks	Frances Parkinson Keyes
B. C. Chatterjee	E. Nesbit	Frank Gee Patchin
Baroness Emmuska Orczy	E. P. Roe	Frank Harris
Baroness Orczy	E. Phillips Oppenheim	Frank Jewett Mather
Basil King	E. S. Brooks	Frank L. Packard
Bayard Taylor	Earl Barnes	Frank V. Webster
Ben Macomber	Edgar Rice Burroughs	Frederic Stewart Isham
Bertha Muzzy Bower	Edith Van Dyne	Frederick Trevor Hill
Bjornstjerne Bjornson	Edith Wharton	Frederick Winslow Taylor

Friedrich Kerst
Friedrich Nietzsche
Fyodor Dostoyevsky
G.A. Henty
G.K. Chesterton
Gabrielle E. Jackson
Garrett P. Serviss
Gaston Leroux
George A. Warren
George Ade
Geroge Bernard Shaw
George Cary Eggleston
George Durston
George Ebers
George Eliot
George Gissing
George MacDonald
George Meredith
George Orwell
George Sylvester Viereck
George Tucker
George W. Cable
George Wharton James
Gertrude Atherton
Gordon Casserly
Grace E. King
Grace Gallatin
Grace Greenwood
Grant Allen
Guillermo A. Sherwell
Gulielma Zollinger
Gustav Flaubert
H. A. Cody
H. B. Irving
H.C. Bailey
H. G. Wells
H. H. Munro
H. Irving Hancock
H. R. Naylor
H. Rider Haggard
H. W. C. Davis
Haldeman Julius
Hall Caine
Hamilton Wright Mabie
Hans Christian Andersen
Harold Avery
Harold McGrath
Harriet Beecher Stowe
Harry Castlemon
Harry Coghill
Harry Houidini

Hayden Carruth
Helent Hunt Jackson
Helen Nicolay
Hendrik Conscience
Hendy David Thoreau
Henri Barbusse
Henrik Ibsen
Henry Adams
Henry Ford
Henry Frost
Henry James
Henry Jones Ford
Henry Seton Merriman
Henry W Longfellow
Herbert A. Giles
Herbert Carter
Herbert N. Casson
Herman Hesse
Hildegard G. Frey
Homer
Honore De Balzac
Horace B. Day
Horace Walpole
Horatio Alger Jr.
Howard Pyle
Howard R. Garis
Hugh Lofting
Hugh Walpole
Humphry Ward
Ian Maclaren
Inez Haynes Gillmore
Irving Bacheller
Isabel Cecilia Williams
Isabel Hornibrook
Israel Abrahams
Ivan Turgenev
J.G.Austin
J. Henri Fabre
J. M. Barrie
J. M. Walsh
J. Macdonald Oxley
J. R. Miller
J. S. Fletcher
J. S. Knowles
J. Storer Clouston
J. W. Duffield
Jack London
Jacob Abbott
James Allen
James Andrews
James Baldwin

James Branch Cabell
James DeMille
James Joyce
James Lane Allen
James Lane Allen
James Oliver Curwood
James Oppenheim
James Otis
James R. Driscoll
Jane Abbott
Jane Austen
Jane L. Stewart
Janet Aldridge
Jens Peter Jacobsen
Jerome K. Jerome
Jessie Graham Flower
John Buchan
John Burroughs
John Cournos
John F. Kennedy
John Gay
John Glasworthy
John Habberton
John Joy Bell
John Kendrick Bangs
John Milton
John Philip Sousa
John Taintor Foote
Jonas Lauritz Idemil Lie
Jonathan Swift
Joseph A. Altsheler
Joseph Carey
Joseph Conrad
Joseph E. Badger Jr
Joseph Hergesheimer
Joseph Jacobs
Jules Vernes
Julian Hawthrone
Julie A Lippmann
Justin Huntly McCarthy
Kakuzo Okakura
Karle Wilson Baker
Kate Chopin
Kenneth Grahame
Kenneth McGaffey
Kate Langley Bosher
Kate Langley Bosher
Katherine Cecil Thurston
Katherine Stokes
L. A. Abbot
L. T. Meade

L. Frank Baum
Latta Griswold
Laura Dent Crane
Laura Lee Hope
Laurence Housman
Lawrence Beasley
Leo Tolstoy
Leonid Andreyev
Lewis Carroll
Lewis Sperry Chafer
Lilian Bell
Lloyd Osbourne
Louis Hughes
Louis Joseph Vance
Louis Tracy
Louisa May Alcott
Lucy Fitch Perkins
Lucy Maud Montgomery
Luther Benson
Lydia Miller Middleton
Lyndon Orr
M. Corvus
M. H. Adams
Margaret E. Sangster
Margret Howth
Margaret Vandercook
Margaret W. Hungerford
Margret Penrose
Maria Edgeworth
Maria Thompson Daviess
Mariano Azuela
Marion Polk Angellotti
Mark Overton
Mark Twain
Mary Austin
Mary Catherine Crowley
Mary Cole
Mary Hastings Bradley
Mary Roberts Rinehart
Mary Rowlandson
M. Wollstonecraft Shelley
Maud Lindsay
Max Beerbohm
Myra Kelly
Nathaniel Hawthrone
Nicolo Machiavelli
O. F. Walton
Oscar Wilde

Owen Johnson
P.G. Wodehouse
Paul and Mabel Thorne
Paul G. Tomlinson
Paul Severing
Percy Brebner
Percy Keese Fitzhugh
Peter B. Kyne
Plato
Quincy Allen
R. Derby Holmes
R. L. Stevenson
R. S. Ball
Rabindranath Tagore
Rahul Alvares
Ralph Bonehill
Ralph Henry Barbour
Ralph Victor
Ralph Waldo Emmerson
Rene Descartes
Ray Cummings
Rex Beach
Rex E. Beach
Richard Harding Davis
Richard Jefferies
Richard Le Gallienne
Robert Barr
Robert Frost
Robert Gordon Anderson
Robert L. Drake
Robert Lansing
Robert Lynd
Robert Michael Ballantyne
Robert W. Chambers
Rosa Nouchette Carey
Rudyard Kipling
Saint Augustine
Samuel B. Allison
Samuel Hopkins Adams
Sarah Bernhardt
Sarah C. Hallowell
Selma Lagerlof
Sherwood Anderson
Sigmund Freud
Standish O'Grady
Stanley Weyman
Stella Benson
Stella M. Francis

Stephen Crane
Stewart Edward White
Stijn Streuvels
Swami Abhedananda
Swami Parmananda
T. S. Ackland
T. S. Arthur
The Princess Der Ling
Thomas A. Janvier
Thomas A Kempis
Thomas Anderton
Thomas Bailey Aldrich
Thomas Bulfinch
Thomas De Quincey
Thomas Dixon
Thomas H. Huxley
Thomas Hardy
Thomas More
Thornton W. Burgess
U. S. Grant
Upton Sinclair
Valentine Williams
Various Authors
Vaughan Kester
Victor Appleton
Victor G. Durham
Victoria Cross
Virginia Woolf
Wadsworth Camp
Walter Camp
Walter Scott
Washington Irving
Wilbur Lawton
Wilkie Collins
Willa Cather
Willard F. Baker
William Dean Howells
William le Queux
W. Makepeace Thackeray
William W. Walter
William Shakespeare
Winston Churchill
Yei Theodora Ozaki
Yogi Ramacharaka
Young E. Allison
Zane Grey